RIGHTS, RISK AND
Restraint-Free Care
OF OLDER PEOPLE

of related interest

Person-Centred Dementia Care
Making Services Better
Dawn Brooker
ISBN 978 1 84310 337 0
Bradford Dementia Group

Enriched Care Planning for People with Dementia
A Good Practice Guide to Delivering Person-Centred Care
Hazel May, Paul Edwards and Dawn Brooker
ISBN 978 1 84310 405 6
Bradford Dementia Group

Decision-Making, Personhood and Dementia
Exploring the Interface
Edited by Deborah O'Connor and Barbara Purves
ISBN 978 1 84310 585 5

Good Practice in Safeguarding Adults
Working Effectively in Adult Protection
Edited by Jacki Pritchard
ISBN 978 1 84310 699 9
Good Practice in Health, Social Care and Criminal Justice

Safeguarding Vulnerable Adults and the Law
Michael Mandelstam
ISBN 978 1 84310 692 0

Person-Centred Counselling for People with Dementia
Making Sense of Self
Danuta Lipinska
ISBN 978 1 84310 978 5

How We Treat the Sick
Neglect and Abuse in Our Health Services
Michael Mandelstam
ISBN 978 184905 160 6

A Practical Guide to Working with Reluctant Clients in Health and Social Care
Maggie Kindred
ISBN 978 1 84905 102 6

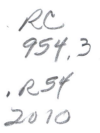

RIGHTS, RISK AND *Restraint-Free Care* OF OLDER PEOPLE

Person-Centred Approaches in Health and Social Care

EDITED BY RHIDIAN HUGHES

Foreword by Baroness Greengross

Jessica Kingsley *Publishers*
London and Philadelphia

First published in 2010
by Jessica Kingsley Publishers
116 Pentonville Road
London N1 9JB, UK
and
400 Market Street, Suite 400
Philadelphia, PA 19106, USA

www.jkp.com

Copyright © Jessica Kingsley Publishers 2010
Printed digitally since 2011

Library of Congress Cataloging in Publication Data
Rights, risk, and restraint-free care of older people : person-centred approaches in health and social care / edited by Rhidian Hughes ; foreword by Baroness Greengross.
       p. ; cm.
   Includes bibliographical references.
   ISBN 978-1-84310-958-7 (alk. paper)
   1. Nursing home patients--Restraint . I. Hughes, Rhidian.
   [DNLM: 1. Health Services for the Aged. 2. Restraint, Physical. 3. Aged. 4. Patient Rights. 5. Patient-Centered Care. 6. Risk Factors. WT 31 R571 2010]
   RC954.3.R54 2010
   362.16--dc22
                              2009023158

British Library Cataloguing in Publication Data
A CIP catalogue record for this book is available from the British Library

ISBN 978 1 84310 958 7
eISBN 978 0 85700 222 8

FOR

Cariad

11 SEPTEMBER 2008

CONTENTS

List of Tables, Figures and Boxes

LIST OF ACRONYMS AND ABBREVIATIONS

AAOS	American Academy of Orthopaedic Surgeons
ACE	Acute care for elders (unit)
ADLs	Activities of daily living
AGS	American Geriatrics Society
APPG	All-Party Parliamentary Group on Dementia
AT	Assistive technology
BGS	British Geriatrics Society
BIHR	British Institute of Human Rights
BPSD	Behavioural and psychological symptoms of dementia
CABG	Coronary artery bypass graft
CAT	Clinical assessment tool
CCTV	Closed circuit television
CHIPP	Community Hospital Integration Program Project
CI	Confidence interval
CMS	Centers for Medicare and Medicaid Services
CSCI	Commission for Social Care Inspection
CSDD	Cornell Scale for Depression in Dementia
CSP	Community Support Planning
DH	Department of Health
EBN	Evidence-based nursing
ECT	Electroconvulsive therapy
FDA	Food and Drug Administration
FOOD	Feed Or Ordinary Diet (trial)
GDS	Geriatric Depression Scale
GP	General practitioner
GPS	Global positioning system
GRADE	Grading of Recommendations Assessment, Development and Evaluation
HCFA	Health Care Financing Administration
HCHC	House of Commons Health Committee
HELP	Hospital Elder Life Program

HRA	Human Rights Act
HSE	Health and Safety Executive
JCHR	Joint Committee on Human Rights
MHRA	Medicines and Healthcare products Regulatory Agency
MMSE	Mini Mental Status Examination
MRI	Magnetic resonance imaging
NHS	National Health Service
NMC	Nursing and Midwifery Council
NPSA	National Patient Safety Agency
OBRA 87	Omnibus Budget Reconciliation Act of 1987
PERT	Psychiatric emergency response teams
PRN	*Pro re nata* (as required)
RCN	Royal College of Nursing
RCT	Randomised controlled trial
RNAO	Registered Nurses' Association of Ontario
RRC	Relation-related care
SIGN	Scottish Intercollegiate Guidelines Network
SSRI	Serotonin reuptake inhibitor
STAT	*Statim* (immediately)
UK	United Kingdom
UN	United Nations
US	United States
WHO	World Health Organization

FOREWORD

The ageing of the world's population is something to be widely celebrated, but we have to acknowledge the fact that it presents us with certain problems that have never before been experienced. We need to learn how to deal with situations which have not been thought about very much until recently. Restraint is one such issue. This is, therefore, an extremely important book. It covers a range of issues in a balanced way, drawing on evidence from various professions and on expertise and experience from many different countries. Restraint is a critically important and often neglected issue, which can take many forms and be used in various situations to control people who are physically ill, those with mental health problems, people in prison or even in their own home, but the book focuses primarily on older people, especially those suffering from dementia and at the particular difficulties they face, as do those people whose role it is to care for them.

The issue of the restraint of older people has been long neglected and this comprehensive publication covers research, policy and practice. It draws on social theory and gives many practical examples, while covering a whole range of ethical issues, including decision making at the end of life.

It is only since the 1980s that this issue has been taken seriously, so focusing on restraint, including whether it is ever permissible and, if so, when, is crucially important, as is an understanding of where the line is to be drawn between restraint and abuse. Attention is drawn to the potential use of the tool of human rights, with its emphasis on dignity and the respect of the individual, which can be very useful in combating the negative attitudes towards older people that sadly often still prevail. The historical thread weaving through the book and the range of views explored remind me of the gradually changing attitudes towards the use of physical restraint and the punishment of children, which have been studied for much longer. These chapters give us the opportunity to decide for ourselves where, in our experience, the danger to an individual older person or the risk to a member of staff might mean that some form of restraint, used in a strictly limited way when a person's behaviour is exceptionally challenging, as a tool of last resort, is legitimate. Similarly, we read about situations where it is never permissible as it has slipped over the boundary into the area of abuse or the denial of an older person's rights as a human being. These difficult boundaries are illustrated in many ways, such as through the use of psychotropic drugs to deal with seriously difficult or violent behaviour. In such situations the boundary between acceptable or abusive treatment is difficult to establish.

A historical perspective throws light on how medicine has often been misused and how frequently various forms of physical restraint have been used in care institutions. The book also demonstrates how legislation that is well thought out can be an important means of combating the misuse of control, which underlies much of the need for restraint. We learn how important good staff training and an effective organisational culture can be in preventing any slip towards abusive behaviour. Above all we gain an understanding of how quality staff leadership, illustrated by many examples, can reduce the need for restraint. The importance of monitoring practice, of increasing transparency and the collection of data to measure improvement, is highlighted.

Above all we learn how a person-centred approach and the building of one-to-one relationships can reduce the excessive use of drugs and other questionable practices.

The ethical basis underlying our values is well illustrated through drawing out the key principles which must guide practice and how care workers must always ask themselves who is intended to benefit from any restraint which is introduced, and whether the beneficiary is the older person or the staff directly involved. The need to work in the best interests of people lacking capacity is rightly emphasised.

Other ethical problems are illustrated and the difficulties when having to restrain people from resisting feeding tubes or using bed rails when attempting to reduce falls, to the danger of infantilising people when blocking their movements, are well demonstrated.

Overall, the book invites us to consider whether the best way to limit the use of restraint is by always considering the motivation of the restrainer. At a time when the numbers of people suffering from dementia and other age-related diseases are fast rising such issues need to be spoken about much more openly. It is only through open debate that we can gain a greater understanding of when such treatment can be justified and how any use of restraint must be set in the context of ageist attitudes which are still so prevalent in our society.

This book should go a long way in helping those at the cutting edge of care services and everyone who considers the future of our ageing society to think deeply about what their response would be if faced with the very difficult situations illustrated in this book. We all need to ensure that our decisions are made in a compassionate and humane way, without in any way seeking to avoid the dilemmas which are inevitably often involved.

I hope this book will be widely read. It encourages us to question our motives if ever we are faced with difficult situations when caring for people to whom it is sometimes very difficult to relate, but who nevertheless need our care and understanding at the most vulnerable period of their lives, as they draw to a close.

Baroness Greengross,
Crossbench Peer, House of Lords, Chief Executive,
International Longevity Centre, UK

PREFACE

In its broadest sense, restraint is about preventing individuals from doing something they wish to do, including placing limits on people's will or ability. There are a host of issues and perspectives to consider if we are to have an intelligent debate about the use of restraint. The practice tends to grab the media spotlight and it is not uncommon for coverage to centre on the abuse of an individual or group of older people, typically living in care or nursing homes, or during a stay in hospital. When we hear or read about the restraint of older people strong feelings can be raised. Few would deny that restraint is a challenging and uncomfortable topic. At a time in older people's lives when they often need to be treated with the utmost dignity and respect, restraint can be viewed as an affront to basic human rights.

A balanced debate about restraint requires a meaningful understanding about the ways in which older people's freedoms are restricted and the effect this has on older people themselves. Crucially, there is an important balance to be struck between care, freedom, safety and risk. Clearly, at the centre of the debate should be the perspectives of older people alongside family members and carers, providers, commissioners and regulators of health and social care.

This book is the first to take a wide view of restraint and to blend reviews and analysis of research and policies, multi-disciplinary perspectives and direct accounts from practice. To these ends the perspectives of those working across health and social care are captured. The contributions cover a great deal of ground but are not standardised, for it is the mix and differences in views, explanations and evidence that are important. The book aims to share what is known, suggests what else needs to be known and where the future might lie in dealing with critical and unresolved issues and tensions. In doing so it is hoped that it will help health and social care professionals, students and those working in research and policy to better understand the complexity of the ethical issues raised.

This book is also important in seeking to redress the balance between the comparably large body of research that is directed to managing disturbed and challenging behaviour in the fields of mental health, learning disabilities and criminal justice when, arguably, much less is known about the issues relating to older people. No one would argue that one group is more important than the other, but there is a growing awareness and call for an equality of attention to be afforded in research, policy and practice to safeguarding issues for older people.

Whilst it is not a book about forming direct international comparisons by virtue of the nations represented in its authorship, it represents a first in bringing together a number of countries' perspectives. It is therefore hoped synergies in restraint reduction and eradication approaches and lessons for policies can be forged to improve health and social care services for older people.

ACKNOWLEDGEMENTS
I am very grateful to all of the authors for their contributions and making this volume possible. A debt of gratitude is also due to the staff at Jessica Kingsley Publishers for their assistance throughout the preparation of this volume. I should also like to acknowledge the support of family and friends, especially Nerys and Meinir, as I brought this book project together.

Rhidian Hughes

Chapter 1

INTRODUCTION

Rhidian Hughes

A BRIEF SKETCH OF ISSUES AND TRENDS

Historical perspectives on restraint largely originate from psychiatry and describe how commonplace restraints were used, including physical restraints, seclusion, sedation and pain-inducing 'treatments' and physical punishments. The non-restraint movement emerged in psychiatry during the second half of the eighteenth century across Europe. This led to a positive shift in values against the use of restraint, which had some success in reducing the use of mechanical restraints in health and psychiatric institutions (Yorston and Haw 2009).

In the United States (US) Evans and Strumpf (1989) note that as far back as 1885 textbooks cautioned against the use of restraint in nursing care. Wang and Moyle (2005) identify references to the existence of restraint of older people since at least the 1900s. In the literature from the 1920s onwards Strumpf and Tomes (1993) point to references about bedboards to prevent older people from getting out of bed.

Antipsychotic drugs, first developed in the 1950s to treat schizophrenia, became increasingly used in long-term care services for older people. Concerns about patterns of prescribing and their long-term effects led to early studies in the US during the 1970s (Kwasny, Hagen and Armstrong-Esther 2005). During the late 1970s and early 1980s awareness heightened about the amount of physical restraint in US nursing homes, ultimately promoting some US witnesses to refer to a 'restraint crisis' (Strumpf and Tomes 1993). A number of developments were crucial in challenging existing philosophies in practice and policies at this time.

First, a programme of early studies and research into the restraint of older people was initiated (Strumpf *et al.* 1998). Before 1983 only one study directly relating to the restraint of older people was identified, and the first systematic review was published in 1989 (Evans and Strumpf 1989).

Second, the US underwent landmark reform of nursing home and long-term care services. The Omnibus Budget Reconciliation Act of 1987 (OBRA 87) set out national minimum standards and a series of rights for people using nursing care services. This included improvements to the regulation of antipsychotic drugs and underlined older people's rights to freedom from physical restraint (Hughes and Lapane, Chapter 3, this volume).

Third, a landmark symposium in 1989, 'Untie the Elderly', was organised by the Kendal Corporation and its partners, and co-sponsored by the United States Senate Special Committee on Aging. The symposium recognised the high levels of restraint that were occurring in the US, which sparked a series of initiatives to critically re-examine the underlying philosophies of care, and set about changing the practices that were driving excessive restraint use (Goldman *et al.*, Chapter 5, this volume; Strumpf, Evans and Schwartz 1990).

Researchers and policy makers in the US were key driving forces in putting restraint clearly on the international agenda. The US experience was characterised by a heightened awareness of the problem of restraint, early research and reviews and a will for policy reform at a time when other countries were only just beginning to become aware of the problem of restraint. Retsas (1998) remarks how Australia looked to the US for evidence about the use of restraint when its first nursing home standards were published. He notes the standards were devoid of any domestic research. The first Australian study on restraint was only published in 1993 (Koch 1993).

It is also notable that, when Evans and Fitzgerald (2002) undertook a systematic review on reasons for physical restraint, no studies from the United Kingdom (UK) were identified. Much less research into the restraint of older people has been undertaken in the UK compared with the US. The UK has, arguably, lagged behind other countries in examining restraint and safeguarding issues for older people. In particular, a number of cross-parliamentary reports have criticised the UK's lack of reliable research in this field, including the use of drugs in the treatment of dementia (All-Party Parliamentary Group on Dementia (APPG) 2008; House of Commons Health Committee (HCHC) 2004; Joint Committee on Human Rights (JCHR) 2007).

There are both differences and similarities between countries in the types of restraint used, which can largely be attributed to cultures and ethos of care internationally (Evans and Strumpf 1989; Leadbetter and Paterson 2009; Royal College of Nursing (RCN) 2008). In the UK the RCN, for example, point to vests, belts and cuff devices that are relatively common across parts of Europe, Australia and the US, but are not acceptable in the UK. Conversely, seclusion is commonly reported as a form of restraint in the UK literature (Commission for Social Care Inspection (CSCI) 2007) but is regarded as an extreme form of restraint that should never be used in the care of older people in Australia (Australian Government, Department of Health and Ageing 2004).

DEFINITIONS

As will be seen throughout this book there are a host of ways in which restraint has been defined. Qureshi (2008) classifies the definitions according to purpose: broad everyday definitions, scientific definitions, and legal and regulatory definitions.

Broad everyday definitions aim to capture the meanings and interpretations of restraint and how restrictions can be placed on people's freedoms. Broad definitions tend to be used to illustrate the range of ways in which older people's freedoms may be curtailed; for example:

- physical restraints – tying or securing someone so they cannot move freely
- physical interventions – moving someone against their will, pushing someone, the use of holding techniques
- covert medication and chemical restraint – the use of drugs to control behaviour or limit freedom in ways that are not treating clinical conditions
- medical restraints – preventing a person from interfering with clinical or medical interventions that are designed to assist and may compromise their clinical care and outcomes (e.g. the use of hand mittens)
- environmental restraints – the design and make-up of environments can limit people's abilities to move freely, such as locked doors, 'baffle' locks, complicated door handles or disguised entrances and exits (e.g. using mirrors)
- seclusion – locking someone in a room
- aversive care practices (also referred to as institutional abuse) – older people's behaviour may be controlled by lights being turned off to discourage certain forms of activities, or threatening or dominant tones of voice to manage someone (e.g. 'where do you think you are going?')
- surveillance – tagging and tracking technology has been proposed as part of a wider debate about the monitoring of

people, especially people with dementia (prone to 'wander walking'). (Hughes 2009)

Scientific definitions are precise descriptions which allow for the incidence of specific activities to be readily established, including for the purpose of research, audit and regulation, whereas *legal and regulatory definitions* set out what is, and is not, permitted by prescribed standards or by law. In this book the plurality of meanings attached to restraint are illustrated in the range of definitions and starting points for individual contributors' chapters.

TOWARDS RESTRAINT-FREE CARE

Some commentators view any form of restraint as an inexcusable violation of human rights. Views that restraint need never be used emphasise the importance of person-centred care. When older people use services, their needs should be put at the centre of all decision making to ensure that it is personalised to meet their needs in ways that maximise their dignity and respect. Thus the early work of Strumpf *et al.* (1998) saw restraint as a symbol of poor quality care and rather than promoting 'alternatives' to restraint they emphasised a preventative and personalised approach to care. 'In our view, the problem of restraint use can be resolved through careful assessment of the client, a focus on "making sense of behavior," and implementation of individualized interventions tailored to specific needs' (Strumpf *et al.* 1998, p.xii). Thus, services that are restraint free are fully personalised and the core elements that support high quality care are in place, including positive staff culture and attitudes, strong leadership, well-resourced services, excellent training and skilled staff.

Many of the chapters in this book demonstrate how restraint needs to be seen within the broader context of care for older people. This includes how services are configured to best meet their needs and preferences. Chapters also show how prevailing attitudes towards older people and organisational norms, cultures, routines and human behaviour and relationships between older people and care staff can work against the provision of truly person-centred care. Yet it is also important not to underestimate the challenges involved in providing care for older people, including disturbed and challenging behaviour, inadequate staff education and training, and a lack of resources that many services face. Beyond these considerations, however, chapters in this book are able to showcase many examples of positive practice and service delivery.

Restraint raises complex legal, ethical and practical dilemmas in the care of older people and there is a question about whether there can ever be a totally 'restraint-free' environment. With all the best prevention work possible, circumstances can arise when an individual may pose a danger to themselves or those around them and staff need to intervene in the best interests of the individual. In these circumstances, restraint becomes a measure of the last resort, which should only ever occur once all other approaches to manage a situation have been tried and found to have failed. This book has taken a hard look at the issue of restraint and encompasses a wide range of perspectives from contributing authors. Views are mixed in how far, if at all, older people should be subject to restraint. These views differ across a spectrum that it is never – sometimes – always justifiable to use restraint. As part of the informed debate about the restraint of older people it is important to recognise that what constitutes restraint for one person may not for another. And, as Hart (2009) has reminded us, restraint can easily turn into abuse.

Differences in opinion on restraint are also reflected in the small body of work that has examined the views of older people who have been restrained (CSCI 2007). Some older people who use services appreciate the need for either themselves or others to be restrained in some circumstances. CSCI (2007, p.5), for example, illustrate a case where an older person was becoming violent, and the sensitive use of restraint helped to calm that individual. 'I was becoming physically violent towards another person and went to physically attack them. The restraint made me feel more calm as if someone else was in control.' However, studies also demonstrate how the use of restraint can leave older people feeling resentful and mistrustful of staff and health and social care services generally. Restraint can leave a deep and lasting effect on people's psychological and emotional well-being, denying people their dignity and damaging their self-respect. There are, therefore, a host of critical and unresolved issues and tensions to be faced in the debate about restraint-free care. The chapters in this book aim to get underneath the issues to better understand and, ultimately, to help make restraint-free care for older people a reality.

COVERAGE AND ORGANISATION OF THIS BOOK

This book is split into three parts to reflect a broad grouping of issues. Part I contains chapters which describe the two main types of restraint. Part II comprises seven shorter chapters which largely draw on issues in health and social care practice. The chapters in Part III are substantive and critically examine ethical, theoretical and methodological issues as well as showcasing innovations in practice and policy.

Following this Introduction, David Evans begins Part I with an overview of physical restraints and medical intervention. He discusses how physical restraint is defined and takes a broad approach to highlighting different forms of physical restraint. He notes the challenges in defining restraint devices and interventions which have legitimate safety or therapeutic benefits, but can also be used inappropriately. Definitions are further blurred because restraint that is reportable (e.g. to management, regulators, etc.) may only include purpose-built devices, and therefore excludes common taken-for-granted restraint such as the use of tables or reclining chairs. Given the range of ways in which physical restraint and medical interventions can manifest, Evans points to the intent of staff as being a key determining factor when considering the definition and methods of restraint.

Carmel M. Hughes and Kate L. Lapane begin Chapter 3 on covert medication and chemical restraint by reminding us that medication has not always been used for positive benefits, and can be misused. They provide a historical sketch of the issues, then describe some trends in the use of drugs prescribed to older people, in ways that enable an individual's behaviour to be easily controlled by staff. Hughes and Lapane highlight the importance of the Omnibus Reconciliation Act of 1987 in the US as a means of providing better regulation of prescribing for older people in nursing homes, and note some successes in the effectiveness of this legislation in reducing over-prescribing. This chapter concludes by pointing to other drivers, such as organisational cultures and person-centred care, that play a crucial role in minimising the use of covert medication and chemical restraint.

The first chapter in Part II is by Gregory M. Smith, Donna M. Ashbridge, Aidan Altenor and Robert H. Davis. It takes a look at the Pennsylvania State Hospital System's approach to restraint reduction. The authors describe, frankly, the high levels of restraint that were employed in the service during the 1990s when there was little monitoring and few review procedures in place. Since that time the hospitals have been transformed and there is now minimal use of restraint. The authors attribute the success of the programme to leadership at all levels within the hospitals; the full involvement of people who use the hospital services and their families; consistent response teams to manage difficult situations; debriefing and witnessing including a focus on prevention; and the introduction of data collection and review processes.

Beryl D. Goldman, Joan Ferlo Todd, Janet Davis and Karen Russell begin the next chapter with a synopsis of the history of the restraint-free care movement in the US and the involvement of the Kendall Corporation. However, whilst noting that the paradigm shift against restraint practice has improved the quality of care and outcomes for older people, they note that this has not been without opposition. The substantive focus of the chapter is on the use of bed rails, seen as a controversial issue in relation to debates about restraint, because bed rails have safety and therapeutic benefits. Equally, however, the authors describe the risks; not least a feeling of restriction, prevention of leaving the bed for some people, and entrapment. A case study, 'Avoid the "quick fix"', illustrates some of the significant decision points in the care of older people and good practice interventions.

In Chapter 6 Jane Williams explores the ethical issues in maintaining enteral (tube) feeding. Clinical-ethical dilemmas are raised when individuals dislodge feeding tubes, which if they remain out of place may seriously compromise individuals' clinical outcomes. Williams notes that there has been little discussion of the clinical-ethical issues in relation to the use of mittens to prevent people from interfering with these tubes. Clinical staff and families and carers often face considerable anxiety and uncertainty during the 'feed or not to feed' decision-making processes. The chapter shows how use of mittens can be acceptable to people when supported by clear policy and practice guidance and decision making that fully involves older people themselves and their families and carers. Throughout the chapter Williams highlights the delicate balance to be struck between restricting people's freedom of movement and maximising clinical outcomes.

Sheena Wyllie, in Chapter 7, looks at strategies to reduce the over-prescription of drugs in care homes for older people living with dementia. The focus of this chapter is on the benefits of the 'Memory Lane' programme, which takes a full person-centred approach to care. At the heart of this work is the view that all behaviour is a form of communication and a number of psychological approaches and therapies are used during one-to-one interventions. Wyllie reviews examples of good practice with regards to the physical (built) environment, the use of pets in therapy and approaches to maximising well-being. This chapter concludes by emphasising how care services need to focus on what older people with dementia can do and how staff, relatives and carers can support the positive aspirations of older people using services.

In the next chapter Jim Ellis draws on personal experience and work as a volunteer companion in a care home for people with dementia. Ellis describes his focused psychological care model with three components: the resident, himself as the personal companion and the content of the meeting or encounter. A series of examples sensitively illustrate the therapeutic benefits to be achieved through simple shared activities including listening to songs, watching DVDs and reading. At the centre of Ellis' approach is a focus on connecting with the person with dementia. Ellis emphasises that these are not one-off encounters, as the benefits in the approach can only be realised in one-to-one relationships that have been forged over time.

The final two chapters in this part of the book take up some broader views; first on health and safety and second on human rights. Stephen Clarke writes from a health and safety perspective, his chapter emphasising the responsibilities employers have to their staff. Clarke argues that organisational cultures and staff attitudes can result in the 'normalisation' of the challenging behaviour of older people. Central to his argument is 'that if a violent or aggressive act were to be redefined as any behaviour that places staff at risk, either on a physical or emotional basis, without the apportionment of blame, strategies to manage the behaviour may be more forthcoming. It also places the behaviour in the realm of health and safety.' Whilst other chapters in the volume underline the importance of prevention, Clarke argues that restraint can sometimes be justified. Clarke emphasises the importance of positive reporting environments to help mitigate the risks staff face at work and that, in turn, reporting can help to foster improvements in assessment and behavioural management strategies.

In Chapter 10 Rhidian Hughes takes a look at restraint through the human rights lens, reviewing and applying these principles to three short case studies. The chapter shows how a human rights approach can help to challenge the negative attitudes held about older people when they use services. Such an approach can also promote highest quality care for all and provides a framework for maximising older people's participation and decision making about their care as well as increasing their independence, dignity and respect.

Chris Gastmans' chapter on clinical-ethical considerations begins Part III of the book. This chapter explores the ethical values and norms that shape the use of restraint and the importance of placing these considerations within the situated context of human behaviour. Gastmans' analysis draws out the psycho-social experiences of restraint from the perspectives of all concerned before going on to weigh up the ethical basis of values and norms in the light of human dignity, autonomy, the promotion of overall well-being and self-reliance. Through these analyses Gastmans explains the importance of a number of key principles for good practice, which are highlighted with examples.

In Chapter 12 Kate Irving draws on social theory, and specifically the work of Michel Foucault, to place restraint within the context of cultures of care practices. The chapter explores discourses underpinning the use of restraint and how these discourses legitimise, justify and maintain the inappropriate use of restraint amongst older people. She majors on three social explanations which hold general acceptance. First, constituting older people as being unable to 'self govern' and the lack of rights afforded to older people who use services compared with the general population. Second, the problematisation of the care environment and the view that in the present system there is little that can be done to avoid the use of restraint. Third, constituting restraint as the only feasible treatment in the circumstances. The exposure of these discourses can help to unsettle the taken-for-granted notions of behaviour and, as Irving argues, provide a platform for staff to critically appraise practice.

In the next chapter Suparna Madan and Pat Rowe explore therapeutic approaches and de-escalation techniques with a special focus on the clinical care of older people living with dementia. The chapter reviews the common causes of disruptive behaviour and the evidence for promoting restraint-free care. The chapter examines the clinical management of delirium, pain, dementia and depression together with fundamental principles of person-centred care approaches. Whilst recognising the barriers towards person-centred care and the factors that can shape restraint usage, they emphasise throughout the importance of knowing the individual. In conclusion they remark that 'treating people who are entrusted to our care with dignity, respect and a touch of humour will make the experience for all worthwhile'.

In Chapter 14 Jan Dewing and Heather Wilkinson discuss 'wander-walking' and people with dementia. They begin by providing an overview on the phenomenon of wander walking, including its attributes, incidence, assessment and management, which can typically involve some form of restraint. Dewing and Wilkinson recognise the diversity of dementia and pay special reference to one neglected group – people with learning disabilities and dementia – and highlight key practice considerations in a detailed case study. They go on to explore the role of assistive technology (AT) and the ethical debates that surround its use in health and social care. Their chapter concludes by highlighting implications for practice and policy and some final thoughts on future research in this area.

Preventing falls and avoiding restraint is the focus of Chapter 15 by Samuel R. Nyman and David Oliver. They begin their chapter with a review of the incidence of falls amongst older people, and go on to critically examine the evidence for the use or removal of restraint to prevent falls. They find many studies are inconclusive and the evidence is weak, not least because of the inherent methodological challenges in conducting research in this field. The use of mechanical restraint, chemical restraint and bed rails are discussed with regards to falls prevention. Underlining their discussion is the importance of non-restraint strategies in the care of older people. The chapter also highlights messages for further research in this area.

Sascha Köpke, Gabriele Meyer, Anja Gerlach and Antonie Haut begin Chapter 16 with the aphorism 'Don't just do something, stand there!' The underlying message here, and throughout the chapter, is that any use of restraint must be of demonstrable benefit to older people themselves. The authors pick up concerns raised earlier in the book about the quality of the evidence base in this field and, in particular, the lack of evidence about the effectiveness, or otherwise, of the use of restraint. The substantive part of the chapter charts the development of evidence-based guidelines for use in care homes. The lessons arising from the production of these guidelines reflect an array of ethical and practical challenges in promoting evidence-based practice in the field of restraint.

The final chapter, by Ingelin Testad and Dag Aarsland, begins with a discussion of the concept of best interests, when people lack capacity to make decisions about their own care. 'To restrain or refrain?' is a central theme throughout this chapter and a case study approach showcases an education and training programme – 'relation-related care' (RRC). The RRC approach emphasises the situated context of behaviour, which includes fundamental human relationships, previous experiences and the wider structural context of care provision including the physical (built) environment. RRC offers a practical framework for staff to improve the relationships between older people and staff and to provider better, personalised care that meets older people's needs.

At the end of the book a selected bibliography draws together some key references. This uses a wide range of sources, and not only literature about older people, as many of the issues, principles and practice implications have resonance across health and social care settings and different 'groups' of people using services.

REFERENCES

All-Party Parliamentary Group on Dementia (APPG) (2008) *Always a Last Resort: Inquiry into the Prescription of Anti-Psychotic Drugs to People with Dementia Living in Care Homes.* London: Alzheimer's Society.

Australian Government, Department of Health and Ageing (2004) *Decision-Making Tool: Responding to Issues of Restraint in Aged Care.* Canberra: Australian Government, Department of Health and Ageing.

Commission for Social Care Inspection (CSCI) (2007) *Rights, Risks and Restraints: An Exploration into the Use of Restraint in the Care of Older People.* London: CSCI.

Evans, D. and Fitzgerald, M. (2002) 'The experience of physical restraint: A systematic review of qualitative research.' *Contemporary Nurse 13,* 2/3, 126–135.

Evans, L.K. and Strumpf, N.E. (1989) 'Tying down the elderly: A review of the literature on physical restraint.' *Journal of the American Society of Geriatrics 37*, 1, 65–74.

Hart, D. (2009) 'The Physical Restraint of Children and Young People.' In R. Hughes (ed.) *Reducing Restraints in Health and Social Care: Practice and Policy Perspectives.* London: Quay Books.

House of Commons Health Committee (HCHC) (2004) *Elder Abuse: Second Report of Session 2003–04. Volume 1: Report, Together with Formal Minutes.* London: The Stationery Office.

Hughes, R. (2009) 'Putting Restraint in Context.' In R. Hughes (ed.) *Reducing Restraints in Health and Social Care: Practice and Policy Perspectives.* London: Quay Books.

Joint Committee on Human Rights (JCHR) (2007) *The Human Rights of Older People in Healthcare: Eleventh Report of Session 2006–07. Volume 1.* London: The Stationery Office.

Koch, S. (1993) 'Restraining nursing home residents.' *Australian Journal of Advanced Nursing 11*, 2, 9–14.

Kwasny, P., Hagen, B. and Armstrong-Esther, C. (2005) 'Use of major and minor tranquilizers with older patients in an acute care hospital: An exploratory study.' *Journal of Advanced Nursing 55*, 2, 135–141.

Leadbetter, D. and Paterson, B. (2009) 'Towards Restraint-Free Care.' In R. Hughes (ed.) *Reducing Restraints in Health and Social Care: Practice and Policy Perspectives.* London: Quay Books.

Qureshi, H. (2008) *Narrative Literature Review on Restraint in Care Homes for Older People.* London: Social Care Institute for Excellence.

Retsas, A.P. (1998) 'Survey findings describing the use of physical restraints in nursing homes in Victoria, Australia.' *International Journal of Nursing Studies 35*, 3, 184–191.

Royal College of Nursing (RCN) (2008) *Let's Talk about Restraint.* London: Royal College of Nursing.

Strumpf, N.E., Evans, L.K. and Schwartz, D. (1990) 'Restraint-free care: From dream to reality.' *Geriatric Nursing*, May/June, 122–124.

Strumpf, N.E. and Tomes, N. (1993) 'Restraining the troublesome patient. A historical perspective on a contemporary debate.' *Nursing History Review 1*, 1, 3–24.

Strumpf, N.E., Robinson, J.P., Wagner, J.S. and Evans, L.K. (1998) *Restraint-Free Care: Individualized Approaches for Frail Elders.* New York: Springer.

Wang, W.-W. and Moyle, W. (2005) 'Physical restraint use on people with dementia: A review of the literature.' *Australian Journal of Advanced Nursing 22*, 4, 46–52.

Yorston, G. and Haw, C. (2009) 'Historical Perspectives on Restraint.' In R. Hughes (ed.) *Reducing Restraints in Health and Social Care: Practice and Policy Perspectives.* London: Quay Books.

PART I
Types of Restraint,
Patterns and Trends

Chapter 2

PHYSICAL RESTRAINT AND MEDICAL INTERVENTIONS

David Evans

INTRODUCTION

Physical restraint has long been used in health and social care to manage a range of challenging situations. Indeed, it has been such a universally accepted approach for the management of confused and aggressive people that it is only in recent times that its appropriateness has been questioned. This unquestioned acceptance has meant some older people have spent extensive periods of time tied to beds or chairs. While there has been a growing call to minimise or abolish the use of physical restraint it is still commonly used in many countries.

It is difficult to determine why physical restraint has become so entrenched in the delivery of care, particularly given that it conflicts with the philosophies of care espoused by all health and social care disciplines. Reasons for its use reported in the literature are varied and often relate to behavioural problems such as confusion, agitation and wandering. Strategies to manage aggressive behaviour have commonly included physical restraint, even though restraint will likely exacerbate the person's anger. However, restraint is probably still used by some staff because it has become a routine part of daily practice. It has become an easy way to manage a range of challenging clinical situations. There is even some suggestion in the literature that staff utilise restraint to be able to complete their duties (Evans and Fitzgerald 2002b). This is particularly important in relation to the management of people who are confused and would otherwise demand more attention than is available in busy health and social care settings.

Maintaining safety has also been commonly cited in both acute and residential care (Evans and Fitzgerald 2002b). However, research suggests that restrained people are more likely to be injured or have poorer outcomes than those people who are not subject to physical restraint (Evans, Wood and Lambert 2003). In fact published reports have linked restraint to injuries such as thrombosis (Hem, Steen and Opjordsmoen 2001), nerve

30

damage (Scott and Gross 1989), asphyxiation (Dube and Mitchell 1986) and death (Miles 2002; Parker and Miles 1997).

From a different perspective, reports in the literature describe the impact physical restraint has upon the restrained person and their family (Evans and Fitzgerald 2002a). One person described physical restraint as 'worse than a jail' (Strumpf and Evans 1988) and for another it was 'just like being harnessed up like a mule' (Hardin *et al.* 1993). Relatives have also made clear statements about restraint. One relative said 'I cried, then felt guilty' (Hardin *et al.* 1993) and another said 'When I saw the restraint, I lost all hope' (Newbern and Lindsey 1994).

It is therefore not surprising, given that restraint does not adequately protect against injury and has a harmful psychosocial impact, that there has been a call to minimise or abolish the use of physical restraint. As part of this interest in restraint minimisation, there has been a growing interest in ways by which challenging behaviour can be managed without having to resort to physical restraint. Initially, the focus of this interest was on the type of devices that were used, rather than on the act of restricting a person's right to freedom of movement. As a consequence there was considerable effort invested into finding more 'socially acceptable' methods of restraint. For example, restraining jackets, wrist restraints and shackles were replaced with such things as tables, sheets and beanbags. The use of bedrails continued, but they were considered to be safety devices rather than restraints. This initial activity highlights the poor understanding of the issues surrounding the use of physical restraint, and also the lack of suitable clinical guidelines and standards to help guide practice.

The search for more 'acceptable' methods of restraint has made it more difficult to determine what is and is not restraint. It is also more challenging to identify restraining devices, given that some devices such as tables and sheets also have legitimate roles in health and social care. Therefore the start point for this chapter is to define physical restraint.

DEFINING PHYSICAL RESTRAINT

Defining what physical restraint is and is not is difficult because restraint can encompass many different devices and interventions. The devices most readily recognised as physical restraint are those that immobilise a person by attaching to a limb, chest or waist and then secured to a fixed object such as a bed or chair. However, other devices restrict a person's movement rather than immobilise, as is done with bedrails. Restraint may also be achieved by confining the person to a specific area, such as by locking a door or through the confiscation of a walking aid or wheelchair. As noted in the introduction to this chapter, the effort to minimise physical restraint devices has resulted in utilisation of a range of different items as restraining devices. Examples of these include tables, chairs and sheets.

It is challenging to identify the boundary between a restraint device and safety device. For example, some staff may view bedrails as safety devices while others see them as a form of restraint. Bedrails have been excluded from studies of restraining devices in acute care (Minnick *et al.* 1998) and residential care (Burton *et al.* 1992; Karlsson *et al.* 1996). Chest restraints are sometimes used to aid posture because they provide support to a person's trunk while they sit in a chair. In this context it may be that they are more therapeutic than restraining. Some wheelchairs have seatbelts, which are generally considered to be a safety feature of the wheelchair. Seatbelts are also used in chairs to stop someone from tumbling from their chair. All these devices sit somewhere between a safety device and a physical restraint.

Furniture is also used to restrict the freedom of people. Reclining chairs and beanbags are sometimes used for older people because it is very difficult for frail individuals to leave the chair. 'Geritables' and lapboards are commonly used in care homes for a variety of legitimate reasons. However, they are also used on occasions to prevent the person from leaving their chair. Because these devices have very practical uses, it is difficult to assess the nature and reasons for their use. Bed sheets are sometimes used in a manner that restrains, or traps, a person's hands below the sheets. Yet sheets are also used for every person in hospitals and residential care in a manner that does not limit their ability to move. Despite the use of all these items to restrict the freedom of people, they are nevertheless a form of restraint.

During hospitalisation someone's mobility may also be restricted by medical devices that provide treatment, such as urinary catheters, wound drains, and intravenous and oxygen therapy. From this perspective, the individual in intensive care is subject to multiple types of restraint due to the invasive nature of their treatment. Similarly, someone may be secured to their bed by cardiac monitoring equipment and in orthopaedics people may be secured by traction. When medical devices are used for people who are confused or forgetful, wrist restraints are sometimes used to protect the integrity of the device and to prevent accidental removal. Sometimes the hands of people are bandaged in a manner similar to that of boxing gloves to prevent tampering with medical devices. At the far end of this spectrum of restraint, some older people are subject to manual physical restraint to force cooperation during procedures.

This discussion highlights the challenge of attempting to define what is and is not physical restraint because it is sometimes difficult to know where the boundary is between restraint and treatment or safety. The seatbelt can be viewed as a safety device, and so its use should be encouraged. However, it may also be a device that limits a person's freedom, and so should be discouraged.

Categorising what is and is not a restraining device is challenging and so there have been a number of definitions proposed. Early definitions of restraint focus on purpose-built devices, restraining vests, belts, harnesses, straps and shackles. These types of devices have been termed 'reportable' methods of restraint. Other methods of restraint using tables, beanbags, reclining chairs, sheets and bedrails have been termed 'non-reportable' methods (O'Connor et al. 2004). These non-reportable methods of restraint were ignored during early attempts to define restraint. However, failure to recognise non-reportable approaches to physical restraint means the prevalence of physical restraint is underestimated.

More recent definitions have taken a broader view of what constitutes physical restraint. These definitions have moved away from the device and focused on the intent of the staff involved. For example, Counsel and Care (2002) argue restraint is 'the intentional restriction of a person's voluntary movement or behaviour'.

The 'intentional' in this definition highlights the fact that physical restraint is a planned and purposeful act, rather than unconscious or accidental action (Royal College of Nursing (RCN) 2008). Another definition that expands on the concept of intent has acknowledged the diverse ways by which restraint may be achieved: 'any manual method or physical or mechanical device, material, or equipment attached or adjacent to the patient's body that he or she cannot easily remove that restricts freedom of movement or normal access to one's body' (Health Care Financing Administration (HCFA) 2000).

This change in focus has had an impact on evaluations of its use in health care. While earlier studies focused on reportable methods of restraint, more recent studies also acknowledge the non-reportable methods of restraint and so now provide a more accurate indication of physical restraint of older people in a range of care settings.

These definitions highlight the importance of focusing on the intent of the actions rather than the device that is used. The purposeful physical restriction of a person's freedom regardless of how it is achieved should be considered to be physical restraint. This focus provides a more appropriate framework for clinical practice, allowing for a more realistic categorisation of what is and is not restraint.

FORMS OF RESTRAINT

As discussed above, there are a range of devices that are used to restrain people who use health and social care services. Some devices are purpose built, while for other devices restraint is not their primary purpose. One approach to the categorisation of restraining devices is reportable and non-reportable methods (O'Connor *et al.* 2004).

Reportable methods of restraint refer to devices that are purpose built for the task of restraining or restricting the freedom of people and include restraint vests, belts and harnesses. This category of restraining devices is the most readily recognisable form of physical restraint. While such devices are found in a variety of forms, all fasten to a person's trunk or limbs and then are attached to a fixed object such as a chair or bed. Common forms that these devices take include:

- *Vest:* As suggested by the name, these restraints are worn like a vest, securing the person's trunk to a fixed object.

- *Belts:* These devices attach to the waist and so take the form of a belt.

- *Cuffs:* These devices are used to restrain limbs, forming a cuff around a wrist or ankle.

Non-reportable methods are those devices used to restrict the freedom of individuals, but that are not purpose-built restraint devices. This category includes:

- *Bedrails:* Bedrails restrict freedom by acting as a barrier for the person in bed. While commonly used to restrict the movement of people, bedrails are sometimes designated as a safety device rather than restraint.

- *Tables:* For the person sitting in a chair, a range of different tables and lapboards are used to create a barrier that prevents them from leaving the chair.

- *Beanbags and chairs:* While beanbags and recliner chairs provide a comfortable support for the frail elderly, their design also means it is difficult for the elderly person to exit without assistance. As a result, they are sometimes used as an alternative form of restraint.

- *Gloves:* Gloves, mitts and bandages around the hand serve as a form of restraint for preventing tampering with the medical device, dressings and wounds.

- *Linen*: Evidence suggests that linen and 'sleeping bag'-type pouches may sometimes be used in such a way as to secure a person in bed and so act as a form of restraint.

REPORTABLE RESTRAINT METHODS

Reportable methods of restraint are the most readily recognisable forms of physical restraint. While they are found in a variety of forms, they all fasten to a person's trunk or limb and then attach to a fixed object such as a chair or bed. Common forms that these devices take include vests, belts and cuffs.

Vests

These devices attach to the person's chest, and are worn as a vest. They are used for people in beds and chairs. The rationale for using these vests is sometimes given as posture support, because they help maintain an upright position while the person sits in a chair. Vests not only prevent a person leaving the bed or chair but also restrict the person's ability to change position. They are more commonly used in residential care than acute care settings. However, the great variability in practice makes it difficult to generalise. There have been numerous reports of injury associated with the use of vest restraints, particularly when they have been applied incorrectly (DiMaio, Dana and Bux 1986; Langslow 1999; Miles and Irvine 1992). Vest restraints have also been linked to brachial plexus injury (Scott and Gross 1989). A review of restraint-related deaths found vest restraints were the most common device involved (Ruben, Dube and Mitchell 1993). However, this may also reflect the frequency of their use.

Belts

These include a range of belts that attach to the waist of a person and then fasten to the sides or underneath a chair or bed. These devices not only prevent a person from leaving their bed or chair but also may limit a person's ability to change position. Seatbelts on wheelchairs fit into this category of restraint. Belt restraints are more commonly used in residential care than in acute care, and one study found that belts are the most common form of restraint when residents sit in a chair (Hamers, Gulpers and Strik 2004). Like other forms of restraint, belt restraints have been linked to various types of harm. One report described a large haematoma that developed on the trunk of a man following repeated use of a soft belt restraint to help support his posture and to prevent him from rising while he sat in a wheelchair (Landi *et al.* 2001). A study of reports of deaths related to restraint devices found that 18 per cent of deaths involved waist restraints (Ruben *et al.* 1993).

Cuffs

These are restraining devices that attach to limbs, most often the wrist. They are lightweight devices not intended to immobilise a person in their bed. They are more commonly used to restrict the movement of a single limb to protect medical devices such as airways, drains and intravenous therapy. Soft wrist restraints are the most commonly used device in the acute care setting (Minnick *et al.* 1998, 2007), particularly in environments such as intensive care (Choi and Song 2003). It has been suggested that, in intensive care, tying an individual's arms loosely to the bed frame is commonly used so that they are unable to use their arms but are still relatively free to move their trunk and legs (Nirmalan *et al.* 2004). In the past, this type of restraint also included leather shackles, used for people considered to be a greater than normal risk to staff or themselves. 'Four-point' restraint has been reported in the mental health literature, described as restraint of both the hands and wrists (Laursen *et al.* 2005). Like all other restraining devices, the literature has reports of harm associated with the use of wrist restraints. Their use has been linked to thrombosis (Steen and Opjordsmoen 2001) and pulmonary embolus following four-point restraint for a period of 13 days (Laursen *et al.* 2005). Ischaemic injury has been reported with the prolonged use of leather wrist shackles (McLardy-Smith, Burge and Watson 1986) and wrist restraints have been implicated with restraint-related deaths (Ruben *et al.* 1993).

NON-REPORTABLE RESTRAINT METHODS

Non-reportable methods of restraint are more difficult to detect because they are not purpose-built devices. It is sometimes difficult to determine if the device is being used for its legitimate purpose, or used to intentionally restrict the freedom of a patient or resident.

Bedrails

The most common devices used to restrict a person from leaving their bed are bedrails, which have long been part of acute and residential care practice. Bedrails are viewed by some as safety devices rather than restraints and so have been excluded from some restraint studies (Lever *et al.* 1994; Whitehead, Finucane and Henschke 1997). In addition, bedrails are also used as an aid for position changes by those recovering from illness, injury or treatment. However, they are also commonly used to restrict people to their bed and so they are another form of physical restraint. A study of four rehabilitation wards found bedrails were the most common form of restraint (Gallinagh *et al.* 2002). Bedrails have been linked to a number of deaths in the literature (Parker and Miles 1997; Ruben *et al.* 1993). One of the dangers with bedrails relates to the risk of the person becoming trapped between the bedrail and the bed, caught at the chest or neck (Miles 2002). There is also concern that bedrails may pose an additional risk for the person exiting their bed, and so may in fact increase the risk of a fall. If a person exits their bed by climbing over the top of the bedrail, then the height of a fall is increased. In relation to this, one study evaluated limiting the use of bedrails in a rehabilitation ward and found there was a reduction in the number of serious injuries and an increase in the number of minor injuries (Hanger, Ball and Wood 1999).

Tables

Various types of tables and lapboards are used in hospitals and residential care facilities during the delivery of normal care. Because these form a barrier, they are sometimes used to restrict the freedom of people. Given that they are not designated restraining devices and so not reportable, they are often excluded from evaluations of physical restraint. Their use is more common in residential care. One evaluation found that, of those residents restrained at the time of the study, geritables accounted for 29 per cent of the restraining devices (Karlsson *et al.* 1996). A Dutch study found that geriatric chairs with a table accounted for 36 per cent of the restraints used on the nursing home residents (Hamers *et al.* 2004). Anecdotal evidence suggests that in the acute setting bed-tables are sometimes used as a barrier in conjunction with bedrails, forming a barrier that encircles people and so increases the difficulty of leaving the bed. However, this also increases the risk of a fall for those who attempt to exit their bed. There is little information on injuries and deaths with the use of geritables and lapboards. This may reflect their safety, or it may be a consequence of them not being a reportable restraining device.

Beanbags and chairs

While beanbags and recliner chairs provide a comfortable support for frail older people, their design also means it is difficult for the people to leave the chair without assistance. As a result, they are sometimes used as an alternative form of restraint. There is also anecdotal information that chairs are used as obstacles besides beds to make it more difficult for patients and residents to exit their bed (Commission for Social Care Inspection (CSCI) 2007). However, the likely outcome of this would be a significantly increased risk to the person should they try to leave their bed. As beanbags, chairs and recliners are not reportable restraint devices they are often excluded from audits and investigations of physical restraint. As a result there is little reliable information on whether they are associated with any form of injury.

Gloves

A range of gloves, mitts and bandages are used to prevent people from tampering with medical devices, dressings and wounds. It has been suggested that wrapping hands in cotton bandages in the form of 'boxing gloves' is commonly used in intensive care areas because it allows free movement of the arms while restricting the use of the fingers (Nirmalan *et al.* 2004). The nature of gloves and mitts means their use is more common in acute care settings as a means of protecting treatments and equipment.

Linen

While there is little information in the literature, anecdotal evidence suggests that linen and 'sleeping bag'-type pouches may sometimes be used in such a way as to secure a person in bed and so act as a form of restraint. In this situation tight-fitting linen traps the person in their bed. However, given that linen is not a reportable restraining device and is used for all older people, this approach to restraint is not normally captured by investigations of restraint use. However, one study of four rehabilitation wards reported that they did not identify any blankets or sheets being used as restraints during the study (Gallinagh *et al.* 2002).

Removal of mobility aids

Restraint may also be achieved by the removal of mobility aids such as wheelchairs and walking frames. For those people dependent on such aids, their removal would severely restrict their freedom. However, given the nature of this approach to restraint, it is unlikely to ever be captured in evaluations of physical restraint use. It is therefore not possible to gauge how often this approach is used in health and social care, although it has been reported.

CONCLUSION

This chapter has highlighted the diversity in the approaches to physical restraint. There are a number of purpose-built devices that are still in use in the health care systems of some countries. However, there are also many other approaches to physical restraint that are more difficult to detect and so some of these will likely still be in use in all health systems. The critical issue that emerges from this difficulty of identifying what is and is not physical restraint is that it is the intent of health and social care staff to restrict the freedom of an individual, not the devices that are used to achieve the restraint.

REFERENCES

Burton, L.C., German, P.S., Rovner, B.W. and Brant, L.J. (1992) 'Physical restraint use and cognitive decline among nursing home residents.' *Journal of the American Geriatrics Society 40*, 8, 811–816.

Choi, W. and Song, M. (2003) 'Physical restraint use in a Korean ICU.' *Journal of Clinical Nursing 12*, 5, 651–659.

Commission for Social Care Inspection (CSCI) (2007) *Rights, Risks and Restraints: An Exploration into the Use of Restraint in the Care of Older People.* London: CSCI.

Counsel and Care (2002) *Showing Restraint: Challenging the Use of Restraint in Care Homes.* London: Counsel and Care.

DiMaio, V.J., Dana, S.E. and Bux, R.C. (1986) 'Deaths caused by restraint vests.' *Journal of the American Medical Association 255*, 7, 905.

Dube, A. and Mitchell, E. (1986) 'Accidental strangulation from vest restraints.' *Journal of the American Medical Association 256*, 19, 2725–2726.

Evans, D. and Fitzgerald, M. (2002a) 'The experience of physical restraint: A systematic review of qualitative research.' *Contemporary Nurse 13*, 2/3, 126–135.

Evans, D. and Fitzgerald, M. (2002b) 'Reasons for physically restraining patients and residents: A systematic review and content analysis.' *Journal of International Nursing Studies 39*, 7, 735–743.

Evans, D., Wood, J. and Lambert, L. (2003) 'Patient injury and physical restraint devices: A systematic review.' *Journal of Advanced Nursing 41*, 3, 274–282.

Gallinagh, R., Nevin, R., McIlroy, D., Mitchell, F., *et al.* (2002) 'The use of physical restraints as a safety measure in the care of older people in four rehabilitation wards: Findings from an exploratory study.' *International Journal of Nursing Studies 39*, 2, 147–156.

Hamers, J.P.H., Gulpers, M.J.M. and Strik, W. (2004) 'Use of physical restraints with cognitively impaired nursing home residents.' *Journal of Advanced Nursing 45*, 3, 246–251.

Hanger, H.C., Ball, M.C. and Wood, L.A. (1999) 'An analysis of falls in the hospital: Can we do without bedrails?' *Journal of the American Geriatrics Society 47*, 5, 529–531.

Hardin, S.B., Magee, R., Vinson, M.H., Owen, M., Hyatt, E. and Stratmann, D. (1993) 'Patient and family perceptions of restraints.' *Journal of Holistic Nursing 11*, 4, 383–397.

Health Care Financing Administration (HCFA) (2000) *Interpretative Guidelines for Hospital Condition of Participation (COP) for Patient's Rights.* Washington: HCFA.

Hem, E., Steen, O. and Opjordsmoen, S. (2001) 'Thrombosis associated with physical restraint.' *Acta Psychiatric Scandinavica 103*, 1, 73–76.

Karlsson, S., Bucht, G., Eriksson, S. and Sandman, P.O. (1996) 'Physical restraints in geriatric care in Sweden: Prevalence and patient characteristics.' *Journal of the American Geriatrics Society 44*, 11, 1348–1354.

Landi, F., Bernabei, R., Trecca, A., Marzi, D., Russo, A., Carosella, L. and Cocchi, A. (2001) 'Physical restraint and subcutaneous hematoma in an anticoagulated patient.' *Southern Medical Journal 94*, 2, 254–255.

Langslow, A. (1999) 'Safety and physical restraint.' *Australian Nurses Journal 7*, 2, 34–35.

Laursen, S.B., Jensen, T.N., Bolwig, T. and Olsen, N.V. (2005) 'Deep venous thrombosis and pulmonary embolism following physical restraint.' *Acta Psychiatric Scandinavica 111*, 4, 324–327.

Lever, J.A., Molloy, D.W., Eagle, J., Butt, G., *et al.* (1994) 'The use of physical restraint and their relationship to medication use in patients in four different institutional settings.' *Humane Medicine 10*, 1, 17–27.

McLardy-Smith, P., Burge, P.D. and Watson, N.A. (1986) 'Ischaemic contracture of the intrinsic muscles of the hand: A hazard of physical restraint.' *Journal of Hand Surgery 11*, 1, 65–67.

Miles, S.H. (2002) 'Deaths between bedrails and air pressure mattresses.' *Journal of the American Geriatrics Society 50*, 6, 1124–1125.

Miles, S.H. and Irvine, P. (1992) 'Deaths caused by physical restraints.' *Gerontologist 32*, 6, 762–766.

Minnick, A.F., Mion, L.C., Johnson, M.E., Catrambone, C. and Leipzig, R. (2007) 'Prevalence and variation of physical restraint use in acute care settings in the US.' *Journal of Nursing Scholarship 39*, 1, 30–37.

Minnick, A.F., Mion, L.C., Leipzig, R., Lamb, K. and Palmer, R.M. (1998) 'Prevalence and patterns of physical restraint use in the acute care setting.' *Journal of Nursing Administration 28*, 11, 19–24.

Newbern, V.B. and Lindsey, I.H. (1994) 'Attitudes of wives toward having their elderly husbands restrained.' *Geriatric Nursing 15*, 3, 135–138.

Nirmalan, M., Dark, P.M., Nightingale, P. and Harris, J. (2004) 'Physical and pharmacological restraint of critically ill patients: Clinical facts and ethical considerations.' *British Journal of Anaesthesia 92*, 6, 789–792.

O'Connor, D., Horgan, L., Cheung, A., Fisher, D., George, K. and Stafrace, S. (2004) 'An audit of physical restraint and seclusion in five psychogeriatric admission wards in Victoria, Australia.' *International Journal of Geriatric Psychiatry 19*, 8, 797–799.

Parker, K. and Miles, S.H. (1997) 'Deaths caused by bedrails.' *Journal of the American Geriatric Society 45*, 7, 797–802.

Royal College of Nursing (RCN) (2008) *Let's Talk about Restraint: Rights, Risks and Responsibility.* London: RCN.

Ruben, B.S., Dube, A.H. and Mitchell, A.K. (1993) 'Asphyxial death due to physical restraint: A case series.' *Archives of Family Medicine 2*, 4, 405–408.

Scott, T.F. and Gross, J.A. (1989) 'Bracheal plexus injury due to vest restraints.' *New England Journal of Medicine 320*, 9, 598.

Steen, H.E. and Opjordsmoen, S. (2001) 'Thrombosis associated with physical restraint.' *Acta Psychiatric Scandinavica 103*, 1, 73–76.

Strumpf, N.E. and Evans, L.K. (1988) 'Physical restraint of the hospitalized elderly: Perceptions of patients and nurses.' *Nursing Research 37*, 3, 132–137.

Whitehead, C., Finucane, P. and Henschke, P. (1997) 'Use of restraints in four Australian teaching hospitals.' *Journal of Quality in Clinical Practice 17*, 3, 131–136.

Chapter 3

COVERT MEDICATION AND CHEMICAL RESTRAINT

Carmel M. Hughes and Kate L. Lapane

INTRODUCTION

The use of medication in older people is a very common occurrence. Indeed, it has been described as one of the most common medical interventions experienced in this population. Medication is usually prescribed or purchased for the relief or control of symptoms in either acute or chronic medical conditions. Furthermore, as the evidence base grows, best practice indicates that for a number of medical conditions, e.g. hypertension and diabetes, more than one medication is required for optimal management and control.

However, medication has not always been used for positive benefits, and there has been a legacy of deliberate misuse of some drugs, notably those which facilitate control of behavioural problems that some patients experience. This has perhaps been best exemplified in the nursing or residential care environment in which some medications have been given to patients (usually known as residents) in order to sedate and subdue them. This deliberate misuse of these drugs has led them to be described as 'chemical restraints'. This chapter will outline the historical context relating to this situation with particular reference to institutional care, the types of drugs which have been used in this way, reasons for such usage, patterns and trends of use across the world, approaches to reducing the use of chemical restraints, and a final discussion on how policy and practice need to respond.

HISTORICAL CONTEXT OF CHEMICAL RESTRAINT USE

The use of medication is the mainstay of medical intervention in many patient populations, perhaps none more so than in older people. For those who live in institutional care, particularly nursing and residential care, prescribing of many drugs, sometimes described as polypharmacy

41

(Hughes *et al.* 2000), is the norm. Table 3.1 shows the average number of medications which have been reported to be prescribed in nursing home residents in a range of countries.

Table 3.1 The average number of drugs received by
nursing home residents in selected countries

COUNTRY	AVERAGE NUMBER OF DRUGS PRESCRIBED FOR RESIDENTS (RANGE)
Norway* (Ruths, Straand and Nygaard 2003)	5.0 (0–19)
Italy* (Bellelli *et al.* 2001)	4.3 (0–13)
Australia** (Snowdon, Day and Baker 2006)	6.84 (not reported)
Northern Ireland*** (Schweizer, Hughes and Curran 2003)	8.5 (0–25)
Republic of Ireland* (O'Grady and Weedle 1998)	4.1 (0–13)
Sweden*** (Bergman *et al.* 2007)	11.9 (not reported)

* not reported if regularly administered only or inclusive of when required (PRN)
** regularly administered only
*** regularly administered and PRN

In terms of medical conditions, residents will also have several active medical diagnoses at any one time, and this partly accounts for the prescribing patterns seen in Table 3.1. Many studies have highlighted the increasing prevalence of cognitive decline such as dementia (Alzheimer's Society 2007), neurological diseases such as Parkinson's disease (de Rijk *et al.* 2000), and mental health disorders such as anxiety and depression (Manthorpe and Iliffe 2006). A wide variety of medications are used to treat the underlying causes of some of these conditions, or some of the symptoms which may arise. In the case of dementia these symptoms can include a range of behaviours which can be viewed as disruptive in an institutional setting. Such behaviours may include anxiety, tension, irritability, wandering, verbal and physical aggression, extreme confusion and sleep disturbance (Ballard, Ayre and Gray 1999). These behaviours may be upsetting to other residents and difficult for staff to manage. A common response has been the use of medications which may control these behaviours, but this approach is now recognised as being inappropriate in many cases and this is illustrated in the case study below.

Case study: Pharmacologic approach

Problematic behaviour: Mary H. is an 88-year-old widow with Alzheimer's dementia. She has been in a nursing home for two months and, in the view of the staff, has been very disruptive. She shouts at staff and other residents, and has attempted to leave the home on two occasions.

Pharmacologic response: Doctors write half the medication orders as PRN, which means 'as needed', to be given at the nurses' discretion. A staff member could give her a psychoactive drug (chemical restraint) 'to calm her down', a frequent justification. The frequent use of the PRN order suggests that the nursing home staff intermittently suppress behaviour rather than treating it as a medical condition.

Many of the medications which have been used to control behaviour are classified as psychoactive or psychotropic. Examples of such drugs include antipsychotics, hypnotics and anxiolytics. Collectively, these drugs have been called tranquillisers. Specific examples are shown in Table 3.2. These drugs have legitimate uses in the treatment of a range of medical conditions which are also summarised in Table 3.2.

Table 3.2 Examples of psychoactive medications
and their licensed indications

DRUG CATEGORY	EXAMPLE	LICENSED INDICATION FOR WHICH THESE DRUGS MAY BE USED
Antipsychotics	Haloperidol, risperidone	Acute and chronic psychosis; mania; schizophrenia
Hypnotics (sedatives)	Nitrazepam, temazepam	Short-term use in insomnia (not more than 3 weeks)
Anxiolytics	Diazepam, buspirone	Short-term use in anxiety (2–4 weeks only)

Information on all medicines taken from the British National Formulary (2009)

However, the literature charts the use of these medications, notably in the nursing home setting, in which there appears to be no clear clinical indication as to why they have been prescribed. The frequency of hypnotic use has been reported to be between 23 and 34 per cent in the nursing home environment (Ingman *et al.* 1975; Kalchthaler, Coccaro and Lichtiger 1977; Morgan, Gilleard and Reive 1982). This is much higher than prescribing rates seen in older people who live in the community and, in fact, there appears to have been a decline in the use of these medications in the community over time (Stewart *et al.* 1989). Similarly, the use of antipsychotic drugs has been extensive in the nursing home setting with rates of up to 50 per cent being reported (Rovner *et al.* 1992) from the United States (US). Indeed, it was the many reports emanating from the US about these prescribing patterns and other concerns about the quality of care in nursing homes which led the US Congress to direct the Institute of Medicine to investigate care provision in its widest sense in this environment (Hughes, Lapane and Mor 1999). The resulting report, published in 1986 and entitled *Improving the Quality of Care in Nursing Homes*, highlighted neglect and abuse leading to premature death, permanent injury, increased disability and unnecessary fear and suffering on the part of many nursing home residents (Institute of Medicine 1986). The report highlighted the extensive use of psychoactive medications and suggested that the differential seen in nursing home residents and people living in their own homes in the community was due to these drugs being used as 'chemical restraints' to sedate and subdue residents, which was more convenient for staff. The report stated that 'understaffed facilities may make excessive use of antipsychotic drugs to substitute for inadequate numbers of nursing staff' (Institute of Medicine 1986).

In addition to the US, other countries have also reported potentially inappropriate use of these medications in older people in care settings. Snowdon *et al.* (1995) found that almost 60 per cent of residents in 46 nursing homes in the Central Sydney area were taking one or more psychoactive drugs (as previously defined), with antipsychotics more likely to be given to residents with great cognitive impairment and more disturbed behaviour; this percentage was among the highest reported in the world at that time. Although the authors did not undertake an analysis of the appropriateness of the prescribing of all of these drugs, they did report that haloperidol (an antipsychotic) was being used in the absence of a supporting clinical diagnosis. Psychoactive drugs have also been used in Dutch nursing homes; Van Dijk *et al.* (2000) reported that 74 per cent of residents from a total sample of 2355 residents in six homes were using these drugs, notably hypnotic agents. Although dosages were low, duration of use was in excess of the recommended time period of 30 days. A similar percentage of residents (73%) in nursing homes (or other types of care settings for older people) in one municipality in Sweden were also using one or more psychoactive drugs (Holmquist, Svensson and Hogland 2003). Again, as with the Australian study, there was a lack of documented diagnosis supporting the use of these medications in half of the cases and treatment had not been evaluated. It was also noteworthy that antipsychotic drugs were being used to treat depression, which is not appropriate. A Norwegian study (Ruths *et al.* 2003) found that prescribing of antipsychotic drugs in over 1300 residents accounted for the greatest proportion of medication problems and 50 per cent of antipsychotic prescriptions were considered to represent an inappropriate choice of drug. Studies in the United Kingdom (UK) have also highlighted excessive use of these drugs (McGrath and Jackson 1996; Oborne *et al.* 2002). In contrast to the US, studies in other countries have not explicitly stated that the use of these drugs effectively represents the implementation of chemical restraints, but the inappropriate use (in terms of choice of drug, lack of diagnosis or excessive duration of use) is recognised. However, reports from organisations such as interest groups, or government inquiries (outside the US), have been more damning in their condemnation. A report from the Joint Committee on Human Rights (JCHR) involving the House of Commons and the House of Lords in the UK which examined the human rights of older people in health care documented 'routine overmedication aimed at keeping older people docile in an effort to reduce staff workload' (JCHR 2007, p.173). This clearly represented the use of chemical restraints. The All-Party Parliamentary Group on Dementia (APPG) published *Always a Last Resort*, which examined the prescribing of antipsychotic drugs to people with dementia living in institutional care (APPG 2008). Again, over-prescribing of antipsychotics was found to be frequent. It was concluded that antipsychotics were prescribed as a way of managing behavioural symptoms such as aggression, shouting and restlessness in residents with dementia.

COVERT MEDICATION

It has also been reported that these drugs have been administered without the knowledge of residents and, on occasion, of their family members (Treloar, Philpot and Beats 2001). This is in the form of covert administration in which medicines have been concealed in food and drink. Current guidance from the main nursing professional organisation in the UK (the Nursing and Midwifery Council (NMC)) on covert administration states that the best interests of the patient or client are paramount and the general principle is as follows:

> As a general principle, by disguising medication in food or drink, the patient/client is being led to believe that they are not receiving medication, when in fact they are. The registrar will need to be sure that what they are doing is in the best interests of the patient/client, and be accountable for this decision. (NMC 2007, p.1)

The guidance also indicates that any decision must not be taken in isolation from the recognition or the rights of the person to give consent, and that in some cases the only proper course of action may be to seek the permission of the court to undertake covert administration (NMC 2007).

The practice of covert administration has been associated with potential abuse and this was reported by Treloar, Beats and Philpot (2000) based on findings from a cross-sectional survey study. Over 70 per cent of respondents (senior staff in nursing and residential homes and National Health Service (NHS) hospitals) stated that they had resorted to covert administration and it was often done secretly, with little discussion. A similar questionnaire was administered to carers who looked after an individual with dementia in the community. Most carers viewed this activity to be acceptable, but also indicated that consultation with a doctor on this issue should be undertaken (Treloar *et al.* 2000). The authors also noted that concealment using food and drink had potential clinical consequences for patients due to potential interactions with the drug or its formulation. Kirkevold and Engedal (2005) collected information from professional carers of patients from a sample of nursing homes and dementia units throughout Norway. For residents in nursing homes, 11 per cent had received medicines concealed in food and drink at least once in the previous seven days, while 17 per cent of people with dementia had been subjected to this form of administration. The practice was documented in 40 per cent of cases. Drugs which were most frequently administered in this way were anti-epileptics, antipsychotics and anxiolytics (Kirkevold and Engedal 2005).

CONSEQUENCES OF PRESCRIBING CHEMICAL RESTRAINTS

As with many drugs, side-effects may occur following prescribing of antipsychotics, hypnotics and anxiolytics. Gurwitz *et al.* (2000) examined nursing home records in 18 homes in Massachusetts, US, and noted that antipsychotics and hypnotics were most frequently associated with adverse events. These included over-sedation, confusion, hallucinations and delirium. Such effects can arise directly because of the pharmacological action of the drugs themselves, but there is extensive documentation to indicate that older people are more prone to the adverse effects of drugs. This may be attributed to age-related physiology and changes in the composition of the ageing body (Turnheim 2004).

It has also been documented that older people are more sensitive to drugs which act on the central nervous system, with chemical restraints exemplifying such agents (Ewing 2002; Kompoliti and Goetz 1998). Effects such as sedation and confusion can increase the risk of falls and, in frail nursing home residents, injuries sustained through falls can lead to further complications and death (Wagner *et al.* 2004; see also Nyman and Oliver, Chapter 15, this volume).

In addition to the side-effects that may manifest from the prescribing of chemical restraints, these drugs may also interact with other medications that nursing home residents may be taking. As shown in Table 3.1, residents may be receiving up to ten drugs, which increase the potential for interactions. For example, a resident may be taking cimetidine, which is used to treat gastric and duodenal ulcers. Cimetidine, by virtue of its chemical structure and how it affects the liver, can prevent the breakdown of other drugs. A case in point is temazepam (a hypnotic), which when given to someone who is also taking cimetidine will not be broken down and its pharmacological action will be more pronounced than would be expected. Therefore they will be more sedated and for a longer period of time. Thus the use of chemical restraints in addition to the other medication received by nursing home residents may lead to a number of drug interactions with serious consequences.

APPROACHES TO REDUCING THE USE OF CHEMICAL RESTRAINTS

There have been a number of approaches taken to reduce the use of chemical restraints. Perhaps the most adversarial is the legislative framework which governs nursing home care in the US which was a response to the Institute of Medicine report previously discussed.

The legislation, the Nursing Home Reform Amendment, is embedded in the Omnibus Budget Reconciliation Act of 1987 (hereafter known as OBRA 87) and was implemented in all US nursing homes in October 1990. The legislation broadly attempted to improve the quality of nursing home care through detailed regulations and standards, inspections and enforcement procedures, with the ultimate sanction being the closure of the nursing home (Elon and Pawlson 1993).

The regulations pertaining to prescribing recognise that there needs to be constant monitoring of the medication received by residents in nursing homes. Residents should not receive 'unnecessary drugs', which have been defined as those used in excessive dose, for excessive duration, without adequate monitoring, or without adequate indications for its use, or in the presence of adverse consequences which indicate the dose should be reduced or discontinued (Tessier 1993).

In relation to chemical restraints, there is a specific regulation which states that 'the resident had the right to be free from any psychoactive drug administered for purposes of discipline or convenience and not required to treat the resident's medical symptoms' (Health Care Financing Administration (HCFA) 1995). In terms of antipsychotic medication the nursing home must ensure that residents who have not used antipsychotic drugs before are not given these drugs unless such drug therapy is necessary to treat a specific condition. In the case of hypnotics and anxiolytics, guidelines are given on the situations in which these drugs can be used, at what dose and for what duration. Detailed documentation is required in resident notes to support prescribing decisions of any psychoactive agent in order to provide justification as to why such drugs are being used. The case study below illustrates a situation which might have led to the use of psychoactive medication for the behavioural problems exhibited, but a non-pharmacologic response is much preferable.

Case study: Non-pharmacologic approach

Problematic behaviour: Mary H. is an 88-year-old widow with Alzheimer's dementia. She has been in a nursing home for two months and, in the view of the staff, has been very disruptive. She shouts at staff and other residents, and has attempted to leave the home on two occasions.

Non-pharmacologic approach: The staff at the home speak with family members and find out that Mary sometimes demonstrated similar behaviour at home before moving into the nursing home. She seemed to respond well to music, so staff install a CD player in Mary's room and family members provide some CDs of Mary's favourite music.

The intensive legislative approach in the US has proved to be effective in reducing the prevalence of prescribing of these drugs and many studies (predominantly observational and retrospective in design) have documented the effect. Interestingly, no other country has replicated the US model, although it has been recognised that the use of these drugs for inappropriate reasons has taken place (Fahey *et al.* 2003; Hughes *et al.* 1999; Snowdon *et al.* 1995; Van Dijk *et al.* 2000). It has also been noted that, if the US regulations were applied to prescribing in some UK homes, these facilities would not meet the required standards (McGrath and Jackson 1996; Oborne *et al.* 2002). However, there are no specific requirements in relation to prescribing of psychoactive medication in UK nursing homes, and the standards which are in place relating to medication are quite generic (Department of Health 2003). There is an emphasis on policies and procedures, record-keeping, storage, administration, seeking advice from a pharmacist when necessary, monitoring residents on medication and initiating a review when required (Department of Health 2003). Similarly, Australia has issued national *Guidelines for Medication Management in Residential Aged Care Facilities* (Commonwealth Department of Health and Ageing 2002) which are very generalist in their approach. One standard in these guidelines encompasses safe administration and storage of medications, incident-reporting mechanisms, legible and available medication orders, and medication review on a regular basis, but there are no criteria laid down for appropriate prescribing for psychoactive medication (Commonwealth Department of Health and Aged Care 1998).

ARE CHEMICAL RESTRAINTS EVER JUSTIFIED?

If chemical restraints are being used simply for the convenience of staff, this could not be deemed as justified use. However, there may be circumstances in which someone is required to undergo an invasive procedure which may cause some distress, e.g. catheterisation, and the use of a chemical restraint may be helpful in ensuring that this procedure is carried out quickly and efficiently. There may also be clinical reasons as to why these drugs may need to be prescribed, e.g. a diagnosis which requires the use of an antipsychotic. Indeed, regulations in the US recognise that there may be occasions when residents could be a danger to themselves or to others (HCFA 1995), in which case prescribing of these drugs is justified. It is documented that 'these regulations...are not meant to cast a negative light on the use of psychopharmacological drugs (antipsychotics, hypnotics and anxiolytics) in long term care facilities' (HCFA 1995). Therefore, the point of the regulations is to encourage an investigation of the underlying causes of symptoms in residents and ensure review and assessment of the appropriateness and need of these drugs (HCFA 1995). The *underlying intent* in the use of these drugs is key. This is illustrated in the case study below.

Case study: A pharmacologic approach to behavioural problems

Problematic behaviour: A resident with a history of dementia and long-standing alcohol abuse was admitted to a nursing home. After a year passed, the woman's behaviour began to *escalate*, to the extent that she now would hit, kick, pinch and make verbal threats to staff when they tried to assist her. For several months staff members attempted various interventions to redirect her behaviour, but were unsuccessful.

Pharmacologic response: During a care conference, the woman's doctor ordered haloperidol (an antipsychotic agent) 0.5 mg be given to her twice daily. The resident was monitored on a regular basis for any adverse effects as a result of starting the medication and, after a week, the dose was reduced to 0.5 mg daily.

Source: Adapted from Williams 2005

Alternatively, depending on the individual and the behaviour manifested, it may be possible to avoid the use of psychoactive medication by using a strategy to distract the resident.

Case study: Non-pharmacologic approach

Problematic behaviour: Mary H. is an 88-year-old widow with Alzheimer's dementia, who attempted to escape from the nursing home every night 'to catch a train home'.

Non-pharmacologic approach: The staff at the home calmed her by telling her, 'The trains have stopped running tonight, but will resume service tomorrow.'

Source: Adapted from Forrest 1990

DISCUSSION

The use of chemical restraints has been a contentious issue, particularly in care homes for older people. Drugs which have been described as chemical restraints also have legitimate uses, and may be the first line of therapy for a number of serious medical conditions. However, as argued above, the use of these drugs to sedate and subdue older people for the convenience of staff represents major abuse. These drugs have been covertly administered (hidden in food and drink), and although covert administration may be permissible in situations where people may be at risk, this form of administration should be very carefully considered.

Approaches to reducing the abusive use of chemical restraints have been varied, from non-specific general guidelines on prescribing of medicines generally, to the adversarial legislation which has been enacted in the US. However, even this legislation appears to be insufficient in tackling the prescribing of these agents. A recent study from the US has reported the highest level of antipsychotic use in nursing homes in ten years (Briesacher *et al.* 2005). It was noted that these drugs (primarily the newer antipsychotics) were being prescribed outside of prescribing guidelines for the management of the behavioural and psychological symptoms of dementia for which they are not licensed. Then, in 2006, a Canadian group reported a point prevalence for antipsychotic use of 32.4 per cent (Rochon *et al.* 2007) while noting a marked variation between homes in the prescribing of these drugs. In the discussion section of the paper, the authors noted '*some environments being more **permissive** about antipsychotic use*' (p.682; emphasis added). This raises the question as to why some homes are more permissive than others, which has led to increasing interest in the role of organisational culture and how it may affect the quality of health care in this setting (Hughes *et al.* 2007).

The term 'culture' has entered the vernacular, but it does have a precise meaning in sociological terms. It has been described as the way things are understood, judged and valued. It encompasses the shared beliefs, attitudes, values and norms of behaviour within an organisation (Mannion, Davies and Marshall 2005). A lay definition which is sometimes used to explain organisational culture is 'the way we do things around here' (Drennan 1992). Svarstad, Mount and Bigelow (2001), using a validated instrument, surveyed US nursing home staff in 16 nursing homes on their views about psychoactive medication (antipsychotics, hypnotics and anxiolytics) and subsequently classified the home as having a resident-centred culture, a traditional culture or an ambiguous culture. The authors define a resident-centred culture as one which promotes individualised assessment of the resident, psychosocial care, multidisciplinary collaboration with other members of staff and other health and social care professionals, e.g. general practitioners (GPs), social workers, etc., and the avoidance of physical and chemical restraints. A traditional-centred culture promotes custodial care, use of physical restraints, use of psychoactive drugs and antidepressants, behavioural control and little collaboration between members of staff and other health and social care providers, e.g. GPs, social workers, etc. An ambiguous culture falls between these two categories. Although this type of classification may be considered superficially useful, the real challenge lies in moving all homes into the category of 'resident-centred' and it is unclear as to how this can be done. Training of nursing home staff on how to manage residents who may exhibit behaviour that is difficult to manage is certainly one way of lessening reliance on medication. Indeed, the APPG (2008) recognised that a lack of dementia care training for staff was one of the contributing factors to the inappropriate use of antipsychotics. The report from this group also noted that a high staff turnover and inadequate leadership may also contribute to excessive antipsychotic use. Much has been written about leadership in nursing, with patient dignity and respect being promoted by leaders in order to deliver best patient care (Kitson 2001). Although beyond the scope of this chapter, consideration needs to be given as to how to promote leadership in the nursing home environment as a means to changing culture and potentially leading to a greater focus on non-pharmacologic interventions.

CONCLUSIONS

The use of drugs in the form of chemical restraints in patients for the sole purpose of greater convenience for staff cannot be condoned. This chapter has reviewed the unfortunate legacy of misuse of such drugs in nursing homes for older people. Concern has been expressed over a number of years about this misuse and the US legislative response has been the most deliberate and focused attempt to eliminate the inappropriate use of these drugs. However, legislation is only one approach and may not be enough to prevent inappropriate usage. A greater consideration of more person-centred care interventions needs to be promoted within the nursing home environment, along with a change in the organisational culture of these services.

REFERENCES

All-Party Parliamentary Group on Dementia (AAPG) (2008) *Always a Last Resort: Inquiry into the Prescription of Antipsychotic Drugs to People with Dementia Living in Care Homes.* London: Stationery Office.

Alzheimer's Society (2007) *Dementia UK.* London: Alzheimer's Society.

Ballard, C., Ayre, G. and Gray, A. (1999) 'Psychotic symptoms and behavioural disturbances in dementia: A review.' *Review of Neurology 155*, suppl. 45, 44–52.

Bellelli, G., Frisoni, G.B., Barbisoni, P., Boffelli, S., Rozzinin, R. and Trabucchi, M. (2001) 'The management of adverse clinical events in nursing homes: A 1-year survey.' *Journal of the American Geriatrics Society 49*, 7, 915–925.

Bergman, A., Olsson, J., Carlsten, A., Waern, M. and Fastbom, J. (2007) 'Evaluation of the quality of drug therapy among elderly patients in nursing homes.' *Scandinavian Journal of Primary Health Care 25*, 1, 9–14.

Briesacher, B.A., Limcango, M.R., Simoni-Wastali, L., Doshi, J.A. *et al.* (2005) 'The quality of antipsychotic drug prescribing in nursing homes.' *Archives of Internal Medicine 165*, 11, 1280–1285.

British National Formulary (2009) *British National Formulary.* London: Royal Pharmaceutical Society of Great Britain and British Medical Association.

Commonwealth Department of Health and Aged Care (1998) *Standards and Guidelines for Residential Aged Care Services Manual.* Canberra: Commonwealth of Australia.

Commonwealth Department of Health and Ageing (2002) *Guidelines for Medication Management in Residential Aged Care Facilities*, 3rd edn. Canberra: Australian Pharmaceutical Advisory Council.

Department of Health (2003) *Care Homes for Older People: National Minimum Standards.* London: Stationery Office.

de Rijk, M.C., Launer, L.J., Berger, K., Breteler, M.M. *et al.* (2000) 'Prevalence of Parkinson's disease in Europe: A collaborative study of population-based cohorts. Neurological Diseases in the Elderly Research Group.' *Neurology 51*, suppl. 5, S21–S23.

Drennan, D. (1992) *Transforming Company Culture.* London: McGraw-Hill.

Elon, R. and Pawlson, L.G. (1993) 'The impact of OBRA on medical practices within nursing facilities.' *Journal of the American Geriatrics Society 41*, 2, 958–963.

Ewing, A.B. (2002) 'Altered Drug Response in the Elderly.' In D. Armour and C. Cairns (eds) *Medicines in the Elderly.* London: Pharmaceutical Press.

Fahey, T., Montgomery, A.A., Barnes and J., Portheroe, J. (2003) 'Quality of care for elderly residents in nursing homes and elderly people living at home: Controlled observational study.' *British Medical Journal 326*, 7389, 580–584.

Forrest, C.B. (1990) 'Nursing homes overuse drugs for restraint.' *New York Times*, 20 January. Available at www.nytimes.com/1990/01/20/opinion/l-nursing-homes-overuse-drugs-for-restraint-133090.html, accessed 6 November 2009.

Gurwitz, J., Field, T., Avorn, J., McCormick, D. *et al.* (2000) 'Incidence and preventability of adverse drug events in nursing homes.' *American Journal of Medicine 109*, 2, 87–94.

Health Care Financing Administration (HCFA) (1995) *State Operations Manual*. Baltimore, MD: HCFA. Available at www.cms.hhs.gov, accessed 6 November 2009.

Holmquist, I.B., Svensson, B. and Hogland, P. (2003) 'Psychotropic drugs in nursing and old-age homes: Relationships between needs of care and mental health status.' *European Journal of Clinical Pharmacology 59*, 8–9, 669–676.

Hughes, C.M., Lapane, K. and Mor, V. (1999) 'The impact of legislation on nursing home care in the United States: Lessons for the United Kingdom.' *British Medical Journal 319*, 7216, 1060–1063.

Hughes, C.M., Lapane, K.L., Mor, V., Ikegami, N. *et al.* (2000) 'The impact of legislation on psychotropic drug use in nursing homes: A cross-national perspective.' *Journal of the American Geriatrics Society 48*, 8, 931–937.

Hughes, C.M., Lapane, K.L., Watson, M.C. and Davies, H.T.O. (2007) 'Does organisational culture influence prescribing in care homes for older people? A new direction for research.' *Drugs and Aging 24*, 2, 81–93.

Ingman, S.R., Lawson, I.R., Pierpaoli, P.G. and Blake, P. (1975) 'A survey of the prescribing and administration of drugs in a long-term care institution for the elderly.' *Journal of the American Geriatrics Society 23*, 7, 309–316.

Institute of Medicine (1986) *Improving the Quality of Care in Nursing Homes*. Washington, DC: National Academy Press. Available at www.nap.edu/catalogue.php?record_id=6A6, accessed 6 November 2009.

Joint Committee on Human Rights (JCHR) (2007) *The Human Rights of Older People in Healthcare*. London: Stationery Office.

Kalchthaler, T., Coccaro, E. and Lichtiger, S. (1977) 'Incidence of polypharmacy in a long-term care facility.' *Journal of the American Geriatrics Society 25*, 7, 308–313.

Kirkevold, O. and Engedal, K. (2005) 'Concealment of drugs in food and beverages in nursing homes: Cross sectional study.' *British Medical Journal 330*, 7481, 20–23.

Kitson, A. (2001) 'Nursing leadership: Bringing caring back to the future.' *Quality and Safety Health Care 10*, suppl. II, ii79–ii84.

Kompoliti, K. and Goetz, C.G. (1998) 'Neuropharmacology in the elderly.' *Neurology Clinics of North America 16*, 3, 599–610.

McGrath, A.M. and Jackson, G.A. (1996) 'Survey of neuroleptic prescribing in residents of nursing homes in Glasgow.' *British Medical Journal 312*, 7031, 611–612.

Mannion, R., Davies, H.T.O. and Marshall, M.N. (2005) *Cultures for Performance in Health Care*. Milton Keynes: Open University Press.

Manthorpe, J. and Iliffe, S. (2006) 'Anxiety and depression.' *Nursing of Older People 18*, 1, 25–29.

Morgan, K., Gilleard, C.J. and Reive, A. (1982) 'Hypnotic usage in residential homes for the elderly: A prevalence and longitudinal analysis.' *Age and Ageing 11*, 4, 229–234.

Nursing and Midwifery Council (NMC) (2007) 'Covert administration of medicines: Disguising medicine in food and drink.' Available at www.nmc-uk.org/aDisplayDocument.aspx?documentID=4007, accessed 6 November 2009.

Oborne, C.A., Hooper, R., Li, K.C., Swift, C.G. and Jackson, S.H.D. (2002) 'An indicator of appropriate neuroleptic prescribing in nursing homes.' *Age and Ageing 31*, 6, 435–439.

O'Grady, M. and Weedle, P. (1998) 'A descriptive study of drug therapy and cost for elderly residents in a nursing home.' *Irish Medical Journal 91*, 5, 172–174.

Rochon, P.A., Stukel, T.A., Bronskill, S.E., Gomes, T. *et al.* (2007) 'Variation in nursing home antipsychotic prescribing rates.' *Archives of Internal Medicine 168*, 2, 676–683.

Rovner, B.W., Edelman, B.A., Cox, M.P. and Schmuely, Y. (1992) 'The impact of antipsychotic drug regulations on psychotropic prescribing practices in nursing homes.' *American Journal of Psychiatry 149*, 10, 1390–1392.

Ruths, S., Straand, J. and Nygaard, H.A. (2003) 'Multidisciplinary medication review in nursing home residents: What are the most significant drug-related problems? The Bergen District Nursing Home (BEDNURS) study.' *Quality and Safety in Health Care 12*, 3, 176–180.

Schweizer, A.K., Hughes, C.M. and Curran, M.L. (2003) 'Is psychoactive medication usage in care homes related to staffing levels?' *International Journal of Pharmacy Practice 11*, R42.

Snowdon, J., Day, S. and Baker, W. (2006) 'Audits of medication use in Sydney nursing homes.' *Age and Ageing 35*, 4, 403–408.

Snowdon, J., Vaughan, R., Miller, R., Burgess, E.E. and Tremlett, P. (1995) 'Psychotropic drug use in Sydney nursing homes.' *Medical Journal of Australia 163*, 2, 70–72.

Stewart, R., May, F.E., Moore, M.T. and Hale, W.E. (1989) 'Changing patterns of psychotropic drug use in the elderly: A five-year update.' *Drug Intelligence and Clinical Pharmacy 23*, 7–8, 610–613.

Svarstad, B., Mount, J. and Bigelow, W. (2001) 'Variations in the treatment culture of nursing homes and responses to regulations to reduce drug use.' *Psychiatric Services 52*, 5, 666–672.

Tessier, E.G. (1993) 'Evaluating Drug Therapy: Principles and Practices for Long-Term Care Providers.' In E.G. Tessier and G. Gaziano (eds) *Geriatric Drug Handbook for Long-term Care.* Baltimore, MD: Williams and Wilkins.

Treloar, A., Beats, B. and Philpot, M. (2000) 'A pill in the sandwich: Covert medication in food and drink.' *Journal of the Royal Society of Medicine 93*, 8, 408–411.

Treloar, A., Philpot, M. and Beats, B. (2001) 'Concealing medication in patients' food.' *Lancet 357*, 9249, 62–64.

Turnheim, K. (2004) 'Drug therapy in the elderly.' *Experimental Gerontology 39*, 11–12, 1731–1738.

Van Dijk, K.N., de Vries, C.S., van den Berg, P.B., Brouwers, J.R. and de Jong-van den Berg, L.T. (2000) 'Drug utilisation in Dutch nursing homes.' *European Journal of Clinical Pharmacology 55*, 10, 765–771.

Wagner, A.K., Zhang, F., Soumerai, S.B., Walker, A.M. *et al.* (2004) 'Benzodiazepine use and hip fractures in the elderly: Who is at greatest risk?' *Archives of Internal Medicine 164*, 14, 1567–1572.

Williams, L. (2005) 'Do you have the "right" to use a chemical restraint?' Available at www.the-freelibrary.com/Do+you+have+the+'right'+to+use+a+chemical+restraint%3F-a0130276071, accessed 6 November 2009.

PART II
Perspectives across Health and Social Care

Chapter 4

PENNSYLVANIA'S NON-RESTRAINT APPROACH to PSYCHIATRIC CARE and SERVICES

*Gregory M. Smith, Donna M. Ashbridge,
Aidan Altenor and Robert H. Davis*

THE PENNSYLVANIA STATE HOSPITAL SYSTEM

The Pennsylvania State Hospital System is the single largest provider of inpatient psychiatric treatment in the state. The system comprises seven government-owned and operated psychiatric hospitals; three forensic units designed to provide psychiatric evaluation and competency restoration to persons with active criminal charges; one treatment unit for adjudicated, juvenile sex offenders; and one nursing home which provides psychiatric care and treatment to people with medical or physical health needs. The hospital system, one of the oldest in the United States (US), is accredited by the Joint Commission on the Accreditation of Healthcare Organizations and is certified by the United States Centers for Medicare and Medicaid.

The structure and operating procedures for the state mental hospitals are defined in Pennsylvania law with the 1966 Mental Health and Mental Retardation Act and the 1976 Mental Health Procedures Act. These laws define the criteria for admission to a state mental hospital whereby an individual, 18 years of age or older with a primary psychiatric diagnosis, must be a danger to themselves or others within the past 30 days to qualify for a time-limited involuntary commitment.

The typical hospital unit comprises 30 beds and is supported on day shift by two licensed nurses, three to five aide staff depending on the type of the care provided, a social worker, psychologist and a psychiatrist who serves as the team leader under a medical model system of care. Other staff such as vocational, recreational, occupational, and physical therapists and a medical physician provide cross-unit coverage. Currently, the seven hospitals provide inpatient treatment to approximately 1750 people: 1400 under a civil commitment order, 220 under a forensic commitment, and

130 residents in the nursing home. Each year the system admits and discharges about 1500 people and approximately 56,000 days-of-care are provided each month.

Approximately 64 percent of the people served in the hospital system are men and 36 percent are women. The average age of those served is 42 and people aged 65 and older account for 17 percent of the hospital population. Schizophrenia and related psychotic disorders is the leading diagnosis of those served, accounting for 72 percent of the hospital census, and 50 percent have a co-occurring substance use diagnosis. People with a diagnosis of mental retardation or a developmental disability account for 10 percent of the hospital population and half of the hospital population have a length-of-residence of two or more years.

People hospitalized in the Pennsylvania State Mental Hospital System are provided with ongoing active treatment programs based upon their individual strengths, needs, and preferences. This individualized treatment approach is outlined in a plan that is designed by the person along with the treatment team to assist in a successful and sustainable discharge from the hospital. An integral component of Pennsylvania's efforts to instill a recovery approach to mental health care is the Community Support Planning (CSP) process. The CSP process is an intensified approach to outlining an individual's recovery plan based upon personal preferences, clinical needs and family involvement.

Over the course of the past 17 years the system has undergone a transformation whereby reliance upon hospitals has been replaced with the expansion of community-based services. In 1992 the first Community Hospital Integration Program Project (CHIPP) was funded to enable the discharge of people served in the state hospitals who had extended lengths of stay and/or complex service needs. Funding to support CHIPP placements involves a shift of state dollars from the hospital budgets to the local community mental health programs. CHIPP-funded opportunities since 1992 have facilitated the discharge of more than 4500 people from the state hospitals to their home communities at a cost of US $200 million annually. This initiative has resulted in the closure of more than 2400 state hospital beds system-wide and four state hospitals.

PENNSYLVANIA'S NON-RESTRAINT APPROACH

The recorded high-point for the use of seclusion in the Pennsylvania State Hospital System occurred in 1990 when more than 90,000 hours were reported. On any day during this year more than ten people were in seclusion around-the-clock. The peak year for the use of mechanical restraint occurred in 1993 when 140,000 hours were reported. On any day during that year more than 16 people were in mechanical restraint around-the-clock. These procedures were widely used and without regard for a person's age (Smith *et al.* 2005).

After 1990 the mechanical restraint and seclusion of people age 65 and older was an uncommon event and accounted for less than 5 percent of all seclusion or restraint events during that span. Current policy for the state hospitals does not preclude the use of these measures with an older person. However, even without specific policy safeguards for older people, the data show that from year 2000 through 2005 mechanical restraint was used only 24 times with people age 65 and older and this restrictive measure has not been used with anyone in this age group since 2005. The secluding of people in this age group has not occurred in the hospital system in ten years.

Throughout the 1990s the unscheduled use of medications given for psychiatric or behavioral indications was not limited or monitored and there were few restrictions on the types of devices that could be used to restrain people in crisis. Physical restraint use was rampant and no efforts were made to monitor or document its use. A "gang" or "all available staff" approach to crisis management was commonly used and was the accepted practice throughout the hospital system.

In 2008 the Pennsylvania State Hospital System used only 11 hours of seclusion and 120 hours of mechanical restraint. Six of the hospitals have discontinued the use of seclusion and half of the hospitals have gone a year or more without using mechanical restraint. Prone physical restraint is no longer permitted and floor restraint of any kind is prohibited. Any form of physical restraint is limited to a maximum of ten minutes after which time the person must be released.

The unscheduled use of medications for psychiatric indications is now limited to a STAT (*statim* or immediately) physician's order only. A physician must approve each use of an unscheduled medication for psychiatric or behavioral reasons (Smith *et al.* 2008). The state policy (Danville State Hospital 2006) that governs the use of these measures is the most restrictive in the US. The use of any restrictive measure is considered a treatment failure.

Pennsylvania's success at reducing and eliminating the use of these measures in its treatment of people with a serious mental illness served by the hospital system can be attributed to all of the following:

Leadership at all levels of the hospital system accounts for the most dramatic decreases in the use of seclusion and restraint during the early 1990s when it was commonly believed that these measures were necessary. Externally, this leadership came from people who have used these services in the past, family members and advocates, including local members of the National Association on Mental Illness and the Pennsylvania Mental Health Association, who were outraged at the rate at which these measures were being used. Initially, they focused their ire on the leadership of specific hospitals. It would take several years for families and advocates to become unified in their approach and direct their efforts at a system change within state government to reduce the use of these measures.

Internally, there were groups of workers (aide staff, nurses, doctors, psychologists, social workers) who challenged the status quo at each hospital regarding the pervasive use of restrictive measures. They advocated for better staff training and safer, more effective measures to support people in crisis (Smith *et al.* 2005).

Response teams involve bringing together a large group of people at the scene of a disturbance to control the person in crisis and has been a long-standing practice throughout the history of psychiatric health care. However, the practice in place at most state hospitals in Pennsylvania is a hybrid of this approach which has the specific purpose and goal of supporting the person in crisis in the least restrictive manner.

Psychiatric emergency response teams (PERT) accomplish this by being highly skilled at verbally deescalating a crisis situation and engaging the person in a therapeutic dialog. While all hospital workers are trained to react in a non-offensive manner to a psychiatric emergency, not all embrace this approach or are competent in its use. PERT team members are highly organized and provide a consistent, positive approach to a psychiatric or behavioral emergency. A successful PERT response is measured by the ability to calm an emergency situation without injury or the use of seclusion or restraint. PERT teams also assure compliance with state policies regarding the use of a restrictive procedure and ensure a thorough debrief post event (Smith *et al.* 2005).

Do-Not-Restrain Orders are used throughout the hospital system by physicians to protect people with a history of trauma or known medical conditions that exposes them to added risk of injury during a restraint event. These lists are reviewed monthly and shared with response team members and unit staff as an added precaution to prevent injury that could occur should a person with this kind of history go into psychiatric or behavioral distress. They involve a written order by a physician restricting or prohibiting the use of a restrictive measure for a specific reason such as trauma or a physical condition. This approach is frequently used with older people served by the hospital system. In those cases where people with special or complex needs present a significant risk of injury to themselves or others, the response team at the scene is more likely to use medication to assist the person to regain control if alternate strategies have failed. Additionally, for people with these conditions who have significant assault histories, the response teams will preplan and practice their approach to supporting this person in crisis.

Proactive Risk Assessments are used with people upon admission to a psychiatric hospital to determine their personal stressors and to hear from them what techniques work best in helping them regain control in a crisis situation. It involves a clinician meeting with the individual within the first few days of their admission to review a menu of activities where the person can identify the issues that cause them the most distress and how best to support them if they go into crisis. They can include soothing music, talking to a family member or friends, pre-selected comfort foods, and minor environmental changes, to name a few. This information is reviewed with nursing staff and response team members as part of a new patient case review. This information is also brought to the scene of a crisis to give team members talking points that can assist with helping the person regain control.

Debriefing and witnessing of psychiatric emergencies are critical elements of a successful seclusion and restraint reduction program. The patient debrief usually occurs within 24 hours of the restraint event or when the individual wants to talk about what happened. The goal of the debrief is to establish what caused the psychiatric emergency and what can be done to prevent the event from reoccurring. Staff debriefs usually occur within an hour of the incident and follow the same format of the patient debrief.

Debriefing of the individual and staff following a crisis situation provides valuable information on what caused the incident and what will prevent reoccurrence. A frequent debrief activity following a psychiatric emergency involves updating the individual's risk assessment to see if there were strategies not considered that could be used in the future to better assist the person in crisis. Witnessing is an effective tool for sensitizing staff at all levels of the hospital on the importance of effective crisis management.

Data collection and transparency of information on the use of seclusion and restraint in the hospital system did not evolve until the latter part of the 1990s. While basic information was collected on the use of these procedures going back to the 1980s, there is minimal evidence that it was being used to measure specific outcomes or the quality of care provided at the hospital.

It was not until the turn of the century that technology caught up with the practice and data systems could be used to demonstrate how harmful the use of seclusion and restraint was or how much psychotropic medication was being administered. Hospital risk management and performance improvement strategies are now working tools used to measure treatment outcomes and determine whether the people being served are receiving effective services. In addition, the quality of care in the hospital system is monitored by providing hospital workers with clinical alerts when patients exceed established treatment outcomes (Smith *et al.* 2005).

Finally, since 2001 the state hospital system has shared its data on the use of restrictive measures, and 30 other performance outcomes, each month with psychiatric health care providers worldwide. This transparency enables other systems of care to benchmark their local efforts with Pennsylvania while providing state hospital leadership with direction on areas in needed of improvement. The hospital system issues a risk management summary report each month that details its use of restrictive measures including other patient-related performance measures. This report can be accessed at the Pennsylvania Department of Public Welfare website (various dates).

CONCLUSION

As a result of the changes in practice in our state hospitals, we have seen reductions in assaultive behavior, injuries, and falls. These improvements, coupled with the reduced exposure to unnecessary psychotropic medications, benefit all who are receiving care. This includes older people who clearly are among the most vulnerable.

If we had to do it all over again, there is no doubt that we would have approached this move away from the use of seclusion and restraint with a greater sense of urgency. We would have listened more closely to people using the services and their families and advocates. We would have done much more to empower staff to do all they can to minimize and eliminate the use of the restrictive and traumatizing measures and to train them to work as a team using noninvasive techniques to support people in crisis. We would have used data to measure the quality of our care and shared it much sooner to ensure its effective use.

We are in absolute agreement with Ashcraft and Anthony (2008, p.1201) that "elimination, rather than reduction, of seclusion and restraint, is a legitimate goal" for all treatment settings. The empirical data which are publicly available provide compelling evidence to support this assertion. We have the technology, services, and supports which will enable and sustain this transformation of our service system. The continuing use of these interventions will only serve to traumatize recipients of our services and reinforce the stigma associated with these practices. As we embrace a recovery-supporting approach to clinical services, the use of seclusion and restraints as "clinical interventions" is being eliminated.

Acknowledgments

The authors wish to thank the Honorable Estelle B. Richman, Secretary, Pennsylvania Department of Public Welfare, and Joan L. Erney, Deputy Secretary, Office of Mental Health and Substance Abuse Services, for their support of this transformational initiative within the Pennsylvania State Hospital System. We also gratefully acknowledge the work and vision of Richard M. O'Dea.

Dedication

The authors dedicate this work to our Pennsylvania advocacy community, the families, former patients, and the thousands of workers in our hospital system who made significant contributions to Pennsylvania's non-restraint approach to psychiatric care and services.

REFERENCES

Ashcraft, L. and Anthony, W. (2008) "Eliminating seclusion and restraint in recovery-oriented crisis services." *Psychiatric Services Journal 59*, 10, 1176–1198.

Danville State Hospital (2006) *Use of Restraint, Seclusion and Exclusion in the State Mental Hospitals and the Restoration Center.* Danville, PA: Pennsylvania Office of Mental Health and Substance Abuse Services.

Pennsylvania Department of Public Welfare (various dates) *State Hospital Risk Management Summary Reports.* Available at www.dpw.state.pa.us/PartnersProviders/MentalHealthSubstanceAbuse/StateHospitals, accessed October 15, 2009.

Smith, G.M., Davis, R.H, Altenor, A., Tran, D. *et al.* (2008) "Psychiatric use of unscheduled medications in the Pennsylvania State Hospital System: Effects of discontinuing the use of P.R.N. Orders." *Community Mental Health Journal 44*, 4, 261–270.

Smith, G.M., Davis, R.H., Bixler, E., Line, H., *et al.* (2005) "Pennsylvania State Hospital System's seclusion and restraint reduction program." *Psychiatric Services Journal 56*, 9, 1115–1122.

Chapter 5

RESTRAINT: THE US NURSING HOME PERSPECTIVE

Beryl D. Goldman, Joan Ferlo Todd, Janet Davis and Karen Russell

INTRODUCTION

Historically, the use of physical restraints in skilled nursing facilities in the US was a long-standing practice in the care of older people. It was not until the mid-1980s that this practice was challenged by advocates who believed that restraint-free care leads to greater independence, the perpetuation of self esteem, and improved strength and stamina; all resulting in fewer incidences of depression, confusion, and slower rate of decline due to pressure ulcers, incontinence, muscle atrophy, and bone decalcification. What sustains this conclusion is the positive outcomes that are achieved when the care of older people is provided without the use of physical restraints regardless of their physical, emotional or cognitive abilities.

In 1986 the Kendal Corporation, a not-for-profit US long-term care provider, known for providing quality care without restraints, began a powerful journey to "Untie the Elderly®," presenting more than 200 programs in 35 states in the US and in Canada on the benefits of care without restraint. In 1989 Untie the Elderly and the US Senate Committee on Aging co-sponsored a Senate symposium on the elimination of physical restraints in the care of older people which created broad recognition and attention for this issue. Reduction in the use of restraints across the country has been largely attributed to the Untie the Elderly initiative and, later, through a Kendal-led subsidiary program in Pennsylvania which has reduced the use of physical restraints in long-term care from 28.6 percent to below 3 percent in that state. Subsequent federal legislation furthered the process of eliminating restraint use.

At a similar time, and due to public demands regarding poor quality of care in the nation's nursing homes, staff of the Centers for Medicare and Medicaid Services (CMS) visited Kendal. (The CMS, formerly known as Health Care Financing Administration (HCFA), administers Medicare, the nation's largest health insurance program, which covers nearly 40 million

US citizens. Medicare is a Health Insurance Program for people age 65 or older and some disabled people under age 65.) The purpose of the visit was to observe the philosophy in practice, and coming away convinced that it was not only possible, but imperative, for all providers to eliminate restraint use. Shortly thereafter, the Federal Omnibus Budget Reconciliation Act of 1987 (OBRA 87) altered the federal regulation. "The resident has the right to be free from any physical or chemical restraints imposed for purposes of discipline or convenience, and not required to treat the resident's medical symptoms" (§483.13(a)). The intent of this revised regulation is to "attain and maintain" each person's highest practicable well-being without the use of physical restraints.

While this paradigm shift in practice has resulted in significantly improved outcomes for older people, it has not been without expressed opposition from some staff and physicians who fear litigation if restraints are not implemented. They often express resistance based on concern about a lack of administrative commitment, lack of knowledge, poor teamworking among staff, staff shortages, and ingrained practices. This concern has been frequently addressed by state and federal agencies overseeing long-term care facilities, emphasizing the requirement that a professional, multi-disciplinary approach is mandatory to determine appropriate interventions on an individual basis. Critical to this collaborative decision-making is incorporating and valuing the input of older people and their family members through participation in care conferences and regular dialogue. Bringing them into the process is essential in reducing the potential for litigation against a facility.

The next section of this chapter presents a relatively newer consideration in restraint elimination – the use of bed rails in hospitals, nursing homes, and home care settings. The chapter concludes with a case study illustrating the importance of a comprehensive approach in looking at the total picture, rather than the "quick fix." The case study is a compilation of experiences reported by representatives of Untie the Elderly.

BED RAILS

The use of bed rails is a controversial issue in the care of older people. For the past 50 years, bed rails have been an integral part of nursing care. Bed rails are available in a variety of shapes and lengths. They may consist of one full-length rail per side or one or more shorter rails per side. Bed rails may be an essential part of the bed frame or removable, and can be a fixed height or adjustable in height, and may move as the head or foot sections of the bed are raised or lowered. Commonly used terms for bed rails include: side rails, grab bars, safety rails, safety sides, or cot sides. There is no universal standard for bed rail design. However, there is an international standard for the medical beds which addresses patient entrapment and identifies general safety requirements. The current medical bed standard is the International Electrotechnical Commission (1999) and a new edition to this international standard, the IEC 60601-2-52, will be published in 2010.

Bed rails serve many purposes. Using bed rails can help a person: turn in bed, provide a handhold for getting in or out of bed, offer a feeling of security, provide easy access to bed controls, or act as a restrictive device. Using bed rails has risks: strangulation or suffocation from entrapment between the bed rail and parts of the bed; more serious injuries from falls when patients climb over the rails; skin bruises, cuts, or scrapes; inducing agitated behavior when rails are used as a restraint; feeling isolated or unnecessarily restricted; and preventing patients who are able to get out of bed from performing routine activities such as going to the bathroom or retrieving an item in their room.

Bed rails are a restraint when it restricts the person's ability to exit the bed or freedom to move. To date, there is no scientific basis to support the efficacy of restraints in preventing injury to nursing home residents (Gutterman *et al.* 1999).

Reports of patient deaths and injuries related to bed rail entrapments to the US Food and Drug Administration (FDA) and in medical literature have cast a spotlight on the hazards of bed rails. Carer providers must re-evaluate the routine use of bed rails in providing care to older people. Between January 1, 1985 and January 1, 2009, the FDA received 803 incidents of people caught, trapped, entangled or strangled in hospital beds. The reports included 480 deaths, 138 nonfatal injuries and 185 cases where staff needed to intervene to prevent injuries. Most older people were frail or confused. The FDA, which regulates medical devices such as beds and their attachments (i.e., siderails), identified seven zones (Food and Drug Administration 2006) in the hospital bed system where there is a potential for patient entrapment. Entrapment may occur in flat or articulated bed positions, with the rails fully raised or in intermediate positions. The seven areas in the bed system where there is a potential for entrapment are identified in Figure 5.1.

Precautions to be taken to reduce bedrail entrapment (Todd 2008) include:

- Familiarize yourself with the seven zones in the hospital bed where entrapment can occur.

ZONE 1—ENTRAPMENT WITHIN THE RAIL

ZONE 2—ENTRAPMENT UNDER THE RAIL, BETWEEN THE RAIL SUPPORTS OR NEXT TO A SINGLE RAIL SUPPORT

ZONE 3—ENTRAPMENT BETWEEN THE RAIL AND THE MATTRESS

ZONE 4—ENTRAPMENT UNDER THE RAIL, AT END OF RAIL

ZONE 5—ENTRAPMENT BETWEEN SPLIT BED RAILS

ZONE 6—ENTRAPMENT BETWEEN THE END OF THE RAIL AND THE SIDE EDGE OF THE HEAD OR FOOT BOARD

ZONE 7—ENTRAPMENT BETWEEN HEAD OR FOOT BOARD AND THE MATTRESS END

Figure 5.1 Drawings of potential entrapment in hospital beds

Source: Food and Drug Administration 2006

- Don't automatically use bed rails. Base any decision about using or removing bed rails on an individual assessment.

- Establish an interdisciplinary group that will be responsible for evaluating existing bed systems (frames, mattresses, and rails) for entrapment risks and taking corrective maintenance and upgrading actions, as needed.

- Make sure that the bed frame, mattress, and rails are compatible with each other. Not all rails and mattresses are designed to work safely with every bed frame.

- Contact the medical bed manufacturer, your best source of information, about the safety of a bed and its accessories, including bed rails.

Case study: Avoid the "quick fix"

Anna (a pseudonym), an 88-year-old woman, was admitted into long-term care. She resides in a 30-bed dementia care unit. Anna has increased confusion and impulsive behaviors, occasional delusions, and episodic outbursts of aggressive behaviors and sundowning. Additional diagnoses include history of cerebrovascular accident with mild residual right-side weakness, history of multiple falls, depression, osteoarthritis, osteoporosis, history of cancer with ileostomy, and recurrent urinary tract infections. Despite her many problems, she often has good days when she is capable of ambulating with a wheeled walker under supervision. The care team determined she is at risk of bed rail entrapment due to her impulsiveness and restless behavior. Her bed rails were removed; she sleeps in a low bed with fall mat and personal bed alarm. The majority of her day is spent in the activity room where she participates in most recreational programs.

Anna has suffered six falls in four months.

April 30, 4:45pm   Found on the floor at the foot of the bed. "I was getting my car from the garage."

May 7, 11:00am   Found on the floor in the dining room. Anna missed the chair while attempting to sit down unassisted.

June 4, 12:50am   Found on the floor in her bedroom next to the bed. Did not know why she was getting up.

June 25, 12:20am   Found on the floor by the bed. "I'm done sleeping." Anna had removed personal alarm device.

June 28, 4:15pm   Witnessed by staff ambulating in living room without walker, she attempted to sit and missed the chair.

July 7, 2:40pm   Found on the floor in the living room, stated, "I missed the chair," pointing to a magazine rack.

Documentation indicated Anna was making attempts to stand and walk unassisted. Due to the ongoing falls and fear of significant injury, the interdisciplinary team made the decision to initiate a clip seatbelt. *This was a critical time for a comprehensive fall assessment. Restraint use should be the last resort.* Documentation related to the clip seatbelt included:

"Anna is very restless this shift and continues to attempt to stand with the seatbelt in place."

"Anna was observed this shift sliding down in her wheelchair attempting to go under the seat belt."

"Anna was found on the floor in front of her wheelchair, seat belt intact; apparently slid under it."

Based on her ability to get out of the seatbelt, a decision was made to use a full tray table attached to her wheelchair. Two days after the tray table was initiated, Anna overturned the wheelchair while attempting to stand. Even though there was documented evidence that described Anna's very unsafe behavior in the seatbelt, an even more restrictive device was put in place. The intention of staff was to create a safer environment but they were not recognizing that restraining Anna in the wheelchair was increasing her risk of more serious injuries as well as increased agitated behaviors due to her dislike of the devices.

It is interesting and important to note that the staff did recognize Anna's risk for entrapment in bed rails due to her impulsive and restless behaviors as well as the configuration of the rails available on the facility beds. A firm decision was made to eliminate all bed rails, place her in a low bed, and provide fall mats and a personal bed alarm.

Untie the Elderly guided staff in focusing their assessment on intrinsic and extrinsic risk factors that may have contributed to Anna's falls and behaviors as well as any trends, i.e., location, time, activity as they relate to incidents. Identifying individual risk factors facilitates the development of a care plan with specific interventions to promote or maintain her highest practicable level of function and well-being.

The areas assessed and interventions added to her care plan are:

1. Assistance with the toilet

- Review medication to identify meds that may contribute to urinary retention or frequency.

- Initiate personal care and "toileting" schedule with attention to higher risk times of day.

- Monitor ileostomy function, as a heavy bag may trigger restlessness.

2. Environmental comfort and safety

- Room temperature set to Anna's comfort.

- Lighting appropriate for time of day.

- Noise levels and odors are minimized (both trigger restless behaviors).

- Sharp furniture corners/edges padded.

- Bed height at level to promote safest transfer.

- Non-skid shoes and floor surfaces.

- Hip protectors to reduce risk for fracture.

- Illuminated call light for night-time use.

- Cooking-timer monitoring method implemented when Anna needs increased supervision, especially when initiating restraint reduction.

  o Directions: Set a cooking timer at 15-minute intervals. Timer is given to first staff person who monitors for 15 minutes, timer rings, is reset, and given to next staff person. Promotes equitable responsibility of staff and ensures supervision.

3. Right-sided weakness/unsteady gait

- Therapy screen for restorative program and range of motion.

- "Personalize" walker with large name plate or decoration to cue Anna to take it with her.

- Support bra for improved posture.

4. Vision (may be deficit from cerebral vascular accident)

- Schedule eye exam.

- Remove objects (i.e., trash can) that may be misinterpreted as seating.

- Adequate lighting.

5. Pain

- Pain assessment for the cognitively impaired; Anna has many "behavioral symptoms" of pain.

- Consider neuropathy as residual effect from the cerebrovascular accident.

- Provide heat and topical agents for osteoarthritis.

6. Medication review for side effects (medications include anti-anxiety, antidepressant, antipsychotic, and histamine receptor antagonists)

- Assess blood pressure for orthostatic hypotension.

- Assess sleeping patterns for possible insomnia/sleep disturbances.

- Assess voiding patterns for urinary frequency, retention, or dysuria.

Since the areas of assessment were completed and more interventions added (support hose, routine analgesic, antipsychotic was discontinued, new glasses), staff report noticeable changes in Anna including a decrease in restless behaviors, improved sleep patterns, and a steadier gait.

CONCLUSION

Documented evidence of psychological damage, severe injury, and death alerted providers, advocates, and regulators to the potential adverse effects of physical restraints that ultimately led to the dramatic reduction in their use in skilled nursing facilities across the US. Based on this understanding, leading experts in the field of restraint reduction have led organizations through a step-by-step, interdisciplinary team process that has and continues to maintain the dignity, self esteem, and empowerment of older people without the use of physical restraints.

REFERENCES

Food and Drug Administration (2006) *Hospital Bed System Dimensional and Assessment Guidance to Reduce Entrapment.* Rockville, MD: Food and Drug Administration. Available at www.fda.gov/MedicalDevices/ProductsandMedicalProcedures/MedicalToolsandSupplies/HospitalBeds/default.htm accessed 6 November, 2009.

Gutterman, R., Altman, R.D. and Karlan, M.S. (1999) "Report of the Council on Scientific Affairs: Use of restraints for patients in nursing homes." *Archives of Family Medicine 8,* 101–105.

International Electrotechnical Commission (1999) *Particular Requirements for the Safety of Electrically Operated Hospital Beds.* Geneva: International Electrotechnical Commission.

Todd, J. (2008) "Waking up to hospital bed entrapment risks." *Nursing 83,* 1, 14–15.

Chapter 6

ETHICAL DILEMMAS IN MAINTAINING ENTERAL FEEDING: THE USE OF HAND-CONTROL MITTENS

Jane Williams

INTRODUCTION

As a student nurse in the late 1970s it was commonplace to see older people with their hands padded and bandaged to prevent them from removing tubes or to use 'tip-back' chairs to prevent people from getting up and 'wandering' and, for those who were very restless, fitting such chairs with a table. It was purported that it was necessary to prevent the people from falling, harming themselves or missing essential treatments. During the intervening years restraint became increasingly taboo and I remember, during a conference I attended over ten years ago in the United States (US), being shocked at the range of physical restraints on display in the exhibition hall. I also remember entering into animated debate with some rehabilitation nurses from the US about their views. Notably the US physical approach was felt to be less harmful than the United Kingdom (UK) approach largely based on drug prescribing and sedation.

More recently, falls in hospital have emerged as a leading risk for older people in the UK. In my own practice, during the recruitment of registered nurses from the Philippines, it became clear that these nurses were very nervous when, in our local induction programme, we talked about the prevention and management of falls. To allow someone to fall was a grievous error in care and they could not understand how people might fall as the use of restraint was commonplace in hospitals in the Philippines. Furthermore, relatives are expected to provide basic care and to ensure that a family member is with the individual at all times. This level of support can help to ensure those who are restless are less likely to fall and less likely to remove or dislodge tubes and lines. These observations raise important questions about which kind of approach is most suitable: the use of sedation to calm individuals and render them incapable of removing tubes, the use of restraint to prevent people being able to reach or move, or the use of family members to watch over their loved one. There is no simple or single answer as complex ethical dilemmas and clinical practice are intertwined with cultural attitudes and personal beliefs. In this chapter I will use the example of working with older people who have had a stroke and their families to explore the use of restraint within acute hospital settings.

STROKE CARE

A stroke occurs when the blood supply to or within the brain is suddenly interrupted. The loss of blood supply leads to permanent damage and the size of the lesion correlates with the severity of the stroke. The development of the World Stroke Organization (www.world-stroke.org) is indicative that stroke is a global issue requiring international recognition and seeks to improve the care stroke survivors receive. Stroke is the leading cause of disability for many western nations. In the UK it costs the National Health Service (NHS) and economy £7 billion per year (Department of Health 2007). The evidence base for effective stroke treatment continues to grow apace across the spectrum of hyper-acute, acute, rehabilitation and long-term care components. People who have had a stroke frequently present with complex physical, psychological, cognitive and behavioural manifestations of the condition which may lead to dilemmas in the provision of treatment.

Within the acute phase of stroke care individuals are frequently restless with fluctuating conscious levels. Aphasia is a communication disability which occurs when the communication centres of the brain are damaged. It is commonly caused by stroke, but also by traumatic brain injury and tumours. Communication impairment with either or both receptive (understanding what is being said to you) and expressive (being able to speak the words you wish to) aphasia will be present in approximately one third of people who have had a stroke (Enderby and Davies 1989) which heightens the distress experienced by individuals themselves as well as their families. It is also estimated that dysphagia (impairment of swallowing) is present in 45–60 per cent of people immediately following a stroke and is associated with poor outcome in terms of survival or functional recovery (Gauwitz 1995; Hayes 1998; Odderson, Keaton and McKenna 1995; Wanklyn, Cox and Belfield 1995). Swallowing problems often resolve over the first or second weeks but some will be left with persistent difficulties (Smithard and Dias 1997) particularly in those with a brain stem stroke or with a history of previous stroke (Horner *et al.* 1991; Veis and Logemann 1985). Dysphagia may be severe and the provision of non-oral food and fluid may be required.

The Feed Or Ordinary Diet (FOOD; Dennis *et al.* 2005) trial, a major multi-national study, reported that early tube feeding is associated with a reduced mortality rate and improved outcome. The trial recommended people with dysphagic stroke should be offered enteral tube feeding via a naso-gastric tube within the first few days of admission. Tube feeding is associated with a range of problems, mechanical blockage, problems with intubation and confirmation of correct placement (National Patient Safety Agency 2005), trauma, gastro-intestinal problems and dislodgement. Naso-gastric tubes become dislodged very easily and people who are confused or have cognitive/perceptual impairments may pull the tube out frequently. Eisenberg, Spies and Metheny (1987) found that 41 per cent pulled out at least one tube. Meer (1987) also found that 40 per cent of people experienced dislodgement of the feeding tube, the majority (91%) being induced by the individual themselves. Ciocon *et al.* (1988) found an even greater number (67%) of people who are tube fed became agitated and self-extubated. The range and types of enteral feeding tubes have developed and fine-bore silicon tubes are more acceptable to the individuals than earlier larger tubes in terms of placement and long-term management but it continues to be acknowledged that naso-gastric feeding may be problematic (Pearce and Duncan 2002). A study undertaken by Quill (1989) in the US found 53 per cent of people had some form of restraint used on them to prevent dislodgement of the feeding tube.

The use of restraint is not generally considered acceptable practice in the UK and is negatively associated with elder abuse (O'Keefe *et al.* 2007). However, despite this, there remains very little discussion about the use of restraint as it relates to enteral feeding.

MANAGING PEOPLE WHO FREQUENTLY DISLODGE NASO-GASTRIC TUBES

People who have difficulties tolerating naso-gastric tubes, in combination with other tube management problems, will experience delays in completing the prescribed feeding regime and recurring problems will create cumulative nutritional deficits (Eisenberg *et al.* 1987; Norton *et al.* 1996; Rogers 1992). It is therefore imperative to ensure that the individual receives adequate fluid and nutrition to realise the best possible outcome for them by maintaining the placement of the naso-gastric tube. This places staff in the position of attempting to discourage people from dislodging their tubes, frequently having to re-pass the tubes and often managing the growing anxieties of relatives and carers who are aware of the importance of maintaining adequate nutrition.

A study exploring the 'feed or not to feed' decision-making process found nurses experienced considerable anxiety whilst managing the tensions associated in such circumstances (Williams 2003). Each clinician has their own views and experiences and may bring these into decision-making discussions for those in their care. It is difficult to suspend one's own thoughts and both nurses and doctors in the study recounted stories of either individuals or their relatives and carers who had faced dilemmas relating to feeding. It was apparent that such cases can be very challenging and can cause disagreement within a team. Using knowledge in this way might 'colour' the discussion and influence the decision through the way information is imparted to relatives. Clearly, tube feeding is charged with emotion and clinicians frequently find themselves in ethically sensitive situations regarding timing, discontinuation, cultural beliefs and personal experiences, both relating to their own lives and those they are caring for. These key themes from the study culminated in the development of a decision-making model centred on the need to share all types of information and knowledge between clinicians and relatives of people who have had a stroke and cannot be involved in decision making themselves.

EXPLORING THE USE OF RESTRAINT TO MAINTAIN TUBE FEEDING

There have been many alternatives produced that attempt to secure naso-gastric tubes; most have been unsightly and involve adhesive fixing systems or, in the past, suturing. The nasal loop has gained support in recent years (Williams 2005). This involves passing a tape internally up and over the nasal septum and securing it to the naso-gastric feeding tube. Whilst this procedure is effective for some it is not suitable for all as it is an invasive and uncomfortable procedure. An alternative method is hand-control mittens (Kee *et al.* 2006; Mahoney *et al.* 2006). These mittens are designed to restrict finger and hand movement and are simple to apply (see Figure 6.1). Mittens may be particularly beneficial with older people with cognitive impairments or altered conscious levels and those with brain injuries as the nasal loop may be unsuitable for these groups who might cause trauma to the delicate structures of the nose by continuing to pull at the tube whilst failing to recognise pain.

Another study explored the acceptability for use of these mittens in clinical practice in hospital (Williams 2008). The main focus of the project

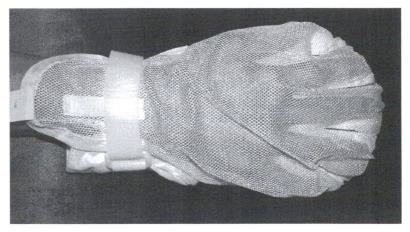

Figure 6.1 Hand-control mitten

was to explore opinions amongst those who have had a stroke and their carers and relatives and the use of various approaches employed to manage the problem of older people removing feeding tubes and their subsequent loss of nutrition. The central premise of the study was that hand-control mittens could have the potential to improve clinical care through the provision of optimal treatment, including enteral feeding, intravenous fluids and medication administration. In all cases people had removed at least two naso-gastric tubes. All family members were very supportive and agreed readily to the application of mittens. Interestingly, it was the physical appearance that caused most discussion and debate amongst staff, relatives and older people themselves. However, appearance was over-ridden by the family concern for ensuring optimal care was provided. One carer remarked: 'The appearance of the mittens is not relevant...life is far more important.' What became evident in this work was the need for a careful and thoughtful decision-making process coupled with clear communication, involving older people and their families and carers in that process. The implications of this work in practice are:

- Hand-control mittens have a place in clinical practice.

- Their use should be supported with clinical policy and guidelines that outline a clear, unambiguous decision-making process for staff to follow.

- Older people and their next-of-kin must be informed about the use of mittens and involved as fully as possible in the decision-making process.

- Staff require education and training to ensure appropriate use of hand-control mittens.

- Audit and evaluation must follow implementation.

CONCLUSION

Ethical dilemmas will always exist in nursing older people, but no objections to the use of hand-control mittens were raised in the studies cited. In fact, ethical dilemmas *should* exist, as they will challenge our practice and assist the avoidance of complacency in the provision of care to older people. The importance of clear clinical decision making and sound communication is pivotal in the reduction of emotional exchanges and will lead to more rational debate and culminate in the provision of optimal care for people.

At the core of any use of restraint in the acute hospital setting are the 'best interests' of the older person (Royal College of Nursing 2008). Nationally, the Mental Capacity Act 2005 serves to protect individuals who lack capacity to make decisions for themselves. It enables staff to take decisions on behalf of older people's best interests. Should any decision to use any form of restraint be made then it must be reviewed frequently (at *least* daily) to respond to the potential changing care needs of the individual. Above all, use of restraint must be open, discussed, disagreements aired, carefully planned and provided in order to minimise the risk to older people themselves as well as to staff.

REFERENCES

Ciocon, J.O., Silverstone, F.A, Graver, L.M. and Foley, C.J. (1988) 'Tube feeding elderly patients: Indications, benefits and complications.' *Archives of Internal Medicine 148*, 2, 429–433.

Department of Health (2007) *National Stroke Strategy.* London: Department of Health.

Dennis, M.S., Lewis, S.C., Warlow, C. and FOOD Trial Collaboration (2005) 'Effect of timing and method of enteral tube feeding for dysphagic stroke patients (FOOD): A multicentre randomised controlled trial.' *Lancet 365*, 9461, 764–772.

Eisenberg, P., Spies, M. and Metheny, N. (1987) 'Characteristics of patients who remove their nasal feeding tubes.' *Clinical Nurse Specialist 1*, 3, 94–98.

Enderby, P. and Davies, P. (1989) 'Communication disorders: Planning a service to meet the needs.' *British Journal of Disorders of Communication 24*, 3, 301–331.

Gauwitz, D. (1995) 'How to protect the dysphagic stroke patient.' *American Journal of Nursing 95*, 8, 34–39.

Hayes, J.C. (1998) 'Current feeding policies for patients with stroke.' *British Journal of Nursing 7*, 10, 580–588.

Horner, J., Buoyer, F.G., Alberts, M.J. and Helms, M.J. (1991) 'Dysphagia following brain-stem stroke.' *Archives of Neurology 48*, 11, 1170–1173.

Kee, K., Brooks, W., Dhami, R. and Bhalla, A. (2006) 'Evaluating the use of hand control mittens in post stroke patients who do not tolerate naso-gastric feeding.' Poster presentation to UK Stroke Forum Conference, Harrogate.

Mahoney, C.M., Rowat, A.M., Horsburgh, D., Taylor, P., Alder, E.M. and Dennis, M.S. (2006) 'The acceptability of interventions used to maintain naso-gastric feeding in acute stroke patients.' Poster presentation to UK Stroke Forum Conference, Harrogate.

Meer, J. (1987) 'Inadvertent dislodgement of nasoenteral feeding tubes: Incidence and prevention.' *Journal of Parenteral and Enteral Nutrition 11*, 2, 187–189.

National Patient Safety Agency (2005) *Reducing the Harm Caused by Misplaced Nasogastric Feeding Tubes.* London: National Patient Safety Agency.

Norton, B., Homer-Ward, M., Donnelly, M.T., Long, R.G. and Holmes, G.K.T. (1996) 'A randomised prospective comparison of percutaneous endoscopic gastrostomy and nasogastric tube feeding after acute dysphagic stroke.' *British Medical Journal 312*, 7022, 13–16.

Odderson, I., Keaton, J. and McKenna, B. (1995) 'Swallow management in patients on an acute stroke pathway: Quality is cost effective.' *Archives of Physical Medical Rehabilitation 76*, 12, 1130–1133.

O'Keefe, M., Hills, A., Doyle, M., McCreadie, C. *et al.* (2007) *UK Study of Abuse and Neglect of Older People: Prevalence Survey Report.* London: National Centre for Social Research and Kings College London.

Pearce, C.B. and Duncan, H. (2002) 'Enteral feeding. Nasogastric, nasojejunal, percutaneous endoscopic gastrostomy, or jejunostomy: Its indications and limitations.' *Postgraduate Medical Journal 78*, 918, 198–204.

Quill, T.E. (1989) 'Utilization of nasogastric feeding tubes in a group of chronically ill, elderly patients in a community hospital.' *Dysphagia 7*, 2, 64–70.

Rogers, P. (1992) 'Ensuring compliance in enteral feeding.' *Nursing Standard 6*, 5, 25–27.

Royal College of Nursing (2008) *'Let's Talk about Restraint': Rights, Risk and Responsibility.* London: Royal College of Nursing.

Smithard, D. and Dias, R. (1997) 'Subjective swallowing difficulties following stroke: A questionnaire survey.' *Clinical Rehabilitation 11*, 4, 350–352.

Veis, S.L. and Logemann, J.A. (1985) 'Swallowing disorders in persons with cerebrovascular accident.' *Archives of Physical Medical Rehabilitation 66*, 6, 372–375.

Wanklyn, P., Cox, N. and Belfield, P. (1995) 'Outcome in patients who require a gastrostomy after stroke.' *Age and Ageing 24*, 6, 510–514.

Williams, J. (2003) 'A relationship based "feed or not to feed" decision-making model for stroke care developed through a grounded theory.' PhD thesis, University of Portsmouth.

Williams, J. (2005) 'Using an alternative fixing device for naso-gastric tubes.' *Nursing Times 101*, 34, 26–27.

Williams, J. (2008) 'Exploring Ethically Sensitive Decision-Making in Acute Hospital Care: Using Hand Control Mittens in Adult Patients.' In T. Shaw and K. Sanders (eds) *Foundation of Nursing Studies Dissemination Series.* London: Foundation of Nursing Studies.

Chapter 7

DO WE NEED DRUGS? STRATEGIES TO REDUCE THE OVER-PRESCRIPTION OF DRUGS IN CARE HOMES SUPPORTING PEOPLE WITH DEMENTIA

Sheena Wyllie

INTRODUCTION

One of the many commonly held beliefs in health and social care is that the development of behavioural problems in people with dementia is inevitable, and all will become aggressive or anti-social due to their dementia. This belief is a myth, and one that can be easily dispelled in a community where antipsychotic drugs are only ever used as a last resort; truly meaning that all approaches have been initiated prior to the use of restraint and restraint is then only used for a short period of time.

Medication is traditionally seen as the solution to help 'aggressive' and anxious behaviours in people with a dementia. Whilst we would not decry the usefulness of medication, the risk is that they are reached for as the panacea and the person who may be communicating feelings through behaviour gets lost and essentially is restrained by chemicals. The drugs that have been designed to help are in fact damaging lives. Much has been written about the side effects of anti-psychotic medication and it does not make for a comfortable read. These side effects include an advance in cognitive decline, increase in the risk of stroke, excessive sedation and unsteadiness leading to higher risks of falls, as well as tremors, rigidity, body restlessness and a reduction in overall levels of well-being. In short the overuse of these medications is not only expensive in monetary terms, but also in the reduction of the individual's quality and length of life.

MEMORY LANE PROGRAMME

Barchester Healthcare has an extensive and varied portfolio of care homes across the United Kingdom (UK), Eire and United States. Memory Lane Communities and the Memory Lane programme have been created and developed to provide creative support for people experiencing dementia.

The Memory Lane programme could easily be viewed, from an initial look, as a traditional nursing home approach, and it may be reasonable to expect the same standard of care that is being experienced by older people in care homes across the UK. These experiences have at best been described as mediocre (Ballard *et al.* 2001). However, Barchester have challenged these expectations in an underpinning philosophy, beliefs and values of the whole home approach that has moved dementia care from the 'warehouse' to home. This approach takes person-centred care to the heart of service delivery. Evidence to support Memory Lane's approach is evident in the number of people being prescribed neuroleptic medication. In the UK it has been estimated that over 40 per cent of people in care homes receive neuroleptic medication (Dempsey and Moore 2005). In an average-sized Memory Lane Community this would mean there would be at least 12 people receiving these prescription medications – however, on average, only two people are prescribed neuroleptic medicines. In these exceptional circumstances the medication is offered as a part of the plan of care for the positive effects for each person rather than being used for control, management or compliance. In many care settings neuroleptics would be introduced at the first signs of any 'behaviours' that staff found challenging. Aside from producing negative side effects, such as cognitive decline and increase in falls (McShane *et al.* 1997), these medications are often used as a covert form of control or restraint to make the staff's lives easier.

IMPROVING SUPPORT IN PRACTICE FOR PEOPLE WITH DEMENTIA

The reduction in the use of neuroleptic medication through the Memory Lane programme has been in no small part due to the understanding of the whole team that all behaviour is seen as a form of communication. Individuals who are experiencing a dementia can display behaviours that challenge, but there is generally a reason and a deeper meaning to the ones that might be traditionally perceived. Behaviours stem from feelings which a person may not be able to verbalise due to cognitive decline – these feelings may be of anxiety, abandonment, loss or anger at feeling powerless and being controlled.

This understanding of individuals' behaviour needs also to come from everyone who provides support, including family, friends and partners as well as from the medical support team. This understanding underpins the unerring belief of the staff that providing a supportive environment and having a can-do approach has enabled people to live with their dementia and not just exist.

There is no one clear model of care that benefits living in a care setting, and the Memory Lane programme is a mixture of many different psychological approaches and therapies. These are fully explored with individuals with the aim of only ever introducing neuroleptics as a last resort, for the benefit of the individual and never for staff convenience.

The approaches employed include:

1. Adapting the environment to make more sense and give cues for the person experiencing a dementia.

2. Recognising and emphasising the importance of an individual's past life – life histories and emotional memories.

3. Staff 'connecting' with people, and being enabled to understand how to communicate in a meaningful way.

4. Providing life-skills and recreating individuals' past jobs, and supporting meaningful occupations.

5. Staff focusing on people's well-being, and finding ways to increase an individual's sense of feeling good about themselves.

6. Staff being able to 'see' the person behind the dementia, and understanding that behaviours need to be interpreted as feelings (Sheard 2008).

7. Having a home that provides comfort and a sense of belonging for individuals, and enables them to feel successful in their daily lives.

8. Staff live in the moment experiencing people experiencing a dementia, understanding and accepting each person's reality – going with the flow.

9. Focus given to supporting people in ways that ensure people experiencing a dementia feel safe and secure inside themselves.

10. Providing a real sense of freedom, and ensuring that people do not feel trapped, and are still in control.

These ten key points form the basis of the approaches within Memory Lane Communities, and are linked strongly to the person-centred work of

Kitwood (1997). These points are not meant to become rhetoric, but to be very real in the everyday lives of the people who live and work in the communities (Dementia Care Matters and Barchester Healthcare 2008).

SPECIFIC EXAMPLES OF SUPPORT IN PRACTICE

The environment

Having sensory spaces outside and the freedom to access these has been really successful in providing the stimulus to unlock memories and provide many pleasant moments. One of our Memory Lane Communities has created a seaside garden, within a courtyard. By making the effort to have sunhats, the sound of the sea playing in the background and team members focused on having fun with people, it has enabled some to describe memories of childhood holidays or holidays with their own families. Spontaneity is often the key to enabling people to be able to express themselves, no matter what their impairment (Alzheimer's Society and Pool 2007).

Pets in therapy

It is often the most simple things that can be the most effective. The therapeutic effect of pets in care homes is well known (Abdill 2000; Crawford and Pomerinke 2003). In one Memory Lane Community, the manager took her Labrador puppy into the Memory Lane, and the puppy's presence had the effect for all of providing the focus to express feelings and memories, both happy and sad. The presence, touch and appearance of this puppy was enough for one previously inactive and isolated gentleman to 'come alive'. As this puppy was placed on his knee and she snuggled into his neck, tears came into his eyes but the smile he had was wide. This simple act brought a meaning back to his life and from that day we managed to find a way to connect with him.

Well-being/ill-being

One last example that can, again, demonstrate the need to understand and interpret individuals' feelings and associated behaviour, and then connect with them, is with Sandra (not her real name), a person experiencing a dementia who had great difficulty in expressing herself through conversation. Sandra was living in a residential home that felt it could no longer meet her needs, as she was managing to get out of the home, going into other residents' rooms and taking and destroying belongings. She had been prescribed antipsychotic medication, and this had been increased over a number of weeks. On initial meeting Sandra could barely open her eyes, could not talk and was described by staff as being 'shell like'. Sandra soon came to live in one of the Memory Lane Communities and it was established in discussion with her daughter that Sandra had been a very glamorous lady and would not go out of her front door without her make up, scarves or a hat. Her daughter had not taken these to her last home as she believed Sandra would not use them. Sandra's daughter was asked to bring them in and also to be part of setting her room up with a mirror and having personal items visible and accessible. The medication was discontinued by the general practitioner and, after a couple of weeks of one-to-one encouragement, Sandra would sit at her mirror and apply her make up, add jewellery, scarves and other accessories and then, after checking her appearance, leave her room and come to the lounge with a big smile, especially if someone told her how nice she looked. Sandra continues to express herself by being supported in making choices that enhance her sense of well-being. She no longer seeks to leave the home or takes other people's possessions.

CONCLUSION

To move forward care homes need to see themselves as a community where everyone has a role to play in connecting with people experiencing a dementia. The focus needs to be on what an individual can do, and how we as supporters 'can make it happen'. The outcome of supporting individuals and not controlling or 'managing' people with dementia in a care home has led to prescribing less medication, maintaining people's mobility and independence, increasing their appetite and an overall increase in well-being for those living in, working in and visiting the home. The provision of a person-centred support programme and the reduction in the use of neuroleptic and debilitating medication is not new. But it does require determined effort and a focus on the individual's needs by the whole team. Our aim is to provide an environment that feeds the individual's spirit and enables the sense of freedom in which they can express themselves freely for who they are – in the moment and feel safe within themselves.

REFERENCES

Abdill, M.N. (2000) *Pets in Therapy: Animal Assisted Activities in Health Care Facilities.* Enumclaw, WA: Idyll Arbour.

Alzheimer's Society and Pool, J. (2007) *Guide to the Dementia Care Environment.* London: Alzheimer's Society.

Ballard, C., Fossey, J., Chithramohan, R. *et al.* (2001) 'Quality of care in the private sector and NHS facilities for people with dementia: A cross sectional survey.' *British Medical Journal 323*, 7310, 426–427.

Crawford, J.J. and Pomerinke, K.A. (2003) *Therapy Pets: The Animal–Human Healing Partnership*. New York: Prometheus Books.

Dementia Care Matters and Barchester Healthcare (2008) *Choosing a Care Home: What's Important for a Person Experiencing a Dementia*. London: Barchester Healthcare.

Dempsey, O.P. and Moore, H. (2005) 'Psychotropic prescribing for older people in residential care in the UK: Are guidelines being followed?' *Primary Care and Community 10*, 1, 13–18.

Kitwood, T. (1997) *Dementia Reconsidered: The Person Comes First*. Buckingham: Open University Press.

McShane, R., Keene, J., Gelding, K. *et al.* (1997) 'Do neuroleptic drugs hasten cognitive decline in dementia?' *British Medical Journal 314*, 7076, 266–270.

Sheard, D. (2008) *Being: An Approach to Life and Dementia*. London: Alzheimer's Society.

Chapter 8

THE THERAPY OF COMPANIONSHIP

Jim Ellis

INTRODUCTION

My wife spent her last four years of early onset dementia in a nursing home where I now work as a volunteer companion. I will draw on this experience substantially in developing a rationale for companionship before going on to discuss some therapeutic interventions. My position owes everything to those who have shown the efficacy of focused psychological care. Of particular interest is research that emerged as a response to the excessive use of neuroleptics for restraint in some nursing homes (Fossey *et al.* 2006). The researchers found that psychological care from trained care assistants could be as effective as neuroleptics in enhancing the well-being of residents.

We should not be surprised by these results since the need for a positive, supportive environment was explored in the pioneering work of Kitwood (1997), recently updated and expanded by Brooker (2007) in her detailed exposition of person-centred care. Her key aspects of care might be a guide for companionship when she writes of valuing people with dementia, recognising their individual rights and needs, appreciating their perspective and providing a positive social environment for them. Supplementing this position we have one which emphasises relationships as the key focus of care (Nolan *et al.* 2008), and Sheard (2007) stresses the importance of relationships, personal qualities and feelings when he characterises person-centred care as 'not something we do but something we feel'.

CONTEXT

I bring Sheard's two concepts 'feeling' and 'doing' together differently in saying that my residents make me 'feel' *as a result of* 'doing'. As I make my way into the lounge of the nursing home expectant faces look up as I acknowledge each one with a smile and a greeting. Many are silent but there are meaningful gestures. A resident waves from the far end of the lounge and as I make my way over to her another resident extends a trembling arm as if to say, 'Do come and hold my hand.' Even before I enter the lounge one resident greets me as he focuses on my bag. 'The bag. I saw the bag,' he says with a satisfied smile and I feel we are on the cusp of another therapeutic adventure.

PERSONALISED COMPANIONSHIP

My therapeutic interventions are part of an ongoing process rather than discrete events. To suggest this I have referred to my interventions as 'offering personalised companionship' (Ellis 2006). It is companionship in the sense that Martin Buber might have had in mind in his dictum 'All real living is meeting' (Buber 1937, p.11). For Buber this is not meeting in any formal sense, more a matter of two people coming together in close harmony and understanding. The relevance for companionship emerges further when Buber explains how one person might relate to another. One form of relating amounts to complete personal involvement, commitment and contact with the very being of another. Quite different is the other relationship marked by objectivity, coolness and engagement without commitment.

I have used 'personalised' to emphasise the quality of the relationship in terms of a person's biography, personality, interests, attitudes, indeed everything that makes each person unique. It is 'offered' because companionship cannot be forced. Sometimes a resident, perhaps more disgruntled and restless than usual, chooses not to engage. Yet he might not want isolation, so we compromise and sit in silence side by side while some kind of osmosis seems to flow and I can almost hear him saying, 'Please give me the peace of silence.'

THERAPEUTIC INTERVENTIONS

Many of our interactions follow a simple routine about personal health, the menu of the day, the weather. Some residents will remember their past and still have sufficient verbal ability to talk about it. Many have short-term memory loss and enjoy going through the same memories time and again. However, it seems important to extend the affective experience of residents as their world contracts. Activity sessions can be fulfilling but they are often pursued with groups of residents and are distinctly different from one-to-one situations arising from residents' declared interests and where the broader concept 'occupation' (Perrin 2002) might better describe the experience.

A particularly effective intervention with one resident arose from using a small portable DVD player for viewing songs from *The Sound of Music* as we sat side by side (Ellis 2007a). She pointed to and touched the screen, looking at me for approval with a breaking smile which I reciprocated. Overall her response was gently joyful but her mood changed appropriately for each song, suggesting a significant level of emotional understanding. Her right hand marked the rhythm and then it fell on my hand. As if compensating for a degree of aphasia she clasped my hand and we were united in rhythm as she carried my hand and hers to beat time. It was a bonding experience for both of us and a deeply felt experience for the resident where her non-verbal behaviour seemed to say, 'I feel and relate, and therefore, I am' (Post 2006, p.233).

The demands of personalised companionship are really tested when there is a discernible change in ability and interactions have to be modified to accommodate the change. We reverted to the tape recorder when the resident lost general awareness and failed to focus on the DVD. I referred to things in her childhood again and she responded appropriately. This is where the continuity of contact over time is qualitatively significant, allowing the companion to draw upon memories that were articulated by the person with dementia when speech was unimpaired.

The portable DVD player was successful with four or five residents but always on a one-to-one basis. Musicals worked very well and we were united even more when I attempted some 'sing along' with the occasional word or two from my companion. A DVD about famous British gardens fascinated a former teacher of botany and led to memories of plants, flowers and shrubs. This experience was extended with illustrated texts where my companion noticed some of the Latin names while admitting to having forgotten most of them as she ran her fingers down the lists of plants.

RHYMES, BOOKS AND PICTURES

Some stimuli need especially sensitive introduction. After developing an extended companionship with one resident, I felt that nursery rhymes might be a source of inspiration (Ellis 2007b). It would be quite inappropriate to impose nursery rhymes, if only for their possible demeaning effect, but again it proved possible to empower the resident as we entered our partnership. I referred to a broadcast I had heard where some mothers and their children knew no nursery rhymes. The resident said, 'Oh', with a little chuckle, and just as I said, 'Three blind mice', she started repeating it with me. Even more significant was 'The noble Duke of York', when she not only spoke some of the words but tapped out the rhythm on the table.

Equally effective has been the sharing of poems and humorous verse. The playful limericks of Edward Lear appeal to many with their repetition, rhythm, rhyme and humour; the accompanying illustrations are a further source of stimulation. The verses are particularly appropriate for my residents who often have a short attention span. Yet I feel even the briefest moments of stimulation take them on an imaginative excursion beyond their restricted world.

Companionship is very much a matter of sharing (Ellis 2007c) and a new series of books especially designed for people with dementia and their carers provide an effective catalyst for shared reminiscence (Bate 2006). The sharing requires positive listening and appropriate verbal restraint on the part of the companion. This was especially so with one resident who went methodically through one of the books initiating comments on several pages where she found links with her interests and experience. She was one of a tiny minority who were capable of holding the book and turning the pages, giving her a tactile, kinaesthetic experience as well as a visual one. One of the more articulate residents was particularly interested in a beautiful reproduction of a nineteenth-century painting showing a milkmaid, a solitary cow and a pail full of milk. He had milked cows by hand, he said, and it was easy. 'You just hold, squeeze and let go properly,' he chuckled. I was able to reciprocate with my own memory of being amazed when, as a young lad, I saw milking for the first time. We went on to share memories of hair cuts after looking at a picture of a mother cutting her son's hair. Keeping your hair short was important, he said, 'because it hangs on your shirt and makes it dirty'. It was a particularly enriching experience for both of us I felt. It became an especially poignant memory when this gentle, happy man died a few weeks later.

DISCUSSION AND CONCLUSIONS

The model described here is a simple one with three components: the resident, the companion and the content. It is a replication of what is taken to be everyday normal life when people meet fortuitously or by arrangement to chat informally. Yet the absence of occupation in nursing homes has been recognised in many reports and researches. Some nursing homes provide a stimulating quality of life and an environment of support and security for residents where activities make a significant contribution. However, the model described here is more difficult to achieve with its one-to-one relationship, long-term consistency and effective bonding between resident and companion. There are clearly implications for the number of staff and volunteers needed to implement an overall one-to-one programme.

The bonding arises partly from the nature of the language used. It is language of the affective domain, defined by Ward (2005) as 'giving out and responding to communication signals at the level of emotion' (p.29). Ward found in his sample of nursing homes that almost 80 per cent of language experienced by residents was functional, dealing with such things as washing, toileting, feeding. The category seems to be akin to one of Buber's relationships, characterised by objectivity and absence of personal commitment. The personalised companionship model thus becomes more than a psychological issue; it is essentially an ethical issue if people are being deprived of an essential feature in their lives. Companionship provides the context within which the most personal human emotion occurs, whether it be humour, nostalgia, regret or sadness. It is the safety valve of human life, especially the life of a person with dementia.

Some of the interventions described here have worked as a calming effect at a particular time but overall the ideal is prevention rather than cure. The principles of person-centred care must be consistent and ongoing so that a volunteer enters an existing ambience of support in the nursing home where residents are engaged in friendly interactions rather than watched from a distance. Residents will continue to be perceived as 'problems' where they are not engaged and stimulated and where little has been done to develop relationships such as we have in the companionship model.

REFERENCES

Bate, H. (ed.) (2006) *Pictures to Share*. Peckforton: Pictures to Share.

Brooker, D. (2007) *Person-Centred Dementia Care: Making Services Better*. London: Jessica Kingsley Publishers.

Buber, M. (1937) *I and Thou*. Edinburgh: Clark (original work published in German, 1923).

Ellis, J. (2006) 'Developing personalised companionship in a nursing home.' *Signpost 11*,1, 36–39.

Ellis, J. (2007a) 'Film viewing one to one.' *Journal of Dementia Care 15*, 5, 12.

Ellis, J. (2007b) 'Volunteer in a dementia-registered nursing home.' *Working with Older People 11*,1, 28–31.

Ellis, J. (2007c) 'Sharing pictures in a nursing home.' *Signpost 12*, 2, 33–35.

Fossey, J., Ballard, C., Juszczak, E., James, I., Alder, N. and Jacoby, R. (2006) 'Effect of psychosocial care on antipsychotic use in nursing home residents with severe dementia: Cluster randomised trial.' *British Medical Journal 332*, 7544, 756–761.

Kitwood, T. (1997) *Dementia Reconsidered: The Person Comes First*. Buckingham: Open University Press.

Nolan, M., Davies, S., Ryan, T. and Keady, J. (2008) 'Relationship-centred care and the "senses" framework.' *Journal of Dementia Care 16*, 1, 26–28.

Perrin, T. (2002) 'Activity, Occupation and Stimulation.' In G. Stokes and F. Goudie (eds) *The Essential Care Handbook: A Good Practice Guide*. Bicester: Speechmark Publishing.

Post, S. (2006) 'Respectare: Moral Respect for Lives of the Deeply Forgetful.' In J.C. Hughes, S.J. Louw and S.R. Sabat (eds) *Dementia: Mind, Meaning and the Person*. Oxford: Oxford University Press.

Sheard, D. (2007) *Being: An Approach to Life and Dementia*. London: Alzheimer's Society.

Ward, R. (2005) 'What is dementia care? An invisible workload'. *Journal of Dementia Care 14*, 1, 28–30.

Chapter 9

HEALTH AND SAFETY PERSPECTIVES

Stephen Clarke

INTRODUCTION

The provision of care to older people whose behaviour may be disturbed or challenging presents a dilemma to care staff. This dilemma occurs in respect of the *duty of care* owed to the individual using services as it contrasts to the *duty of care* owed to the provider of care by the employer. It has to take account of the ability, health and capacity of the individual, and may be complicated in the mind of staff by an emotional assessment that there may be no intent, or that the behaviour is an inherent part of the individual. These issues are further complicated in the provision of care of older people with reduced capacity, including people with dementia. Staff attitudes that 'they don't mean it', or recognition that 'it might be me one day', strongly affects the responses by staff in practice. However, how, and crucially why, staff respond can have a significant effect on their own well-being, both physical and psychological (Denney 2005; Paterson, Leadbetter and Bowie 1999).

It is therefore essential that staff realise that behaviour does not have to be intentional to pose a risk, and that management of the behaviour does not necessarily create blame. Perhaps replacing the terms 'violence' and 'aggression' with expressions such as 'inappropriate behaviour' or 'risk behaviour' would assist in this change of attitude. This would represent an important step in providing ethical care to those individuals who present with behaviour that may be especially difficult or challenging to deal with. It is also essential to ensure proper approaches, including policies and procedures, are in place to reduce the need to restrain older people.

UNDERSTANDING CHALLENGING BEHAVIOUR

Large numbers of people living in care homes have some form of dementia. In the UK, estimates suggest that two-thirds of all people living in care homes have some form of dementia (National Audit Office 2007). About one-third of care home places are registered to provide specialist dementia care (Commission for Social Care Inspection (CSCI) 2009).

> The challenging behaviour of older people with dementia and other impairments can be formulated as a communication of unmet need... this highlights the interactive nature of challenging behaviour. The responses of carers to challenging behaviour may be seen as mediated by the beliefs that carers have about the reasons for and appropriate responses to such behaviour. (Dagnan, Grant and McDonnell 2004)

The Royal College of Nursing (RCN) (2008) emphasise that the occurrence of 'the violent incident', in the sense understood in health and safety terms, is not so much the issue, as the existence of a range of 'violent' behaviour. Violent behaviour is widely defined and can include physical and non-physical behaviour (Department of Health 2001; McCreadie 2002; RCN 2008).

A clear understanding of what constitutes challenging and violent behaviour is a basic step in beginning to address this situation. The problem with words like 'disturbed' or 'challenging behaviour', 'violence' and 'aggression' is that they are subject to individual interpretation, based upon life experience and events the individual has encountered. One individual may interpret a behaviour as manageable, whilst another may find it extremely difficult. In the provision of care this interpretation may be affected by a normalisation process whereby behaviour that is encountered regularly becomes tolerated. Such tolerance can also lead to complacency or even bad practice. Staff need to understand that, although they may not personally feel threatened or at risk from a behaviour, others may. Any definition needs to take this into account and be supported through staff training and in management responses to incidents. This is particularly the case where the treatment of staff is in the form of singling individuals out at an emotional or psychological level. It can be the most serious behaviour in terms of long-term effects of stress on staff health and welfare (Paterson *et al.* 1999). These behaviours are also the most difficult for staff to describe, as they may have to reveal their own emotions when recording the incident. Physical and non-physical challenging behaviours can take many forms, as the examples in Table 9.1 illustrate.

ENSURING HEALTH AND SAFETY
The perspectives and care needs of older people and their families and carers and the duty of care that must be afforded to staff by their employers are two sets of issues raised within the context of an informed debate about

Table 9.1 Examples of physical and non-physical challenging behaviours

PHYSICAL VIOLENCE	NON-PHYSICAL VIOLENCE
Assault causing death	Verbal abuse
Assault causing serious injury	Racial or sexual abuse
Minor injuries	Threats (with or without weapons)
Kicking	Physical posturing
Biting	Threatening gestures
Punching	Swearing
Use of weapons	Shouting (or screaming)
Use of missiles	Name-calling
Spitting	Bullying
Scratching	Insults
Sexual assault	Innuendo
Deliberate self-harm	Deliberate silence

Source: Bibby 1995; see also Bibby 1994

the restraint of older people. Other chapters in this book examine the perspective of older people. Here I argue that if a violent or aggressive act were to be redefined as any behaviour that places staff at risk, either on a physical or emotional basis, without the apportionment of blame, strategies to manage the behaviour may be more forthcoming. It also places the behaviour in the realm of health and safety. Internationally employers have responsibility to ensure the health, safety and welfare of the employee. In the UK these responsibilities are enshrined in the Health and Safety at Work Act 1974 (Her Majesty's Government 1974). The Act specifies the employer's duty that has a particular relevance to the management of high-risk behaviours. These responsibilities include the:

- preparation of written policies covering the arrangements for dealing with foreseeable risks
- provision of a safe working environment
- provision of safe systems of work
- provision of information, instruction, training and supervision.

The Act also places important obligations upon employees. An employee must take 'reasonable care for the health and safety of himself and of others who may be affected by his acts or omissions at work' and 'as regards any duty or requirement imposed by his employer...to co-operate with him in so far as is necessary to enable that duty or requirement to be performed or complied with' (Her Majesty's Government 1974, section 7).

The Management of Health and Safety at Work Regulations (Her Majesty's Government 1999) place planning and knowledge in a legal perspective. Employers are responsible for ensuring suitable and sufficient assessment of:

- the risks to the health and safety of employees to which they are exposed whilst they are at work
- the risks to the health and safety of persons not in his employment arising out of or in connection with the conduct of the undertaking. (Health and Safety Executive (HSE) 2000)

Health and safety guidance indicates that this must include effective planning, organisation, control, monitoring and review (HSE 2006a). If the risks discovered identify the need to protect employees from exposure to reasonably foreseeable violence then appropriate steps need to be taken. The implications of this for the care of older people is that as soon as risk behaviour become obvious or foreseeable, then a risk assessment must be put in place. The principles underpinning risk assessment first require employees to consider who might be at risk (HSE 2006b). If an employee is at risk, then steps must be taken to remove, reduce or manage that risk. Those steps must include a plan that makes it clear to the employee as to how to deal with the individual, whilst still providing and meeting the care needs of the older person.

This leads on to the problem of recording and collating risk incidents. The Reporting of Incidents, Diseases, Dangerous Occurrences Regulations 1995 require the reporting of defined incidents (HSE 1999). This will involve all incidents that result in the loss of three or more days' work. However, this is a legal minimum and good practice suggests that all employers should have an effective reporting and recording system that allows them to respond to *all* staff safety incidents. If the reporting is linked to risk assessment employers will be better able to demonstrate 'due diligence' in law.

These health and safety considerations need to be understood within the context of care and services for older people, especially when older people exhibit disturbed or challenging behaviour (Berry 2006; Terri and Logsdon 2000). Berry (2006), for example, surveyed the extent and nature of aggression amongst people with dementia living in 197 care homes. The results from the care homes participating indicated that:

- 73 per cent had records of a person with dementia being verbally or physically aggressive in the past three months; 22 per cent reported more than ten incidences during this period

- 35 per cent reported that a member of staff had been injured as a result

- 89 per cent reported staff being distressed by people with dementia's behaviour and many staff suggested that the recorded incidences were the tip of the iceberg.

It is essential that employers create a positive reporting environment. It should be recognised that the information and patterns of behaviour identified by effective reporting following core health and safety principles creates a positive caring environment for both people using the service and staff. Such an approach helps to reduce unplanned and potentially inappropriate responses. To ensure this outcome, employers should have a clear 'violence at work' policy and a clear definition within their workplace of what violence means to an individual (HSE 2000). The policy and definition should be supported by training and instruction and upheld with strong leadership in the service.

The Healthcare Commission (2008) note insufficient reporting within health services, with many concerns about safety being left unaddressed:

A higher level of reporting, paradoxically, indicates a stronger culture of safety. It increases the potential for learning and the prevention of further harm. It is important that even incidents that lead to no harm are reported, so that risks, hazards and good practice can be identified before harm occurs. (Healthcare Commission 2008, p.36)

Once a clear reporting ethos is developed it is then possible to use the reports to establish a risk assessment strategy. Every report of violent or risk behaviour should lead to a risk review of the individual. This should be in addition to, or complement, detailed care and nursing plans. The risk assessment could be described as the staff safety assessment of the individual displaying the behaviours. It should include a plan which sets out staff responses and prevention strategies, enabling them to respond consistently to the individual and with confidence that they are responding in a manner that has been identified in consultation with older people themselves and their family members and carers as appropriate.

Behaviour management also relies on the clarity of information provided, and requires staff to have training and knowledge in areas such as conflict management, assertiveness, communication skills and defusing techniques. Such knowledge will include details and information on human responses such as body language and recognising the signs and symptoms of aggression, including its triggers and cues. Equally important here is that it should also encourage recognition of the needs of the individual.

Behaviour management also has to take account that the behaviour may not be in the moment. It could be as a result of an act which has just happened or, in the case of older people with dementia, relate to something that has happened in the past. Therefore it is important that reporting procedures describe what was happening at the time of the incident, what was happening prior to the incident, and how this might fit with the history of the individual. It should enable the identification of patterns of behaviour, so that the whole process is geared to avoiding creating situations and circumstances that lead to inappropriate behaviour. Staff need to foster good one-to-one relationships with those in their care, trying to understand the experience from the perspective of the older person (CSCI 2007). Unfortunately, life is more complex than it is possible to be able to record, therefore behaviour management cannot predict every eventuality. However, staff can be trained to be more aware of their own needs if they are supported by a positive management culture.

As soon as behaviour presents a challenge and a risk, it is necessary to consider how to respond to that behaviour. As indicated, it should primarily be about prevention. But, as many of the behaviours described are physical, it is also necessary that physical responses are considered as the last resort. Therefore staff need clear guidelines and policies as to what they can and cannot do and what should be referred to more senior staff.

All organisations providing care should have a physical intervention policy setting out their approach to aggressive or risk behaviour. It is not enough to state that the organisation has a non-restraint policy. Here I point out that restraint-free care is unattainable – there will always be situations when restraint may need to be planned and, as a last resort, employed.

What should be in place is a policy with clear information about how and when physical responses are appropriate and ethical. This will also require that staff have a level of appropriate training in this area. In the UK good guidance is given on this subject from the field of learning disability and provides advice and information on the use of physical interventions in different service settings (Harris *et al.* 2008). Resources from the field of learning disability are helpful in distinguishing between:

- *planned intervention*, in which staff employ, where necessary, pre-arranged strategies and methods which are based upon a risk assessment and recorded in care plans, and

- *emergency or unplanned* use of force which occurs in response to unforeseen events.

The scale and nature of any physical intervention must be *proportionate* both to the behaviour of the individual to be controlled and the nature of the harm they might cause. These judgements have to be made at the time, taking due account of all the circumstances, including any known history of other events involving the individual to be controlled.

The use of restrictive physical interventions should be minimised by the adoption of primary and secondary preventative strategies. Whenever it is foreseeable that an individual might require a restrictive intervention, a risk assessment should be carried out which identifies the benefits and risks associated with the application of different intervention techniques with the person concerned (British Institute of Learning Disabilities 2006). Where the use of self-harm prevention devices is indicated, staff should be fully trained in their usage.

CONCLUSION

The care of older people needs to be managed in an ethical manner, irrespective of the way individuals may act or behave. Care should also be delivered in ways that put older people at the centre of all decisions about their care. These principles should not conflict with, but should rather complement, the legal entitlements of staff. Health and safety principles and procedures need to be brought together with high quality care delivered to ensure that positive approaches to difficult behaviour are maintained. The principles and perspectives outlined in this chapter should provide a better understanding of the reasons underpinning an individual's difficult or challenging behaviour. In turn this will lead to an environment where staff are informed and prepared for situations which will enable them to act confidently, competently and consistently.

REFERENCES

Berry, R. (2006) 'Survey on challenging behaviour in care homes.' *Journal of Quality Research in Dementia 2*. Available at www.alzheimers.org.uk/downloads/Issue_2_May_2006.pdf, accessed 6 November 2009.

Bibby, P. (1994) *Personal Safety for Social Workers*. Farnham: Ashgate, in association with the Suzy Lamplugh Trust.

Bibby, P. (1995) *Personal Safety for Health Care Workers*. Farnham: Ashgate, in association with the Suzy Lamplugh Trust.

British Institute of Learning Disabilities (2006) *BILD Code of Practice for the Use of Physical Interventions: A Guide for Trainers and Commissioners of Training*, 2nd edn. Kidderminster: British Institute of Learning Disabilities.

Commission for Social Care Inspection (CSCI) (2007) *Rights, Risks and Restraints: An Exploration into the Use of Restraint in the Care of Older People.* London: Commission for Social Care Inspection.

Commission for Social Care Inspection (CSCI) (2009) *The State of Social Care in England 2007–08.* London: Commission for Social Care Inspection.

Dagnan, D., Grant, F. and McDonnell, A. (2004) 'Understanding challenging behaviour in older people: The development of the controllability beliefs scale.' *Behavioural and Cognitive Psychotherapy 32*, 4, 501–506.

Denney, D. (2005) 'Hostages to fortune: The impact of violence on health and social care staff.' *Social Work and Social Sciences Review 12*, 1, 22–34.

Department of Health (2001) *NHS Zero Tolerance Campaign.* Government campaign tackling violence against staff in the NHS.

Harris, J., Cornick, M., Jefferson, A. and Mills, R. (2008) *Physical Interventions: A Policy Framework*, 2nd edn. Kidderminster: British Institute of Learning Disabilities.

Health and Safety Executive (HSE) (1999) *A Guide to the Reporting of Injuries, Diseases and Dangerous Occurrences Regulations 1995*, 2nd edn. London: HSE.

Health and Safety Executive (HSE) (2000) *Management of Health and Safety at Work*, 2nd edn. London: HSE.

Health and Safety Executive (HSE) (2006a) *Violence at Work: A Guide for Employers.* London: HSE.

Health and Safety Executive (HSE) (2006b) *Five Steps to Risk Assessment.* London: HSE.

Healthcare Commission (2008) *State of Healthcare 2008.* London: Stationery Office.

Her Majesty's Government (1974) *Health and Safety at Work etc. Act 1974.* Chapter 37. London: Her Majesty's Stationery Office.

Her Majesty's Government (1999) *The Management of Health and Safety at Work Regulations 1999* (Statutory Instrument 1999 No. 3242). London: Stationery Office.

McCreadie, C. (2002) *Review of Research on Violence towards Social Care Staff with Special Reference to Services for People with Alzheimer's Disease: Research Review.* London: King's College London.

National Audit Office (2007) *Improving Services and Support for People with Dementia.* London: Stationery Office.

Paterson, B., Leadbetter, D. and Bowie, V. (1999) 'Supporting staff exposed to violence at work: The role of psychological debriefing.' *International Journal of Nursing Studies 36*, 6, 479–486.

Royal College of Nursing (RCN) (2008) *Let's Talk about Restraint: Rights, Risks and Responsibility.* London: Royal College of Nursing.

Terri, L. and Logsdon, R.G. (2000) 'Assessment and management of behavioral disturbances in Alzheimer's disease.' *Comprehensive Therapy 26*, 3, 169–175.

Chapter 10

HUMAN RIGHTS PERSPECTIVES

Rhidian Hughes

Where, after all, do universal human rights begin? In small places, close to home – so close and so small that they cannot be seen on any maps of the world. Yet they are the world of the individual person; the neighbourhood he lives in; the school or college he attends; the factory, farm or office where he works. Such are the places where every man, woman and child seeks equal justice, equal opportunity, equal dignity without discrimination. Unless these rights have meaning there, they have little meaning anywhere.
Eleanor Roosevelt
(Office of the High Commissioner for Human Rights 1997)

INTRODUCTION

Older people who use health and social care services are free to live their lives, doing as they wish within the law, unless their freedom to do so is constrained by legislation. In the broadest terms these principles are recognised by the 1948 Universal Declaration of Human Rights and associated covenants and treaties, such as the International Covenant on Economic, Social and Cultural Rights and the Convention on the Rights of Persons with Disabilities. In 1950 the Council of Europe established the European Convention on Human Rights and Fundamental Freedoms.

In most countries conventions are automatically enshrined in law. The United Kingdom (UK) is different, because its parliamentary process requires an act of parliament for human rights to be dealt with in its domestic courts. The 1998 Human Rights Act (HRA) was one of the first pieces of legislation the then new Labour government enacted, and it came into force in 2000. The HRA is a statute that enables human rights to be directly enforced in UK courts and provides the bedrock for all new legislation to be HRA compliant. It also makes it easy to take a human rights case to court in the UK – prior to the HRA cases were heard at the European Court of Human Rights.

In recent years human rights have been afforded increased attention in relation to health and social care services (Gruskin *et al.* 2005; Marks 2006), older people (Butler 2006; Harding 2005; Joint Committee on Human Rights 2007) and specifically restraint (Koch, Nay and Wilson 2006; Nay and Koch 2006). In Australia Koch *et al.* (2006) found that nurses reported considerable tension between protecting older people in care homes and preserving their human rights as individuals. Nay and Koch (2006) took forward a specific definition of restraint that conceptualises restraint in human rights terms rather than solely as a clinical issue.

This chapter considers the different types of human rights, before going on to look at some illustrative case examples of restraint through the human rights lens.

HUMAN RIGHTS IN HEALTH AND SOCIAL CARE

Fairness, respect, equality, dignity, autonomy, universality and participation are core values that underpin human rights. Whilst no one can have their human rights completely withdrawn, rights can be differentiated by their type:

- *Absolute rights* are fundamental and should never be restricted in any way, e.g. freedom from torture, inhuman and degrading treatment and punishment.

- *Limited rights* can be limited in strictly defined circumstances, e.g. right to liberty and security.

- *Qualified rights* can be qualified in the interests of proportionality in relation to the rights of others and wider societal interests, e.g. right for respect to private and family life.

Human rights are minimum standards, are the responsibility of the state and can require public bodies to:

- *respect* and refrain from infringing certain rights, e.g. right to life

- *protect* individuals from the actions of others, e.g. freedom from discrimination

- *fulfil*, to ensure human rights are positively incorporated into the reality of people's lives. (British Institute of Human Rights 2008)

The right not to be tortured or treated in an inhuman or degrading way: The case of mechanical restraint

The state has a positive obligation to protect individuals from infringements of absolute rights, including the prohibition of torture and inhuman or degrading treatment. One of the reasons staff give for using physical restraint is their concerns about the safety of older people (Koch *et al.* 2006; Nay and Koch 2006). A careful balance needs to be struck between risk and safety. Staff clearly face dilemmas between balancing safety and freedom in relation to the use of mechanical restraints (e.g. lap belts) to prevent falls, as indicated in the case study below. The example illustrates the kind of situation that might breach the right not to be treated in an inhuman or degrading way – defined as treatment which is humiliating and undignified – and illustrates the importance of staff seeking to work in ways that treat older people with the utmost dignity and respect.

Case study: Protecting dignity: Older woman strapped into her wheelchair against her wishes

A consultant came across an older woman on a hospital ward in London who was crying out in distress. The woman was in a wheelchair and when the consultant lifted up her blanket, she discovered that the woman had been strapped in and that this was why she was so upset. Staff explained that they had fastened her into the wheelchair in order to stop her walking around because they were fearful she might fall over and hurt herself. The consultant told staff that while their concerns were understandable, strapping her into a wheelchair for long periods was an inappropriate response because her human rights had not been taken into account. She pointed out that this could be considered degrading treatment given the impact on the woman. Staff quickly agreed to unstrap her and, after she was assessed by a physiotherapist, they were encouraged to support her to improve her mobility.

Source: British Institute of Human Rights 2008, p.6

The right to liberty: The case of 'best interests'

The right to liberty is a right which can be limited in strictly defined circumstances, such as to detain someone or ensure compliance with a medical treatment. In the UK recent mental capacity legislation makes illegal the restriction of someone's liberty of movement, regardless of whether they resist (2000 Adults with Incapacity Act (Scotland); 2005 Mental Capacity

Act (England and Wales)). Mental capacity legislation is particularly important in the care of older people who lack capacity, including people living with the moderate to advanced stages of dementia.

Mental capacity protection sets out how restraint should only occur to prevent harm to the person being restrained, and the amount and type of restraint, including the time it lasts, should be proportionate to the likelihood and seriousness of the harm needing to be prevented. Guidance is clear: restraint should not be used for convenience nor to ensure that someone can do something more easily (Department for Constitutional Affairs 2007). The European Court of Human Rights has identified a number of cases which have inappropriately deprived people of their liberty, as shown in the cases below.

Case study: Restraint and deprivation of liberty

- Restraint was used, including sedation, to admit a person into care who was resisting this measure.

- Professionals exercised complete and effective control over care and movement for a significant period.

- Professionals exercised control over assessments, treatment, contacts and residence.

- The person would be prevented from leaving if they made a meaningful attempt to do so.

- A request by carers for the person to be discharged to their care was refused.

- The person was unable to maintain social contacts because of restrictions placed on access to other people.

- The person lost autonomy because they were under continuous supervision and control.

Source: Department for Constitutional Affairs 2007, p.110

The right to respect for private and family life, home and correspondence: The case of electronic surveillance

The right to respect for private and family life, home and correspondence is broad ranging. A number of issues are relevant in health and social care in relation to restraint, including privacy, participation in recreational activities and independent living. It is a qualified right which may therefore be interfered with when serving lawful and legitimate purposes and – crucially – when actions are deemed proportionate.

There is a debate to be had about the use of electronic surveillance in the care of older people, including closed circuit television (CCTV) and tagging devices (Hughes 2008). Electronic surveillance is often discussed in relation to 'wandering', or persistent walking, associated with dementia that risks people becoming lost or being involved in accidents. It can be of great concern to people with dementia, their carers and professionals. However, it is important to recognise that walking can be an enjoyable experience for people with dementia and provides an important form of healthy recreation (Marshall and Allan 2006). A human rights approach, illustrated in the case study below, demonstrates the principle of proportionality and the importance of individualised care arrangements rather than blanket monitoring in care homes.

Case study: Privacy versus safety and the use of CCTV

A care home takes a decision to have a blanket policy of placing CCTV in the bedrooms of all residents, for safety reasons.

Outcome
This interferes with the right to respect for private life of all residents.

Alternative
A decision is made that only residents who pose a risk to themselves and/or others will have CCTV placed in their rooms. This decision will be made on a case by case basis.

Outcome
Some residents have their right to respect for private life interfered with for their own safety or the safety of others; other residents do not have their right to respect for private life interfered with.

Source: Department of Health 2008, p.14

Equality issues

The British Institute of Human Rights (2009) has raised concerns that the traditional equality strands – that is, race, sex and disability – are taken more seriously than human rights. They point out the additional benefits that a human rights framework can bring to attaining equality.

- Greater protection against discrimination: equality is integral to human rights and is a fundamental human right which prohibits discrimination on *any* grounds regardless of impairments older people may have.

- Protection against universally bad treatment: an important consideration with regards to the use of restraint and its close connection to institutional abuse of older people.

- Protection against other forms of ill-treatment.

- Discrimination legislation in the UK takes up issues in relation to specific equality strands whereas human rights adopts a truly holistic perspective.

Take, for example, attitudes faced by older people with dementia. They may typically be viewed by society as 'vulnerable', 'challenging' or those whose voices are seldom heard or listened to and can be seen as problems to be managed. In the later stages of dementia they may be regarded by society as 'non-persons' without the rights and attributes that full citizenship implies. When someone with dementia moves into a care home it can accentuate views that those with dementia are not full citizens and certain freedoms are not as important for them as they are to the rest of society. The human rights 'lens' shows how these kinds of views are unfair and discriminatory.

CONCLUSION

The abuses older people face tend to be more invisible to society when compared with other groups (House of Commons Health Committee 2004) and their invisibility is no less apparent in relation to human rights (Joint Committee on Human Rights 2007). A human rights focus in the care of older people, especially in relation to restraint, provides the bedrock to ensuring that people are treated with maximum dignity and respect, are fully involved in decisions about their care and are not subject to discrimination by virtue of age, impairment or any other factor.

A human rights approach provides a framework for practice which encourages staff to ask a number of questions about their practice, such as:

- Does this impact on anyone's human rights?

- If so, which rights and who do they belong to?

- How should my practice, decision or response reflect this? (Department of Health 2008)

The case examples presented in this chapter illustrate the importance of adopting a human rights approach to maximise outcomes for older people and avoiding the unnecessary and inappropriate restraint. However, the HRA – in the UK at least – has not provided the powerful catalyst for change that was expected as restraint still remains routinely used in many areas of health and social care practice.

REFERENCES

British Institute of Human Rights (2008) *The Human Rights Act – Changing Lives*, 2nd edn. London: British Institute of Human Rights.

British Institute of Human Rights (2009) *Human Rights and Equality.* London: British Institute of Human Rights.

Butler, F. (2006) *Rights for Real.* London: Age Concern.

Department for Constitutional Affairs (2007) *Mental Capacity Act 2005 Code of Practice.* London: Stationery Office.

Department of Health (2008) *Human Rights in Healthcare: A Short Introduction.* London: Department of Health.

Gruskin, S., Grodin, M.A., Marks, S.P. and Annas, G.J. (eds) (2005) *Perspectives on Health and Human Rights.* New York: Routledge.

Harding, T. (2005) *Rights at Risk: Older People and Human Rights.* London: Help the Aged.

House of Commons Health Committee (2004) *Elder Abuse: Second Report from Sessions 2003–04. Volume 1 – Report, Together with Formal Minutes.* London: Stationery Office.

Hughes, R. (2008) 'Safer walking? Issues and ethics in the use of electronic surveillance of people with dementia.' *Journal of Assistive Technologies 2*, 1, 45–48.

Joint Committee on Human Rights (2007) *The Human Rights of Older People in Healthcare: Eighteenth Report of Session 2006–07. Volume I – Report and Formal Minutes.* London: Stationery Office.

Koch, S., Nay, R. and Wilson, J. (2006) 'Restraint removal: Tension between protective custody and human rights.' *International Journal of Older People Nursing 1*, 3, 151–158.

Marks, S.P. (2006) *Health and Human Rights: Basic International Documents*, 2nd edn. Cambridge, MA: Harvard University Press.

Marshall, M. and Allan, K. (2006) *Dementia: Walking not Wandering – Fresh Approaches to Understanding and Practice.* London: Hawker.

Nay, R. and Koch, S. (2006) 'Overcoming restraint use: Examining barriers in Australian aged care facilities.' *Journal of Gerontological Nursing 32*, 1, 33–38.

Office of the High Commissioner for Human Rights (1997) *The Universal Declaration of Human Rights: A Magna Carta for All Humanity.* Geneva: Office of the High Commissioner for Human Rights. Available at www.udhr.org/history/Biographies/bioer.htm, accessed on 6 November 2009.

PART III
Issues and Innovations

Chapter 11

CLINICAL-ETHICAL CONSIDERATIONS ON THE USE OF PHYSICAL RESTRAINT

Chris Gastmans

INTRODUCTION

In caring for older people, it is sometimes necessary to carry out actions that limit their freedom of movement. Usually, this is done for reasons of good care; sometimes practical considerations or necessity play a part. Empirical research has given us a better idea of the prevalence, the reasons behind and the physical consequences of restraint use among older people. What is less well known are the psychological and social consequences of physical restraint use. Until now, the ethical values that might come into conflict when applying physical restraint have scarcely received any serious attention.

This chapter will identify certain values and norms which must be borne in mind in an ethical evaluation of physical restraint. These values and norms are the basis for a number of recommendations that can support staff in their clinical and ethical decision-making concerning physical restraint.

THE ETHICAL MEANING OF PHYSICAL RESTRAINT

The work of care providers always takes place in a human context. Consequently, there can always be conflicting expectations, desires and emotions at play. These are usually based on ethical values and norms upheld by those involved. In the effective provision of care services this means that conflicts can arise between the expectations, desires and emotions of the care provider and those of the other people involved. The following case is a striking example of this.

Case study: Mr Janssens

Mr Janssens has had a good life. An 82-year-old, he retired as a successful businessman almost 20 years ago. During those 20 years he has enjoyed numerous hobbies and contacts. Now he is in a hospital with advanced prostate cancer. Metastases already have affected the bone tissue and, because of a prolapsed vertebra, his legs are partially paralysed. There is nothing to be expected from cytostatics any more and the treatment focuses primarily on pain relief and preventing more fractures and decubitus. Doctors and nurses do not expect that he will live much longer.

Mr Janssens himself feels very tired and nauseous. In addition, because of the medication he is often drowsy and confused. In between, he is repeatedly rebellious, wants 'out', refuses to eat and resists care. Communication with him is scarcely possible. He often seems scared, looks bewildered and calls for his wife who died many years ago.

During a visit, his only son discovers that his father is tied to the bed with a Swedish belt. Outraged, he calls a nurse who tells him that this is necessary because Mr Janssens continuously wants to get out of bed. 'It would be really irresponsible to let him do this. He doesn't really know what he is doing, he would surely fall and break something and we cannot be with him all day! At night we secure his bed, just in case, because he is very restless!'

The son does not appreciate this. 'Of course he is restless if you tie him down! You cannot do that to somebody who has been active his whole life. Until recently, he was still living on his own. And he's been afraid of small spaces ever since he got stuck in a lift. I find this inhumane and I demand that you find some other solution. If he is allowed out every now and then, he will become more at ease.'

The nurse explains again that his father's level of consciousness, physical weakness and metastases in the bones require him to stay in bed. Finally, he promises to speak to the nursing team again.

The nurse judged the situation in the above case based first of all on the physical condition and the safety of Mr Janssens. For him, there did not at first appear to be a problem. He takes measures to restrict Mr Janssens' freedom, probably in accordance with the nursing standards and institutional guidelines for the protection and safety of people using health and social care services. Furthermore, he acted with a view to the quality of care considering the individual's safety. He believes the well-being of Mr Janssens will be improved by restraint use. Well-being he understands first of all to be an end of life that is as comfortable and painless as possible.

However, the measures taken by this nurse take place in a human context which means that other people may have a different opinion of well-being. This appears from the confrontation with Mr Janssens' son, who understands his father's well-being to be to protect him from bad memories of the past and to achieve as much freedom and independence as possible. Following the contribution from Mr Janssens' son, the situation suddenly does become problematic.

Apart from his physical disorders, Mr Janssens clearly expresses the problematic nature of his 'confinement to the bed' through rebelliousness, fear and signs of regression. Until recently, he had indeed been very active with many contacts in his environment. This experience contrasts strongly with his current situation. The stay in the hospital does not correspond with his personal history until that moment and he rebels against it, intuitively, as it were. That is further enforced by a negative experience in the past, namely, being stuck in a lift. A similar experience is triggered by the protective device on the bed. Mr Janssens' son knows the personal history of his father and therefore disagrees with the view of the nurse.

It appears that the nurse was not fully informed of Mr Janssens' personal history, or he considers it of secondary importance to the problem of his safety, which, in turn, is classified and resolved as a technical nursing issue. Mr Janssens' rebelliousness, protests and fears he considers are normal reactions and not at all something problematic. One could call this 'callous': because of the circumstances, the nurse overlooks the perceptions and experiences of Mr Janssens. It is only with reluctance that the nurse in the case is then willing to acknowledge the problem as perceived by Mr Janssens and his son.

The conversation with Mr Janssens' son reminds the nurse again that people's health must not be considered only from a medical-technical perspective but also from a broader perspective: health also relates to the general well-being of people. This latter perspective on health implies that the nurse is no longer the sole specialist; Mr Janssens' son is at least as much an expert as he is. The dialogue between both people breaks open the nurse's perspective, as a result of which Mr Janssens' well-being comes back into view. The nurse is then challenged to find out what can concretely be done to serve Mr Janssens' well-being best. This search process indicates that an ethical issue is also involved.

PSYCHOSOCIAL EXPERIENCES
As we saw in the previous section, there are differences in opinion about restraint use among the elderly in the hospital or in a home. This section

will briefly touch on the way restraining measures are experienced by older people themselves, their relatives and care providers (mainly nurses and geriatric staff).

Older people

Older people report mixed feelings about their experience with physical restraint (Gallinagh *et al.* 2001). For some, these methods (e.g. bedside rails or wheelchair bars) have a positive significance. They can lend a feeling of security and stability ('I feel safer with bed rails'). Dependence is not always experienced as something negative by older people. Many of them greatly appreciate the assistance being offered. One could say that in these cases there is a positive reception of care ('I don't feel that it really restricts me. I don't actually think about it much. If I want to stand up, they help me. But I need it for my pillows; otherwise my arm slides away. I think it's a good idea').

In general, however, physical restraint is not experienced as something positive (Gallinagh *et al.* 2001). On the contrary, in the experience of many older people, the use of these methods has more of a traumatic than a therapeutic character. This is accompanied by feelings of shame, loss of dignity and self-respect, loss of identity, anxiety and aggression, social isolation and disillusionment. Many older people express feelings of imprisonment ('I feel like a bird in a cage') and restriction of their freedom of movement ('I can't even bring my two hands together'). They worry about the possibility of injury in their attempts to escape from physical restraint. Others express feelings of depression and apathy concerning the use of these methods (Cohen-Mansfield 1986; Dawkins 1998; Evans and Strumpf 1989).

Relatives

From the limited research into the relatives' experience of physical restraint it can be seen that restraint is primarily associated by relatives with the idea of finality — a sense of the beginning of the end of life as these people had known it ('When I saw the restraint, I lost all hope'; 'Seeing the restraint makes it so real to me. It is so real, that we can never do the things we planned'). Restraint symbolizes the inevitably finite and limited nature of human life (Newbern and Lindsey 1994). Other meanings ascribed to restraint include: control of the situation ('I don't want him to fall'), denial ('if I don't see the restrictions on movement, then everything is all right'), anger ('I don't think they are doing it to help him') and disillusionment ('because of the restrictions, it seems as if he no longer has all his mental faculties'). Most of the relatives express the need for emotional support on the part of older people and their relatives.

Care staff

The application of physical restraint brings about a certain structure. The failure to apply these methods of restraint would put this structure at risk, increasing the chance of chaos (Fairman and Happ 1998). This has led to a situation where the application of restraint has, in certain circumstances, become a kind of ritual which rather meets the needs of staff for a fixed structure than older people's therapeutic needs.

In addition, staff often have the impression that applying methods of restraint affords them a measure of control over older people; they experience it as a way of maintaining order (O'Connor 1998). It is noteworthy in this respect that some staff use a child-like language to structure the experience of older people. This sort of approach is often regarded by older people as a humiliating experience (infantilization) and is often intended to sustain existing relations of power (Van Dongen 1997).

For some staff, the application of physical restraint gives the feeling that they can escape legal proceedings (Janelli, Dickerson and Ventura 1995). Nevertheless, various inner conflicts can also be observed among carers, such as frustration, ambivalence and feelings of guilt about the use of physical restraint (Lamb et al. 1999; Lee et al. 1999; Quinn 1993).

These emotions can play an important role in identifying and assessing ethically irresponsible situations. For instance, the application of restraining measures on people with dementia without considering a greater sense of well-being induces aversion. Precisely that emotion leads us to define the problem in ethical terms. Yet, the discussion of ethical problems must exceed the level of emotions. We must evolve to the level of ethical arguments, weighing values and norms. For this ethical line of reasoning, some basic ingredients are provided in the section below.

ETHICAL ASSESSMENT OF VALUES AND NORMS

Clinical ethicists must interpret clinical reality in the light of human dignity (Janssens 1981; Selling 1988). In more concrete terms, clinical ethics is about weighing up ethical values and norms which serve as guidelines for clinical actions. Values express what staff must aim at in order to attain greater human dignity; norms express concrete rules of behaviour which are generally accepted as responsible and adequate for giving human dignity to care. In what follows, we explain some of the values and norms which are important for an ethical evaluation of physical restraint.

Respect for the dignity of older people

As a first value, we could state that every older person should be treated as an individual. Being an individual constitutes human dignity. This dignity is grounded in the fact that everyone is a unique individual who becomes more and more human by contact with others, thus taking part in society as a whole (Janssens 1981; Selling 1988). Human dignity cannot be relinquished, not even through illness, impairment or an approaching death.

This value gives rise to the ethical norm that health and social care staff must give priority to respect for the dignity of older people.

Respect for autonomy

As a second value, one should always consider older people as responsible individuals. A human being is not an object like the material things that surround us; he or she is one normally called to be conscious, to act according to his or her conscience, in freedom, and in a responsible manner (Janssens 1981).

The ability of human beings to make choices must always be respected in the context of physical restraint (Cheung and Yam 2005). From this derives the ethical norm that staff, in cases where physical restraint is being considered, should inform competent older people and their relatives as much as possible about the various options. They should provide information, as objectively as possible and in a way that is understandable for older people and their relatives, about the various treatment possibilities, their nature and aim, their pros and cons, effects and risks. Health and social care staff, older people and their relatives should attempt to arrive at a well-considered choice on the basis of this information. The application of physical restraint to a mentally competent individual without his or her consent is unacceptable (Dodds 1996; Moss and La Puma 1991). Even mentally incompetent older people should be involved as much as possible in the decision-making procedure, since the loss of cognitive functioning – usually a gradual process (e.g. dementia) – does not necessarily mean that an individual can no longer make their own choices and decisions (Cheung and Yam 2005). Staff should ask relatives to make an attempt to determine what the individual lacking mental competence would want.

Promoting overall well-being

In the practice of care, the physical aspects of well-being are often a main focus because they can be translated most easily into objectifiable complaints, and physical restraint is often used in order to prevent physical harm (Evans and Strumpf 1989). However, when considering older people as full individuals, we must accept that care for the older people's well-being involves more than just preventing physical harm. Respect for overall well-being is the third value that must be protected. In certain cases, this value can come into conflict with the value of physical integrity (Dodds 1996). Although the protection of physical integrity can be considered as a fundamental value, one cannot claim that this value always takes priority over all other values. In certain cases, the choice of another value can be justified, even though it may entail risks for physical well-being. During their lives, people pursue many kinds of activities with the aim of attaining values they find important, even though it may cause harm to their physical integrity. There is no reason to suppose that the lives of individuals must be dominated by the protection of their safety and physical integrity.

From the choice of overall well-being as a priority value, we can derive the norm that, when making decisions about physical restraint, not only older people's physical well-being should be taken into account, but also the social (possibility for contact), psychological (experience of older people and their relatives) and moral (respect for autonomy, informed consent) dimensions of the individual's well-being. Just from the perspective of this norm, the behaviour of the nurse in the case of Mr Janssens can be criticized.

Promoting self-reliance

The fourth ethical value gives priority to optimal support for older people's ability to do things independently (self-reliance). Creating a home-like atmosphere for those who may be disoriented or ill at ease (e.g. a quiet room, lighting during the night, contacts with volunteers and relatives), providing support to people with mental degeneration by setting a clear daily routine (e.g. fixed appointments, an activity calendar), organizing group activities (e.g. movement exercises), etc. – these are all care interventions with a great psychological and social significance, both for the older person and for the staff.

Case study

An older person was strapped down in bed with a belt around the waist and the bed's side rails because she was very restless and was often lying with her legs over and through the bed's side rails. At night, she would also often remove her adult continence pad. By helping the individual to bed in an unhurried fashion, however, she calmed down to such an extent that the use of a strap around her waist became unnecessary.

Concern for 'ordinary' daily activities deserves the highest priority, not only for its human value but also because it can, in a great many cases, postpone or even preclude the need to apply physical restraint (Brower 1991). However, this requires expert assistance for the older people's behaviour (see Box 11.1).

Box 11.1 Examples of interventions to reduce physical restraint

- Specific measures: lower bed, mattress placed on the ground, bed/chair alarms, relatives/sitters/volunteers/hospice workers, shock-absorbing floor covering, hip protectors, non-slip floor and footwear, walking aids, strategic placement of patients (compatibility, location)
- Measures to optimize the environment: balancing environmental stimulation to prevent/minimize sensory overload/under-stimulation, familiar surroundings and orientation, ample lightening without glare, correct/adjust glasses, allow 'wandering', etc.
- Individualized care: continuity of care; clear, meaningful, communication that reflects courtesy and respect; active listening, documentation and analysis of behaviour; encourage visits from relatives; description and explanation before therapeutic interventions; therapeutic touch; encourage participation in physical activities; regular rest periods to compensate for fatigue and loss of reserve energy
- Preventing/minimizing predisposing and precipitating factors for falls and delirium: nutrition and hydration management, pain management, routine toileting, elimination/minimization of unnecessary medication, cognitive stimulation, use of sensory protocols, management of postural hypotension, balance and gait training and strengthening exercises

Sources: Brower 1991; Capezuti *et al.* 2002; Evans, Wood and Lambert 2002; Gallinagh, Slevin and McCormack 2002; Geusens *et al.* 2003; Milisen *et al.* 1998. Adapted and reproduced from *Journal of Medical Ethics* (2006) *32*, 148–152 and used with permission from BMJ Publishing Group.

With a view to optimally supporting older people's self-reliance, we would put forward the norm that the application of physical restraint methods should only be considered in exceptional cases whenever it would pose a serious risk to themselves or to others, and only if the abovementioned means (see Box 11.1) of avoiding physical restraint are unsuccessful.

CLINICAL-ETHICAL DECISION-MAKING

On the basis of the normative interpretation just given, we can now sketch some examples of good clinical-ethical decision-making with respect to physical restraint.

The benefits should outweigh the shortcomings

For staff, it is often not clear if physical restraint should be applied or if it would be pointless. The application of physical restraint is only justified if the benefits outweigh the shortcomings. The benefits can be physical, psychological or social in nature. So physical restraint methods should only be considered if older people's health, integrity or living and caring environment would be seriously damaged by not using them. As far as form, duration and frequency are concerned, the staff team must carefully assess which procedure is most appropriate for attaining their goals and which is best adapted to individuals' needs and wishes. The least restrictive methods should always be tried out first. Individuals' freedom should not be restricted any longer, or to any higher degree, than is strictly necessary. In other words, there should be a reasonable or proportionate relation between the physical restraint and the harm it intends to avoid (Moss and La Puma 1991).

Case study: Using waist straps

An older person was secured to a seat with a dinner tray in order to prevent her from falling. Initially, the staff believed this measure to be a good solution. The resident, however, thought differently and started yelling continuously, knocking on the table and throwing everything within reach. By replacing the dinner tray with a waist strap which was much less confronting to the woman, peace returned and both parties were relieved. Before, feelings of guilt and incapacity were predominant amongst staff.

Starting from a concern to avoid unnecessary physical restraint, we propose that the application of physical restraint methods can only be considered when:

- specific benefits are envisioned
- there is a reasonable expectation that these benefits can be attained through physical restraint (effectiveness)
- there are no practical alternatives to physical restraint (see Box 11.1)
- the application of physical restraint hinders the individual as little as possible.

Every method should be individualized

The choice to use or not to use physical restraint should be based on an individualized comprehensive assessment (e.g. cognitive, physical, mobility and sensory state; drug therapy; past history and environmental issues) (Evans *et al.* 2002; Gallinagh *et al.* 2002). If physical restraint is applied, then certain additional measures need to be applied in order to respect older people's human dignity as much as possible and to avoid complications (see Box 11.2).

Box 11.2 Recommended measures when using physical restraint

- Continuous monitoring of physical health status (e.g. skin colour, extremity movement and sensation) and personal needs (e.g. toileting, food and fluids).
- Maximum protection of privacy and optimizing psychosocial comfort.
- Interruption of physical restraints at regular intervals.
- Re-evaluate the justification for physical restraint at regular intervals.

Sources: Evans *et al.* 2002; Sullivan-Marx *et al.* 1999. Adapted and reproduced from *Journal of Medical Ethics* (2006) *32*, 148–152 and used with permission from BMJ Publishing Group.

Open discussion with all involved should be organized

Dealing with physical restraint involves a difficult decision-making process, in which everyone must participate on the basis of their own expertise.

Management

Dealing with physical restraint requires an organizational policy supported by the daily management of the healthcare institution. The key points in such an organizational policy are vision, guidelines, operational policy, training and communication (Cheung and Yam 2005; Evans *et al.* 2002).

- Management must develop an *ethical view* with respect to physical restraint. A policy based on ethical values can serve to motivate staff.

- The application of methods of physical restraint should, ideally, take place in accordance with previously established evidence-based *guidelines* which are recognized by management and staff and applied consistently.

- The reduction of physical restraint requires an *operational policy*. Elements of such a policy would include: adaptation to environmental factors (e.g. architecture, choice of materials), allocation of resources, an interdisciplinary approach (including the individual and his or her relatives), registration of the use of physical restraint, communication about the policy pursued, and so on.

- The development of an ethical view, guidelines and a policy goes hand in hand with a continuous *staff training* in the application of methods of physical restraint, its ethical and legal aspects, the risks and indications of physical restraint, alternatives, etc.

- Finally, good *communication* must ensure that all parties involved are aware of the institutional policy with respect to physical restraint.

Staff team

Staff should pose critical questions of one another about the responsible use of physical restraint. The search for new ways of promoting older people's well-being is part of the task of an ethically motivated expert caregiver. That search is not merely a question of individual expertise, however; it is much more a collective undertaking by people who are open to one another's input. The various responsibilities could be summed up as follows:

- Every nurse and doctor can resort to the application of physical restraint methods on the basis of observation.

- The request is discussed within the interdisciplinary care team. The team supervises compliance with the institutional policy.

- Whenever there is a necessity to apply physical restraint 'unexpectedly and quickly', then prolongation of, or alternatives to, the method should be considered as soon as possible.

- The care team informs all parties involved about their decision.

Older people

The care team must involve older people as much as possible (even in cases of cognitive decline) in the decision-making process (Cheung and Yam 2005). Staff should provide accessible information to individuals about treatment possibilities so that he or she can make real choices. In this, it is not so much the quantity of information that is important but what the individual can do with the information. It is essential to the decision-making process that the individual's wishes are taken into account as much as possible (Vassallo *et al.* 2005).

Relatives and carers

The care team assists the relatives and informal carers by informing them, at an early stage (e.g. when admitted), about the institution's policy concerning physical restraint (Vassallo *et al.* 2005). Although the aim is to involve relatives in the decision-making process about the older person, it must be stressed that the ultimate decision is taken by the care team, and they retain full responsibility for their decision. Often, relatives are under great stress due to being confronted with the process of the individual's clinical decline, and they should not be made to feel responsible for the entire process of care as well, since this could give rise to guilt feelings.

Feelings of guilt can be combated by, as far as possible, involving the relatives directly (according to their ability and capacity to deal with it) in the caring process which aims at the avoidance of physical restraint. Through a more intense contact with their familiar environment and with familiar people, the individual will be given cognitive, physical, psychological and social stimulation, whereby disorientation, aggressive behaviour and feelings of boredom can in many cases be reduced. Moreover, the mere presence (supervisory function) of older people's relatives can serve to avoid physical restraint (Gallinagh *et al.* 2002). This inclusion in the care process can heighten the feeling, for the individual and their relatives, that the situation is a meaningful one. Of course, it goes without saying that the relative must be able to freely choose whether or not they want to participate in the caring process.

CONCLUSION

This chapter has dealt with two problems related to the physical restraint of older people. First of all, there is sufficient empirical evidence to support the idea that, in many cases, physical restraint causes more harm than benefit. In addition, the application of physical restraint methods often goes together with a disproportionate infringement of the principle of respect for the autonomy of older people. This does not preclude the use of physical restraint methods in exceptional cases; however, the emphasis should be on finding adequate alternatives. In this way attempts are made to protect older people as much as possible from harm, on the one hand, and to respect as much as possible their personal freedom, on the other.

REFERENCES

Brower, T. (1991) 'The alternatives to restraint.' *Journal of Gerontological Nursing 17*, 2, 18–22.

Capezuti, E., Maislin, G., Strumpf, N. and Evans, L.K. (2002) 'Side rail use and bed-related fall outcomes among nursing home residents.' *Journal of the American Geriatrics Society 50*, 1, 90–96.

Cheung, P.P.Y. and Yam, B.M.C. (2005) 'Patient autonomy in physical restraint.' *International Journal of Older People Nursing* in association with *Journal of Clinical Nursing 14*, 3a, 34–40.

Cohen-Mansfield, J. (1986) 'Agitated behaviors in the elderly II: Preliminary results in the cognitively deteriorated.' *Journal of the American Geriatrics Society 34*, 10, 722–727.

Dawkins, V.H. (1998) 'Restraints and the elderly with mental illness: Ethical issues and moral reasoning.' *Journal of Psychosocial Nursing 36*, 10, 22–27.

Dodds, S. (1996) 'Exercising restraint: Autonomy, welfare and elderly patients.' *Journal of Medical Ethics 22*, 3, 160–163.

Evans, D., Wood, J. and Lambert, L. (2002) 'A review of physical restraint minimization in the acute and residential care settings.' *Journal of Advanced Nursing 40*, 6, 616–625.

Evans, L.K. and Strumpf, N.E. (1989) 'Tying down the elderly: A review of the literature on physical restraint.' *Journal of the American Geriatrics Society 37*, 1, 65–74.

Fairman, J. and Happ, M. (1998) 'For their own good? A historical examination of restraint use.' *HEC Forum 10*, 3–4, 290–299.

Gallinagh, R., Nevin, R., McAleese, L. and Campbell, L. (2001) 'Perceptions of older people who have experienced physical restraint.' *British Journal of Nursing 10*, 13, 852–859.

Gallinagh, R., Slevin, E. and McCormack, B. (2002) 'Side rails as physical restraints in the care of older people: A management issue.' *Journal of Nursing Management 10*, 5, 299–306.

Geusens, P., Milisen, K., Dejaeger, E. and Boonen, S. (2003) 'Falls and fractures in postmenopausal women: A review.' *Journal of the British Menopause Society 9*, 3, 101–106.

Janelli, L.M., Dickerson, S.S. and Ventura, M.R. (1995) 'Focus groups: Nursing staff's experiences using restraints.' *Clinical Nursing Research 4*, 4, 425–441.

Janssens, L. (1981) 'Artificial insemination: Ethical considerations.' *Louvain Studies 8*, 1, 3–29.

Lamb, K.V., Minnick, A., Mion, L.C., Palmer, R. and Leipzig, R. (1999) 'Help the health care team: Release its hold on restraint.' *Nursing Management 30*, 12, 19–23.

Lee, D.T.F., Chan, M.C., Tam, E.P.Y. and Yeung, W.S.K. (1999) 'Use of physical restraints on elderly patients: An exploratory study of the perceptions of nurses in Hong Kong.' *Journal of Advanced Nursing 29*, 1, 153–159.

Milisen, K., Foreman, M.D., Godderis, J., Abraham, I.L. and Broos, P.L.O. (1998) 'Delirium in the hospitalized elderly: Nursing assessment and management.' *Nursing Clinics of North America 33*, 3, 417–439.

Moss, R. and La Puma, J. (1991) 'The ethics of mechanical restraints.' *Hastings Center Report 21*, 1, 22–25.

Newbern, V. and Lindsey, I. (1994) 'Attitudes of wives toward having their elderly husband restrained.' *Geriatric Nursing 15*, 3, 135–138.

O'Connor, B. (1998) 'Culture and the use of patient restraints.' *HEC Forum 10*, 3–4, 263–275.

Quinn, C.A. (1993) 'Nurses' perceptions about physical restraints.' *Western Journal of Nursing Research 15*, 2, 148–162.

Selling, J. (ed.) (1988) *Personalist Morals: Essays in Honor of Professor Louis Janssens.* Leuven: Leuven University Press.

Sullivan-Marx, E.M., Strumpf, N.E., Evans, L.E., Baumgarten, M. and Maislin, G. (1999) 'Predictors of continued physical restraint use in nursing home residents following restraint reduction efforts.' *Journal of the American Geriatrics Society 47*, 3, 342–348.

Van Dongen, E. (1997) 'Ongelukjes en niet-ongelukjes: Infantilisering en het oude lichaam.' *Medische antropologie 7*, 1, 41–60.

Vassallo, M., Wilkinson, C., Stockdale, R., Malik, N., Baker, R. and Allen, S. (2005) 'Attitudes to restraint for the prevention of falls in hospital.' *Gerontology 51*, 1, 66–70.

Chapter 12

CHANGING RESTRAINT USE: DISCOURSES ON RESTRAINT

Kate Irving

INTRODUCTION

This chapter is concerned with restraint use that continues in practice but is ethically and legally problematic. For this reason, for the purposes of this chapter restraint use is defined as *any physical or chemical treatment carried out with the intention of limiting the mobility of a patient for any reason other than during a medical procedure.* Some treatments such as intravenous infusion pumps, skin traction or external fixators can constrain movement. The difference is that such *constraint* is an unwanted side effect of a medical intervention and is not directly *intended.* Some definitions of restraint focus on the effect of an intervention or the ability of an individual to choose an intervention but these definitions do not always help to identify those incidences of restraint that are ethically problematic.

There is a thin line between appropriate restraint, when someone asks for a bedrail to make them feel secure or when a drug is prescribed to treat anxiety, and inappropriate restraint where the individual's rights are violated. Car seatbelts can be considered a restraint, but one would not suggest they were unethical in the same way a straitjacket may be considered unethical. It needs to be clear to all care providers that there is a mode of restraint that is problematic, and it is this type of restraint that should be addressed in research and practice. Thus, any definition of restraint should facilitate the identification of inappropriate restraint, not merely count the number of people who are taken to be restrained according to some pre-specified criteria.

CHANGING RESTRAINT USE

Eliminating this kind of restraint use seems to defy a straightforward educational approach where people using restraint are taught about the damage it causes and thus cease to use it. Therefore this chapter examines the contradiction between the continued use of physical and chemical restraints, the empirical evidence of the harm they cause (Evans, Wood and

Lambert 2003) and professionals' aspirations for evidence-based practice (Soukup and McCleish 2008). There is a need to develop an understanding of the factors inhibiting restraint reduction. One explanation, based on an understanding of the work of Michel Foucault, is that restraint use is socially bound in the complex discourse and culture of health care. Authoritative accounts of the work of Foucault include Burchell, Gordon and Miller (1991) and Dean (1994). It is not my intention to give a detailed account of his wide-ranging projects or ideas; however, I will attempt to explain aspects of his work which underpin the arguments made. Primarily this chapter is influenced by his work on genealogy and his later work on ethics.

The aims of this chapter are to explore:

- what explanations care staff give in respect to the use of restraint
- what social explanations (discourses) underpin these explanations
- how such discourses function to legitimise, justify and maintain the practice of restraint.

DISCURSIVE PRACTICES

Discursive practices are not just spoken words but other practices, visible in the care of people who become restrained. The issues and discourses raised here are contested and I seek no claim to have the 'right' answer about why restraints are used, only to provide an explanation which provokes new forms of thinking about the way we care for people such as the gentleman in the case study I will make reference to. My endeavour is underpinned by the proposition that language is not merely a transparent medium for the relay of information between individuals or groups (Hazelton 1999). The way we choose to refer to people is aimed towards a socio-political end point; the choice of words is not mere chance but a strategic decision on the part of the speaker to represent themselves and the subject to the world in a particular way.

In illustrating these discourses I will call on a case study based on my experience as a general nurse in the care of older people. However, it is my belief that some parts of these discourses will be recognisable to any staff where any type of restraint that meets the definition above takes place.

The following case is based largely on a person I cared for while working as a staff nurse in an acute medical ward in Australia. The work was part of my initial training for PhD data collection. The name used is a pseudonym. Restraint use in Australia has been the subject of intense publication in the last ten years with the result that there have been changes in practice since this case occurred. According to recent Australian guidelines and regulations one form of restraint used here, a vest (posey) restraint, is considered extreme restraint (Commonwealth of Australia 2004) and not recommended for use.

Case study: Joe's case

The clinical details below give some background information on Joe. It is worthy of note that Joe was independent on admission. Joe was suffering from Lewy Body Dementia which is frequently associated with more extreme psychological and behavioural symptoms than other dementias. It is characterised by fluctuations in mood and mental state and by Parkinsonian features and in this respect Joe was typical.

Joe was calm and not restrained for the first day after admission, however, when he begins to realise he cannot easily get out of the hospital he becomes more determined to leave and this gives rise to the first instances of restraint. He was chemically restrained first but later had a 'special' who sat with him to keep him contained; he also had bed rails and at times a vest restraint. Although the 'special' was considered a benevolent act by the staff, he frequently remained restrained while the special was there. The reason given for the restraint was risk of falling and risk of absconding. Joe was under a 'section' of the Mental Health Act for the first 24 hours of his stay. However, following this he had the legal right to leave the hospital. I frequently saw him walking around with the chair which he was restrained to on his back. I also found him in the car park as I was coming into work once.

CLINICAL DETAILS

Admission diagnosis: Acute confusional state for management.

Age: 74   **Marital status:** Married

Residence: Home

Past medical history: Ischaemic heart disease (CABG) [coronary artery bypass graft]. 8-year history of Parkinson's disease; however, the diagnosis following MRI [magnetic resonance imaging] scan is Defuse Lewy Body Dementia.

Drug history: Sinemet, Zocor, Asprin, Tenomin

Psychiatric history: 3–4-year history of night-time hallucinations worsening in the last year. Relieved with reduction of Sinemet. Admitted with altered mental state following violence towards his neighbour and running away down a busy road. MMSE (Mini Mental State Examination): 17 on admission.[1]

Functional status: Fully independent on admission

[1] A score of 23 or lower is indicative of cognitive impairment

NURSING AND MEDICAL NOTES
Nursing Note 1
Assisted with ADLs [activities of daily living] requiring constant supervision becoming aggressive violent and extremely agitated lashing out pacing +++. Haloperidol given 1mg given IMI as ordered. Dr is aware. May have 1–2mg 8/24, placed in restraint as bashing self into the walls continues to be agitated.

Pt [patient] extremely agitated still trying to break restraint, chair or himself. 2 mg haloperidol given. Graduate RN

Medical Note 1
ATS [asked to see] re-:agitation. Patient apparently violent, agitated – needs 4–5 people to restrain – freed himself from posey – walking all over the place – very aggressive on being approached. D/W [discussed with] and S/B [seen by] neuro, plan – 1–2mg haloperidol 8/24 – RMO [resident medical officer] to be called if agitated despite haloperidol – higher doses of sedation/haloperidol risky as pt has diffuse Lewy Body Disease (clinical working diagnosis).

Nursing Note 2
Pt became aggressive when told to go back to room he grabbed next patient's razor out of locker and slashed at my arm when registered nurse and I tried to clam him down he then grabbed my two wrists and squeezed them till they hurt then he pulled at my blouse and would not let go until male CN [clinical nurse] calmed him down.

Discourse in action
Three discourses are described here: constituting the person as unable to self govern; constituting an appropriate environment; and constituting an appropriate treatment. I argue that these discourses are used to justify using restraints despite the difficulties their use precipitates.

Constituting the inability to self govern
The first discourse, 'constituting an inability to self govern', is a central feature of discursive practice regarding people who are restrained. This discourse concerns the way ordinarily, one citizen cannot restrain another citizen without consequences. For example, if I were to decide to lock

my students into the lecture theatre to ensure they listen to the class, this would be considered false imprisonment in our legal system and I could, quite rightly, face punishment from various authorities for my actions. However, restraint in a care environment is legitimised and regularly has no consequences for the people who use it. One of the differences between my students and people in care environments is that they are 'constituted' (i.e. there is general acceptance and support for the idea by those living and working around them) as individuals who are capable of living within the bounds of what is considered socially acceptable. Because they conform to these ideals we afford them certain human rights; for one, they have the right to certain freedoms. It is imperative, if one wants to restrain a person, to constitute that person as not able to self govern. This may seem reasonable; if people are unable to self govern, other responsible people should govern them – I do not dispute this. The issue here is that this constitution is based on varying degrees of fact about the person. My students may engage in behaviour that is socially unacceptable but are able, because of the freedoms they are afforded, to conceal these behaviours. In this way the 'us' and 'them' distinction between my students and people who become restrained is less stark than we might like to think.

One powerful way of legitimising restraint was to establish certain truths about the individuals seen as needing restraint. The staff had a range of ways of establishing these truths. One potent means was to describe the behaviour of the subject in isolation from the context in which it took place.

For Joe, this involved presenting in full and graphic detail the nature of his behaviour as exemplified in Nursing Note 1, but ignoring the possibility that, to some extent, restraint use reinforced these behaviours. Words such as 'requiring constant supervision' reinforce how he thwarted the best efforts of the staff to treat him humanely.

In the light of such extreme risk to Joe and to others the idea of restraints as both inevitable and humane is made easy. For example, 'needs 4–5 people to restrain' (Medical Note 1) is a powerful statement; however, careful observation of what he was doing to require restraint by 4–5 people was revealing. Joe was attempting to escape the restraint the staff had already subjected him to. In this way restraint itself justifies more restraint. In Nursing Note 2, Joe is referenced as having slashed at the nurse's wrists with a razor. This sounds very dramatic; however, the razor was a disposable razor and thus not easy to do damage with. Also Joe had marked Parkinsonian features so the nurse was obviously very close to him if he slashed at her, as there was always a few seconds' warning that he was going to move since there was a delay in his ability to initiate gross movement. It is clear to me that the nurse was, at the time of this incident, invading Joe's space and different behaviour by her could have avoided this situation. However, it is Joe and his behaviour that is problematised, not the skill of the nurse in question who, it would seem, is not exercising research-based de-escalation techniques. The nursing note makes reference to Joe's behaviour but to no positive intervention on her part. This omission is not questioned by the team who later deconstructed his behaviour in fine detail.

There is a certain problematisation of what the person is and how they behave in relation to how a person should behave prescribed by tradition and education, and this can be called an ontology. The ontology of people in hospital is not based on the average person with dementia and places unrealistic expectations on how people should behave. Importantly, people with dementia do not get better as people are supposed to do in hospital and hence they are already exceptional. This ontology is governed by a deontology or set of 'rules' that set out the appropriate intervention under specific circumstances such as the use of restraints in exceptional cases. This in turn conditions the ontological construction of the 'what is' of the individual with dementia because in order to use restraint certain conditions must be present, and the staff, through their assessments, must prove these circumstances. Also in operation is an aesthetic or a sense of the look and feel of an intervention, and this too must be manipulated to legitimise restraints. There is a need for a general impression of progress towards a more aesthetically pleasing 'patient' so as to legitimise the role of the hospital. Older people wandering around or calling out threaten this aesthetic value.

This examination of abnormal behaviours is what Foucault would call a 'technology of normalisation'. The examination as an exercise of power is a major focus of *Discipline and Punish* (Foucault 1991, p.184) where Foucault describes the examination as functioning to 'transform the economy of visibility into the exercise of power' (1991, p.187). It reaffirms the coherence of the normal and homogeneous as 'us' and the others as 'them'.

These assertions have practical functions; they have an effect which, although unstable and unpredictable, can be traced through the analysis of current practices. The consideration of Joe's behaviour in isolation from the interventions of the staff represents a total marginalisation of his narrative. It forms the basis for the view that Joe's narrative is irrelevant, irrational or deviant. His behaviour is neatly packaged as a symptom of illness and the legitimacy of his actions is denied. Foucault argues that the examination that 'places individuals in a field of surveillance also situates them in a network of writing; it engages them in a whole mass of documents that capture and fix them' (Foucault 1991, p.189).

The case notes are not an adjunct to the selfhood of the patient, but for the staff using them they actually become part of the 'patient's self' (Irving 2002, p.410). Therefore, the examination makes possible the production of subjects who can be compared and constituted in a range of ways.

> This form of power that applies itself to immediate everyday life categorizes the individual, marks him by his own individuality, attaches him to his own identity, imposes a law of truth on him that he must recognize and others have to recognize in him. It is a form of power that makes individuals subjects. There are two meanings of the word 'subject': subject to someone else by control and dependence, and tied to his own identity by a conscience or self-knowledge. Both meanings suggest a form of power that subjugates and makes subject to. (Foucault 1997, p.331)

In order to demonstrate 'insight' and competence Joe has to accept the restraint positively. However, Joe does not have the ability to see that his acquiescence may lead to the removal of restraint and so he reacts by fighting against the restraints and anyone who seeks to impose them. Joe's presumed lack of ability to make minute decisions about his day-to-day functioning is providing the possibility for staff to become paternalistic and create 'docile bodies' (Foucault 1991, p.135).

The second part of this discourse is the demonisation that runs alongside the absent cause of behaviour. In this instance Joe is portrayed in ways that give his behaviour exceptional qualities. Joe, for instance, was labelled 'Houdini' after his ability to escape the restraining vest, which is on the surface just a funny name for him. Implicit in this nickname however is an image that is beyond comprehension, slightly disturbing, somebody who is extraordinary at resisting control. This image bears little relation to the vulnerable person presented in the introduction to Joe. This demonisation reinforces the dichotomy of 'us' and 'them', distancing the subject from the perception of a human being with the same rights as the person applying or ordering the restraint.

Joe is disqualified from the right to leave the ward. This negated right preserves the perception of the need for control, which is crucial to justification of restraint. Also in action is a discourse aimed at the unsuitability and unaccommodating nature of the environment.

Constituting an appropriate elsewhere

This discourse functions to alter the responsibility for the restraint in as much as the environment places certain pre-existing realities on the staff. This practice of discussing the environment as a 'problematisation' is directly influenced by Foucault. It is not a criticism that aspects of an individual's care are problematised. Problematisations make way for new ways of behaving but can equally delimit what can be said and done. For example, wards are often ideally designed for those who can use a nurse call buzzer. This presumption of ability to appropriately use the nurse call system is somewhat anomalous if we consider the proportion of people accommodated in hospital wards who, like Joe, are unable to use the nurse call system. The presence of numerous exits with no barriers also demonstrates the assumption that all are obedient and stay in their appropriate place. This is not a presumption based on reality. In other words, we are setting both people in hospital and the staff up to fail in their reciprocal tasks of receiving and providing humane care. Possibly because of these inherent structural obstacles staff are aware that there might be an 'elsewhere' more appropriate for their 'problem care-awaiting patients' as I heard one nurse manager refer to 'patients like Joe'. For Joe this discourse was extensively problematised until the pursuit of an alternative place (the old-age psychiatry ward) became the goal of care for some time.

It was the skills of the staff on the old-age psychiatry ward which the general nurses seemed to think they lacked. The effect of bringing into question the old-age psychiatry ward was to constitute an appropriate elsewhere, geographically distant from the current ward. It had the effect of diminishing the possibility of delivering humane care in the current environment. On the other hand, removal of the subject removes the problem for the ward, and in this way this discourse adds to a marginalisation of such individuals.

This discourse has one assumption at heart, which I argue is fundamentally flawed. The assumption is that there was a right place for Joe; that there is a space in which his care is unproblematic, or at least so much less problematic that restraint is no longer required. Without arguing, contrary to the literature, that environment has an effect on behaviour, the function of this discourse is to render the staff helpless in their current situation, thereby contributing to the legitimisation of restraint use. As a result these subjects end up in what I have heard called the 'too hard basket' or the 'hole in the system', which inevitably ends in nursing home placement.

The hospital is treated as a kind of 'warehouse' for these subjects. This is implied in hospital staff's familiar discourse such as 'problem care-awaiting patient' or 'bed blocker'. It also implies that there is a particular trajectory in dementia care, i.e. an expectation that there can be no recovery and that there, necessarily, must be decline. This again appears normal and natural, but if one considers the effect of this on the subject, it is not negligible as it negates the trial of alternatives.

It is becoming apparent that there are certain rules governing the use of restraints. One of these rules is that there must be a lack of clarity in deciding the 'proper course of events'. This lack of direction is contributed to by the first discourse, which demonstrates the extraordinary nature of the subject, the second, which demonstrated the unsuitability of the environment, and by the next discourse, which demonstrates the difficulty in deciding on a course of treatment.

Constituting an appropriate 'other' treatment

Staff I have worked with seem to identify two approaches to caring for people such as Joe, the psychosocial or the biomedical. There is tension between the two that can create conflict for individual staff members. Staff members do recognise the over-reliance on the biomedical model and offer some resistance to it, identifying when behaviours may have a physical discomfort cause, such as needing the toilet or being hungry. The staff seem all too aware of the dangers of using restraints. They are aware that individuals can escape and that in Joe's case he can walk around with the chair strapped to his back by the restraint. At the same time, they are forced to justify restraint, as it is the only accepted visible method they are familiar with that is legitimate for use in such cases.

Chemical restraint is also interesting as its availability and the responsibility for its use is somewhat dispersed. Although the doctors prescribe it, the nurses may exercise an amount of discretion in the administration because it is frequently prescribed as an 'as required' medication. 'As required' medications are available, quick and legitimate. Often no other measures are written down as possibilities for intervention. The visibility of the 'as required' medications as opposed to other measures here reinforces chemical restraint, which in turn increases the visibility of chemical restraint as a measure of care.

This is a way of packaging the solution as standard, and it is important that treatments are seen to be standard or protocol. At the same time it is obvious that the medications for people such as Joe (and any practising nurse would be able to relate instances where medications were unhelpful) do not have predictable or standard effects on behaviour. Just as there was a perception of a good or desirable space in which to care for Joe, there is an illusion that there is a good or desirable way to control his behaviour. It constitutes another treatment regime under which Joe, for example, becomes manageable and is still treated humanely. It is quite possible that there is no perfect way of controlling behaviour; perhaps some of the behaviours just have to be tolerated. By problematising the need for control the possibility of using restraint is introduced. My question is, why have techniques such as promoting comfort, hydrating, feeding or validation become subordinate to medications? It seems that these alternative strategies suffer the serious drawback of being too basic for the behaviours that have already been constituted as 'extreme'. The effects of this 'truth' and its dominance in the discourse are evident in their ability to delimit other treatments and interventions.

Underlying this discourse is the assumption that hospitals are places people go to for cures and that they can deal with whatever is thrown at them from nursing homes or homes in crisis from carer burnout. There is an expectation that the hospital will always be of benefit to a person. However, a century ago people went into hospital to die and it was generally accepted that few people came out alive.

There is a striking disjunction between the academic or research-based discourse on restraints and the discourse of the staff on the wards. I argue that, in terms of what happens to patients with regards to restraint, the ward-based discourse is more influential than the academic discourse.

Summary of discourses

Three discourses were identified, constituting the subject as unable to 'self govern', constituting an appropriate environment, and constituting an appropriate treatment. These discourses are so powerful and damaging to the subject that their existence seems to imply that the subject has no rights to any of the normally expected options. Individuals staying in hospital are no longer allowed to make choices about small things such as how much or when to eat, much less as to where they will be discharged. Not only are the factors leading to this characterisation established as truth, these truths establish a number of other truths about the subject, which further serve to support the original truth that the subject is unable to 'self govern'.

Second, the discourse involved an intense problematisation of the environment with the effect of constituting another environment distant from the present where care can be given appropriately, where staff would be free from the physical manifestations of their inappropriate environment.

The staff I talk to frequently know very little about how this environment would differ from the current one. In fact, this ideal environment seems to be almost mythical but can lead the spectator into the view that there is little that the staff can do to eliminate restraint use in their environment. Thus the responsibility for restraint use is shifted to a somewhat ephemeral group of people not present.

The third discourse of importance involves constituting restraints as the only treatment that is realistic and sensible. This discourse includes traces of the last discourse in that it includes reference to an ideal treatment, which is not easily pinned down by those who espouse it. This discourse also systematically rules out the trial of alternatives by a number of persuasive arguments which are damaging to the identification of alternatives to restraint use.

These discourses do not fit into a neat scheme but form a network or capillary system whereby one does not need, in a hierarchical sense, to have power to contribute to the longstanding use of restraints.

CONCLUSIONS

These discourses in no way represent a full and comprehensive analysis of the ways we talk about people who are restrained, but it is my hope that they are recognisable to people who are caring for people where restraints are sometimes deemed necessary. It is also my hope that people using restraints will think critically of my arguments and come up with alternative discourses they think explain the continued use of restraint. Essentially this chapter challenges the notion of the 'objective assessment' and highlights the functions it serves which are perhaps not objective but orientated to very specific socio-political goals. The preceding section may not lead directly to clear guidelines about what to do to prevent inappropriate restraint use. This is because the understandings laid out here do not stem from a belief that overarching theories presented as the 'truth' on a particular topic are a good platform for moving practice forward in contested areas such as restraint use.

It is possible to see the lack of overarching theories referred to as an advantage rather than a flaw. Falzon (1998, p.4) suggests that the alternative to overarching world-views is not fragmentation but an opening up:

> By freeing ourselves from the illusion that there is some absolute standpoint, and recognising that all our concepts of knowledge, truth and right action are 'local' or historically specific, we will help open up a space for diversity, for otherness, for other forms of life.

The passage of time between the arrival of an anti-restraint discourse, and their continued use in the present day, shows us that mere knowledge of the damage restraints cause does not change practice. In a logical world identification of best practice results in a change in that practice. I argue that, because of the complex and static social discourses that surround restraint use, their continuance is possible, and examination of these discourses can lead to an appropriate way forward. We must open up a space for diversity, and 'local' or historically specific understanding of the phenomena of restraints.

My argument is that this approach is more informative to care practice than one that imposes false structures from the beginning. This approach implies the need for never-ending attention to the ways we conduct ourselves, as history does not stop at some logical best practice point, but continues to service the present in its language and design. Language is not a total and innocent representation of consciousness; care staff are speaking subjects positioned within a socio-political context.

We need to constantly probe the way in which views about people's behaviour of any kind are constructed. Foucault refers to this never-ending vigilance thus:

> My point is not that everything is bad but that everything is dangerous, which is not exactly the same as bad. If everything is dangerous, then we always have something to do. So my position leads not to apathy but to a hyper and pessimistic activism. I think that the ethico-political choice we have to make everyday is to determine which is the main danger. (Foucault 1990, p.262)

It is clear that in order for alternative points of view to be heard, the language needed to express them must be available for reflection and analysis. Through making these views visible in text it is possible to make available to staff who feel uncomfortable about restraint use, other points of view and ways of expressing them which undermine the commonly perceived inevitable necessity of restraint use.

> Discourse analysis enables the expanding of possibilities for the framing and shaping of practices by making visible the invisible power relations embedded in texts. In so doing it offers the opportunity for those in health care to conceive of other possibilities. (Lupton 1992, p.149)

In this manner this chapter has the potential to unsettle the taken-for-granted nature of the current practice of restraining patients. The coherence and fruitfulness of my arguments will be judged by the reader.

Acknowledgements
I would like to acknowledge the support and guidance of Professor Michael Clinton during the development of the ideas expressed here.

REFERENCES
Burchell, G., Gordon, C. and Miller, P. (eds) (1991) *The Foucault Effect: Studies in Governmentality.* London: Harvester Wheatsheaf.

Commonwealth of Australia (2004) *Decision-Making Tool: Responding to Issues of Restraint in Aged Care.* Canberra: Australian Government, Department of Health and Ageing.

Dean, M. (1994) *Critical and Effective Histories: Foucault's Methods and Historical Sociology.* London: Routledge.

Evans, D., Wood, J. and Lambert, L. (2003) 'Patient injury and physical restraint devices: A systematic review.' *Journal of Advanced Nursing 41*, 3, 274–282.

Falzon, C. (1998) *Foucault and Social Dialogue.* London: Routledge.

Foucault, M. (1990) *The Care of the Self: History of Sexuality*, trans. R. Hurley, vol. 3. New York: Pantheon. (Original work published in French, 1984.)

Foucault, M. (1991) *Discipline and Punish: The Birth of the Prison*, trans. A. Sheridan. New York: Vintage Books. (Original work published in French, 1975.)

Foucault, M. (1997) 'The Subject and Power.' In J.D. Faubion (ed.) *The Essential Works of Michel Foucault: 1954–1984*, vol. 3. London: Penguin Books.

Hazelton, M. (1999) 'Psychiatric personnel, risk management and the new institutionalism.' *Nursing Inquiry 6*, 4, 224–230.

Irving, K. (2002) 'Governing the conduct of conduct: Are restraints inevitable.' *Journal of Advanced Nursing 40*, 4, 405–412.

Lupton, D. (1992) 'Discourse analysis: A new methodology for understanding the ideologies of health and illness.' *Australian Journal of Public Health 16*, 2, 145–150.

Soukup, S.M. and McCleish, J. (2008) 'Advancing evidence-based practice: A program series.' *Journal of Continuing Education in Nursing 39*, 9, 402–406.

Chapter 13

THERAPEUTIC APPROACHES AND DE-ESCALATION TECHNIQUES

Suparna Madan and Pat Rowe

Case study: Mr Sparks

Mr. Sparks is an 87-year-old retired baker with mild to moderate Alzheimer's Dementia and a remote history of alcohol abuse. He lives at home with his wife and his medications include a cholinesterase inhibitor. Two weeks ago he started getting out of bed at night and his wife worries he might fall and hurt himself or wander out of the house. During the day he attempts to help with meal preparation but he can no longer follow a recipe and he gets irritable if his wife corrects him. Once while his wife was having an afternoon nap he turned the oven on and then forgot about it. His wife asks their doctor if there is a stronger 'sleeping pill' that can help him sleep at night and also asks where she can buy a bed with side rails like she's noticed in the hospitals.

INTRODUCTION

Disruptive behaviours are defined by Rossby, Beck and Heakcock (1992, p.99) as 'behaviour resulting in negative consequences for the resident, or other residents' and staff, and include behaviours such as psychomotor or verbal agitation and aggression towards self or others. As described in other chapters in this book, physical restraint (such as bed rails or wrist restraint) and chemical restraint (including antipsychotics and sedatives) are associated with poor outcomes when used to manage disruptive behaviours. Therefore, restraint should only be used as a last resort to address immediate safety needs of the older person or staff. Effectively using alternatives to physical restraint, however, can be a challenging endeavour that requires recognition of the underlying source of behaviour and a multifaceted individualized approach to management.

Ayalon *et al.* (2006) propose that underlying sources of disruptive behaviours include unmet physical or emotional needs (e.g. assistance with personal care including personal care such as going to the toilet, boredom or feeling too warm in bed), reinforced or learned behaviour (i.e. the individual learns they can get attention for the behaviour) environmental triggers (such as hearing a dog bark or an uncomfortable mattress) or, as Hall and Buckwalter (1987) propose, result from an individual's reduced ability to process information from their environment as they become cognitively impaired, leading to a reduced stress threshold. In the case study Mr Sparks' stress threshold was probably exceeded with the demands of cooking which led to his irritability.

Similarly, management of disruptive behaviours can be divided into categories that address unmet needs, environmental triggers and a reduced stress threshold. For example, a bedtime snack, ear plugs and a personal care regimen might encourage Mr Sparks to remain in bed at night. Mrs Sparks should also be advised about ways to minimize risk of injury for her husband. Potential environmental modifications include lowering the bed so it is closer to the floor or padding the floor with cushions if he is prone to falling out of bed, using a bedside commode, lowering the bedroom temperature, and installing safety locks on exterior doors.

Providing education to families and friends on managing behaviours may be an effective means of addressing an individual's reduced stress threshold. For example, a controlled community-based study by Gormley, Lyons and Howard (2001) educated families and friends on the non-cognitive aspects of dementia and identification of environmental factors that may contribute to behaviours (including precipitating factors, communication methods, distraction techniques and acceptance of inappropriate statements or requests). There was a positive trend to showing this behavioural education approach reduced disruptive behaviours (Gormley et al. 2001).

A behaviour log is a helpful tool for staff to critically assess and explore treatment options for disruptive behaviours (e.g. see GERO T.I.P.S. Online Learning 2009). For one example of a behaviour mapping tool refer to Figure 13.1. A behaviour map is an objective way of recording the type of behaviour and the number of times it occurs in a time frame. To use a behaviour map, start by identifying the three (or fewer but not more) behaviours you most want to eliminate or modify. All staff should be aware of what the behaviour is (i.e. describe the behaviours clearly and specifically) and each behaviour can be assigned a letter or number for ease of charting. Staff may choose to highlight the behaviours in different colours to more visibly demonstrate the time and frequency of occurrence. It is important to record behaviour around the clock, so if the behaviour only occurs on one work shift others have the opportunity to assist in care planning. It is also a useful tool to communicate the frequency and timing of the behaviours to family and medical personnel so optimal interventions may occur.

Patient Name: Mr. Sparks

List three difficult behaviours encountered with the resident:

A. Wandering

B. Hitting

C. Screaming "Help Me"

Date	0700	0800	0900	1000	1100	1200	1300	1400	1500	1600	1700	1800	1900	2000	2100	2200	2300	2400	0100	0200	0300	0400	0500	0600
July 26	C	C	B	C		A	A	A					C	B	B	C								
27	C	C	C	B		A	A	A					C	C	B	C								
28	C	B	C	C		A		A					C	C	B	C								
29	C	C	B	C		A	A	A																
30	C	B	C			A	A	A					C	B	C									
31						A	A	A	A															
Aug 1						A	A	A																
2																								
3																								

Comments:

Hitting & screaming during AM & PM ADLs
Analgesic changed on July 31
New after-lunch activity program
started Aug 2

Figure 13.1 Behaviour mapping tool

In the case study confrontations in the kitchen caused by a decreased stress threshold could be de-escalated by ensuring Mrs Sparks understands that her husband's cognitive limitations may influence his ability to organize and perform tasks. Instead of expecting him to be able to follow a recipe, his wife could give him a simple task such as kneading dough at the kitchen table while she works in the kitchen and she could unplug the stove when she is not available to supervise him.

This chapter will review some common causes of disruptive behaviours (including delirium pain and depression) and evidence for restraint-free pharmacological and non-pharmacological treatment options.

Case study

Mr Sparks slipped on an icy pavement while walking his dog, Misty, and fractured his hip. Following surgical repair of his hip, his wife informs hospital staff that her husband is more confused, especially in the evenings. He sometimes doesn't recognize who she is and picks at the air. Nurses are growing frustrated that he has pulled out his intravenous line twice and his Foley catheter once since being admitted to hospital.

MANAGING DELIRIUM

In older people with or without an underlying dementia, delirium should be considered whenever there is an acute change in someone's behaviour that results in disruptive behaviour. Delirium is a life-threatening, often under-recognized, medical condition characterized by a change in cognition (memory, language, orientation) or perceptual disturbance and an altered level of consciousness with reduced ability to maintain or shift attention (Meagher 2001). Symptoms tend to develop acutely over hours to days, may fluctuate over the course of the day and have evidence of an aetiological cause (Meagher 2001). A mnemonic that can assist with identifying possible aetiologies of delirium is 'NO RESTRAINT' (see Figure 13.2).

N	Neurological conditions (such as strokes, seizures, subdural hematoma)
O	Oxygenation (Is the person hypoxic?)
R	Retention (constipation, urinary retention)
E	Endocrine (including thyroid, parathyroid, adrenal imbalances)
S	Surgery (consider post-operative delirium, pain)
T	Toxins (heavy metals, drug intoxication, drug withdrawal)
R	Replace (sensory deprivation – replace hearing aids, visual aids)
A	Acute metabolic disturbances
I	Infections (urinary tract, pneumonia, sepsis)
N	No restraint
T	Teach (educate staff on recognizing delirium and deirium prevention)

Figure 13.2 NO RESTRAINT mnemonic

Beeping machines, intravenous tubing and oxygen masks may be unfamiliar, uncomfortable or even scary to an older adult, even in the absence of delirium, causing them to be non-compliant with care. Re-inserting a Foley catheter on multiple occasions is certainly one option; however, if the older person is not tolerating the medical equipment, it might be more helpful to ask, 'Is there a less invasive way to offer care?' For example, if the person is drinking and taking medications orally, can the intravenous feeding be discontinued? Can an incontinence pad be used instead of a Foley catheter?

If invasive medical equipment is necessary, camouflaging the equipment, for example covering intravenous tubing with a long-sleeved shirt or hiding a carotid line from view with a turtleneck top, might help. Distracting people by giving them a job to do such as folding towels or 'helping' the nursing staff by untangling knotted tubing may also help divert their attention.

An 'elder-friendly' unit (including carpeting, handrails, large clocks and person-centred care) may encourage people to be more independent in the basic activities of daily living (Landefeld *et al.* 1995). An environment that minimizes injury risk would probably lessen the temptation for staff to use restraint.

A delirium room refers to a four-bed room within an acute care for elders (ACE) unit. It is staffed with 24-hour nursing care and multidisciplinary interventions focused on identifying and treating underlying causes of delirium and can provide closer observation for people with cognitive impairment or fall-risk factors (Flaherty *et al.* 2003). During a one-year pilot delirium room study by Flaherty *et al.* (2003), no physical restraint was used although 29 per cent of older people received a chemical restraint such as a sedative or antipsychotic.

While distraction techniques and 'elder-friendly' units may reduce restraint need, implementing protocols for delirium prevention should not be overlooked. Inouye *et al.* (1999) conducted a prospective-matched controlled study of 852 older people at Yale University Hospital. An interdisciplinary protocol targeting six risk factors for delirium (cognitive impairment, immobility, vision and hearing impairment, dehydration and sleep deprivation) was shown to reduce delirium rates from 15 to 9.9 per cent ($p = 0.02$, odds ratio 0.60) and the total number of days older people had delirium decreased from 161 to 105 ($p = 0.02$) (Inouye *et al.* 1999). The above protocol, referred to as the Hospital Elder Life Program (HELP), has been successfully adapted to several hospitals that report improved outcomes for older people, and increased client and staff satisfaction with implementation of the protocol (Inouye *et al.* 2006). Vollmer, Rich and Robinson (2007) describe a similar delirium protocol that addresses sensory impairment, mobility and cognitive impairment and found that delirium rates reduced from 37.5 to 13.8 per cent.

In summary, delirium is a common but often under-diagnosed source of agitation and aggression in the community and in hospital; however, implementing protocols for prevention, early recognition and treatment of delirium in combination with creative 'distractions' to provide needed care may minimize the need for restraint while providing essential medical care.

Case study

Mr Sparks stopped pulling out his intravenous line once it was camouflaged by a long-sleeved shirt and his physician discontinued the Foley catheter. However, he remains more confused than pre-admission and refuses to participate with the rehab programme for the repair of his hip. He shouts and strikes out whenever nursing staff try to bath or mobilize him. The nursing staff request his physician order haloperidol to address these behaviours.

MANAGING PAIN

The severity of discomfort in people with dementia as indicated by facial expression, vocalization and body language has been shown to be significantly related to verbally aggressive behaviour and non-aggressive physical behaviour (Pelletier and Landreville 2007).

Rating scales or relying on an individual with dementia to communicate their discomfort may not provide reliable information. For people with significant cognitive impairment (e.g. with Mini Mental Status Exam (MMSE) scores below 15) observational or visual pain scales may be more helpful (Savoie 2008). The Mahoney Pain Scale is an example of a scale that prompts staff to consider the presence of medical conditions that may be associated with pain, affect, breathing, body language and changes in people's behaviour and 'vegetative' signs (Mahoney and Peters 2008).

A cross-sectional study of long-term care residents showed that people with severe dementia may experience significant pain and yet tend to receive the least pain treatment (Husebo *et al.* 2008). This study emphasizes the importance of having a high degree of suspicion for pain as a source of disruptive behaviours in people who are unable to communicate their discomfort and ensure that there is adequate analgesic treatment.

Case study

Once his delirium cleared, Mr Sparks returned home with his wife. In the following two years his dementia progressed and his wife noted a gradual escalation of behaviours such as swearing, shouting and hitting. Mrs Sparks was reduced to tears when behavioural interventions she was previously taught were no longer effectively averting his angry outbursts. A medical work-up was negative for delirium and he was on a regular analgesic regime. He was admitted to the long-term care facility due to staff 'burnout'.

At the care facility Mr Sparks shouts and strikes out at staff when they encourage him to eat meals and two staff members are needed to physically restrain him while a third nurse baths and dresses him. His wife is shocked by his behaviour since her husband was never physically aggressive with her at home. A team conference has been arranged with Mrs Sparks to discuss how these behaviours can be best managed.

MANAGING DEMENTIA

Aggressive and disturbed behaviours are common in the mornings, when staff may be seen to violate an individual's personal space while assisting them with activities of daily living (ADLs) such as assistance with personal care including going to the toilet, bathing, dressing and eating (Ryden, Bossenmaier and McLachlan 1991; Schreiner 2001). One possible explanation for this is that, as dementia progresses, behaviour becomes a way of communicating feelings and needs and regaining control of a confusing world.

Institutional care tends to revolve around schedules and 'task' completion; however, while schedules are needed to provide care in a timely fashion, in our clinical experience, educating staff to critically assess how they deliver care with a focus on the individual and their individual needs is a necessity to providing restraint-free care.

Making daily care routines similar to experiences from the past will help to reduce anxiety and diminish disruptive behaviours. For example, staff should be aware of people's previous routines including frequency and time of bathing, preference for showers, tub baths or sponge bathing. Assigning specific staff to do the bathing allows for more person-centred care approaches to be built up over time. Including people in decisions and providing choice about when to have their bath, undressing them in the privacy of the bathroom and promoting a calm, quiet and warm environment will help to reduce or eliminate the need for restraint. The more 'homelike' the experience, the greater the satisfaction for older people and staff.

When there is a transition from care in the community to a care home or hospital, family or friends should be encouraged to communicate to staff the likes and dislikes of the individual, their previous career, and how they communicate physical needs such as hunger, boredom, fatigue, need to use the bathroom and so on. Understanding what makes people an 'individual' is a key preliminary step to developing an effective behavioural and restraint-free approach for disruptive behaviours. A ten-day placebo controlled trial by Cohen-Mansfield, Libin and Marx (2007) showed that individualized, non-pharmacological interventions significantly decreased disruptive behaviours. Examples of non-pharmacological interventions include music therapy, animal-assisted therapy and other recreational activities.

Raglio et al. (2008) conducted a 16-week randomized controlled trial of music therapy in 59 individuals with moderate to severe dementia and showed a significant improvement in certain behavioural and psychological symptoms including delusions, agitation, abnormal motor activity, night-time disturbances, anxiety, apathy and irritability. Interestingly, the reduction in disruptive behaviours continued for one month following the completion of the study.

Brotons and Pickett-Cooper (1996) conducted group music therapy sessions for 20 people with dementia in a nursing home and found that residents were significantly less agitated during music therapy sessions and this was independent of whether or not they had a musical background. Tabloski, McKinnon-Howe and Remington (1995) used a quasi-experimental design, where each subject served as their own control, and found that calming music significantly reduced agitation in the nursing home residents they studied. Denney (1997) found that there was a 46 per cent decrease in verbally agitated behaviours and physically non-aggressive behaviours when quiet music was played during lunchtime. Goddaer and Abraham (1994) used a repeated measures design to expose nursing home residents to relaxing music during mealtime. They found significant reductions in total agitated behaviours, physically non-aggressive behaviours and verbally agitated behaviours; however, there was no change in aggressive behaviours and hiding/hoarding behaviours. Ragneskog et al. (1996) played three different types of music (pop music, Swedish tunes and soothing music) for two-week periods during meal times at a nursing home. During all music periods, residents ate more food in total, possibly because staff were serving the residents more food. In addition they found residents appeared less irritable and anxious, especially when soothing music was played.

Thomas, Heitman and Alexander (1997) observed 14 residents during three baseline bathing episodes, three treatment (music intervention) periods and three post-treatment bathing episodes. They found significant reductions for aggressive behaviour, but not for hiding/hoarding behaviour or physically non-aggressive behaviour, during music treatment sessions. Clark, Lipe and Bilbrey (1998) observed 18 residents during ten bathing episodes with their own preferred music and ten bathing episodes without music and found a reduction in aggressive behaviours during the music condition. In addition, staff reported more cooperation from residents. Gerdner (2000) used a repeated-measures, crossover design to compare the effects of classical 'relaxation' music versus familiar or 'individualized' music on agitated behaviours in demented long-term care residents. It was found that both music conditions reduced agitated behaviours; however, the effect was stronger for the individualized music.

Nguyen and Paton (2008) reviewed 11 randomized studies of aromatherapy in older people with behavioural and psychological symptoms in dementia. Although some of the studies were suggestive of reduction in negative behaviours, overall data to support the efficacy of aromatherapy is limited. The potential for adverse effects needs to be considered when this therapy is initiated and to date there are no clear recommendations on the type of oil or optimal method of administration. Animal-assisted ('pet') therapy studied in a nine-week pilot study involving 15 care centres showed a statistically significant decline in agitation in comparison to baseline (Richeson 2003).

Limitations of much of the literature examining non-pharmacological interventions include small sample sizes, lack of blinded study designs and reductions of agitation without clear clinical correlates (e.g. evidence of reduced need for restraint was not documented in the majority of studies). Nevertheless, there is a clear trend suggesting individualized interventions that place an emphasis on understanding individuals' past and current preferences in the context of their present cognitive and physical limitations can be promising alternatives to restraint. Furthermore, these interventions are often simple, inexpensive and non-invasive means of improving the quality of life for older people.

Case study

Three years later, Mr Sparks' dementia has progressed to a moderately severe stage. His wife died four months ago and Mr Sparks' sister has taken over visiting him in the care centre on a weekly basis. His sister is worried that Mr Sparks no longer perks up when she brings his dog,

Misty, to visit. She has also noticed that his clothes are looser and staff confirm that he is no longer eating his entire meals. He used to keep busy on the unit wiping down the countertops as he was in the habit of doing at the bakery he worked at, but now he seems anxious and either sits in a chair wringing his hands or paces to the exits of the unit saying 'Oh no' or 'Help me' over and over. Nursing staff worry that he might elope from the unit and also find him to be more irritable when they try to engage him in recreational activities.

MANAGING DEPRESSION

Verbally disruptive behaviours including singing, screaming, using threatening or obscene language, talking constantly, repeated requests for 'help' or other repetitive attention-seeking words or phrases are a heterogeneous group of behaviours with frequencies reported as high as 66 per cent (von Gunten *et al.* 2008). In our experience, these behaviours are frustrating for staff and commonly lead to requests for chemical restraint by staff.

Prior to considering pharmacological treatment of these behaviours, it is important to clarify the source of the verbally disruptive behaviour. Factors such as over or under-stimulation in the environment, a primary psychiatric disorder (such as psychosis or a mood disorder), pain, hunger or other types of physical discomfort all need to be considered and addressed (von Gunten *et al.* 2008).

It may be a simple matter of asking people 'What is wrong?' Issues such as loneliness could be addressed by relocating people to a chair close to the nursing station; if someone is bored they could be given a meaningful activity to do; and physical discomfort or pain can be treated as appropriate. Sometimes people can be too cognitively impaired to verbally communicate their concerns. In this situation, determining if there is a pattern of behaviour, for example via behaviour mapping, may be helpful in determining possible cause. (See, for an example, the Behavioural Vital Signs Tool, Canadian Academy of Geriatric Psychiatry 2008 or figure 13.1.) Increased agitation around meal times might signal hunger as a cause for calling out whereas agitation later in the day or around unit shift changes may suggest sundowning or over-stimulation. Remaining vigilant for pain, as discussed earlier, is also crucial.

Environmental modifications, reframing of disruptive vocalizations in more positive ways, educating staff to approach people in a calm and soothing manner (thereby encouraging the person with dementia to mirror their behaviour), positively reinforcing non-disruptive behaviour and engaging older people in individual specific activities (such as music therapy or other sensory stimulation) are all possible means of reducing verbally disruptive behaviour, although to date these interventions lack rigorous research evidence to support their efficacy (von Gunten *et al.* 2008).

Psychiatric symptoms can often be difficult to elicit, especially in those with moderate cognitive impairment due to impairment with memory and verbal skills. However, given the high prevalence of psychiatric illnesses such as depression in people with Alzheimer's Disease and other neurodegenerative disorders (Migliorelli *et al.* 1995; Shanmugham *et al.* 2005), a high degree of suspicion is needed to diagnose these disorders. Diagnosis of a psychiatric illness that may be contributing to disruptive behaviours in this population often relies on interviewing family members and friends, knowledge of the individual's personal and family history for mood or other psychiatric disorders and evidence of a cluster of symptoms that represent a change from the person's norm.

The presentation of depression in dementia can have a different constellation of symptoms than typical depression. For example, people with dementia and depression may present with irritability, social withdrawal and aggression (Olin *et al.* 2002). Lyketsos *et al.* (1999) studied the relationship between physical aggression and depression in 541 people with dementia living in the community. Moderate to severe depression was associated with physically aggressive behaviour. Interestingly, sleep disorders, delusions and hallucinations were not shown to be associated with aggression when depression, impairment in activities of daily living and gender were controlled for. There are various tools to assist with diagnosis of depression in older people. For example, the 30-item Geriatric Depression Scale (GDS) has a sensitivity of 84 per cent and specificity of 91 per cent in care home residents with a MMSE greater than 15 (Aging Clinical Research Center's (2008) GDS; McGivney, Mulvihill and Taylor 1994).

The Cornell Scale for Depression in Dementia (CSDD) involves a semi-structured informant interview of mood, vegetative and behavioural symptoms of depression in dementia. It has a sensitivity and specificity of 93 and 97 per cent and has been shown to retain validity in dementia (Kørner *et al.* 2006). (See Cornell University 2002). If depression is confirmed as the possible source of irritability and aggression in people with dementia, several non-restraint options are available for management, including psychotherapy, pharmacotherapy for depression and electroconvulsive therapy (ECT).

Psychotherapy can be limited by the degree of cognitive impairment in people with dementia; however, individuals with mild impairment may benefit from a modified cognitive-behavioural approach or structured recreational activities. For example, a significant decrease in depressive symptoms was found in a review of randomized control trials of non-pharmacological interventions for depression such as peer volunteer intervention, group cognitive behavioural therapy, bright light therapy and staff-assisted exercise programme (Snowden, Sato and Roy-Byrne 2003).

There is little research on the use of antidepressants in dementia. In the seven randomized controlled trials to date, some authors report positive effects of antidepressants; however, these studies are limited by small sample sizes and large placebo effects (Bains, Birks and Dening 2002) and much of the research doesn't include commonly available medications. Recommendations for pharmacological management of depression include starting with an serotonin reuptake inhibitor (SSRI), such as Citalopram 10 mg, increasing to 20 mg if tolerated. If an SSRI is ineffective, mixed mechanism antidepressants could be tried, although due to their significant adverse effect potential, tricyclic antidepressants should be avoided in this population if possible. Rozzini *et al.* (2007) conducted an uncontrolled 16-week study of 135 people with and without depressive symptoms and found that treatment with cholinesterase inhibitors resulted in an improvement in mood four months later, independent of cognitive improvement.

If psychotherapy and pharmacotherapy trials are ineffective, ECT remains an option. Although people with dementia are at greater risk for interictal confusion, ECT has been shown to be effective in the treatment of depression in dementia (Rao and Lyketsos 2000). In addition to non-responders to other treatments, we tend to use ECT in those who have previously showed positive response to ECT, poorly tolerate medications or would benefit from quick resolution to their symptoms.

This section of the chapter has focused on depression diagnosis and management, but other psychiatric conditions, such as psychosis and anxiety disorders, can also present with disruptive behaviours in older people. Remaining vigilant for psychiatric illness and treating symptoms whenever possible can result in less need for the use of restraint as a last resort.

CONCLUSION

The barriers to providing restraint-free care are still numerous. Lack of knowledge about the negative impact of restraint, lack of restraint alternatives, poor communication among staff, low staff-to-client ratios and limitations of the physical environment are just a few examples of barriers to restraint-free care voiced by staff (Moore and Haralambous 2007).

Fortunately, there is evidence that educating staff can lead to reduced restraint use by at least 54 per cent (Testad, Aasland and Aarsland 2005). Implementing policy changes on restraint use, 'restraint reduction kits' and encouraging open discussion among staff are good examples of techniques that can cultivate a restraint-free environment for older people (Markwell 2005).

Knowing the person you are caring for as an individual, preserving them as a person and maintaining their dignity will ultimately lead to restraint-free care. Awareness of potential underlying sources of disruptive behaviours, including psychiatric illness, delirium, pain and unmet emotional and environmental needs, will offer further clues to an effective treatment plan. In conclusion, explore all possibilities to meet the challenge of providing restraint-free care. Entrust staff with the education, tools and the opportunity to be creative in managing disruptive behaviours. At the end of life, treating people who are entrusted to our care with dignity, respect and a touch of humour will make the experience for all worthwhile.

REFERENCES

Aging Clinical Research Center (2008) *Geriatric Depression Scale.* Stanford: Aging Clinical Research Center. Available at www.stanford.edu/~yesavage/GDS.html, accessed 6 November 2009.

Ayalon, L., Gum, A.M., Feliciano, L. and Areán, P. (2006) 'Effectiveness of nonpharmacological interventions for the management of neuropsychiatric symptoms in patients with dementia.' *Archives of Internal Medicine 166*, 20, 2182–2188.

Bains, J., Birks, J.S. and Dening, T.R. (2002) 'The efficacy of antidepressants in the treatment of depression in dementia.' *Cochrane Database of Systematic Reviews 4*, CD003944.

Brotons, M. and Pickett-Cooper, P.K. (1996) 'The effects of music therapy intervention on agitation behaviors of AD patients.' *Journal of Music Therapy 33*, 1, 2–18.

Canadian Academy of Geriatric Psychiatry (2008) *Behavioural Vital Signs Tool.* Toronto: Canadian Academy of Geriatric Psychiatry. Available at www.cagp.ca/Content/Documents/Document. ashx?DocId=27068, accessed 6 November 2009.

Clark, M.E., Lipe, A.W. and Bilbrey, M. (1998) 'Use of music to decrease aggressive behaviors in people with dementia.' *Journal of Gerontological Nursing 24*, 7, 10–17.

Cohen-Mansfield, J., Libin, A. and Marx, M.S. (2007) 'Nonpharmacological treatment of agitation: A controlled trial of systematic individualized intervention.' *Journals of Gerontology Series A – Biological Sciences and Medical Sciences 62*, 8, 908–916.

Cohen-Mansfield, J. (2008) 'The relationship between different pain assessments in dementia.' *Alzheimer Disease and Associated Disorders 22*, 1, 86–93.

Cornell University (2002) *Cornell Scale for Depression in Dementia.* Available at www.qualitynet.org/dcs/ ContentServer?cid=1116947564848&pagename=Medqic/MQToolsToolTemplate&c=MQTools, accessed on 6 November 2009.

Denney, A. (1997) 'Quiet music: An intervention for mealtime agitation?' *Journal of Gerontological Nursing 23*, 7, 16–23.

Flaherty, J.H., Tariq, S.H., Raghavan, S., Bakshi, S., Moinuddin, A. and Morley, J.E. (2003) 'A model for managing delirious older inpatients.' *Journal of the American Geriatrics Society 51*, 7, 1031–1035.

Gerdner, L.A. (2000) 'Effects of individualized versus classical "relaxation" music on the frequency of agitation in elderly persons with Alzheimer's disease and related disorders.' *International Psychogeriatrics 12*, 1, 49–65.

Goddaer, J. and Abraham, I. (1994) 'Effects of relaxing music on agitation during meals among nursing home residents with severe cognitive impairment.' *Archives of Psychiatric Nursing 8*, 3, 150–158.

Gormley, N., Lyons, D. and Howard, R. (2001) 'Behavioural management of aggression in dementia: A randomized controlled trial.' *Age and Ageing 30*, 2, 141–145.

Hall, G.R. and Buckwalter, K.C. (1987) 'Progressively lowered stress threshold: A conceptual model for care of adults with Alzheimer's disease.' *Archives of Psychiatric Nursing 1*, 6, 399–406.

Husebo, B.S., Strand, L.I., Moe-Nilssen, R., Borgehusebo, S., Aarsland, D. and Ljunggren, A.E. (2008) 'Who suffers most? Dementia and pain in nursing home patients: A cross-sectional study.' *Journal of American Medical Directors Association 9*, 6, 427–433.

Inouye, S.K., Baker, D.I., Fugal, P. and Brandley, E.H. (2006) 'Dissemination of the Hospital Elder Life Program: Implementation, adaptation, and successes.' *Journal of the American Geriatrics Society 54*, 10, 1492–1499.

Inouye, S.K., Bogardus, S.T., Charpentier, P.A., Leo-Summers, L. *et al.* (1999) 'A multicomponent intervention to prevent delirium in hospitalized older patients.' *New England Journal of Medicine 340*, 9, 669–676.

Kørner, A., Lauritzen, L., Abelskov, K., Gulmann, N. *et al.* (2006) 'The Geriatric Depression Scale and the Cornell Scale for Depression in Dementia: A validity study.' *Nordic Journal of Psychiatry 60*, 5, 360–364.

Landefeld, C.S., Palmer, R.M., Kresevic, D.M., Fortinsky, R.H. and Kowal, J. (1995) 'A randomized trial of care in a hospital medical unit especially designed to improve the functional outcomes of acutely ill older patients.' *New England Journal of Medicine 332*, 20, 1338–1344.

Lyketsos, C.G., Steele, C., Galik, E., Rosenblatt, A. *et al.* (1999) 'Physical aggression in dementia patients and its relationship to depression.' *American Journal of Psychiatry 156*, 1, 66–71.

McGivney, S.A., Mulvihill, M. and Taylor, B. (1994) 'Validating the GDS Depression Screen in the nursing home.' *Journal of American Geriatrics Society 42*, 5, 490–492.

Mahoney, A.E. and Peters, L. (2008) 'The Mahoney Pain Scale: Examining pain and agitation in advanced dementia.' *American Journal of Alzheimer's Disease and Other Dementias 23*, 3, 250–261.

Markwell, S. (2005) 'Long-term restraint reduction: One hospital's experience with restraint alternatives.' *Journal of Nursing Care Quality 20*, 3, 253–260.

Meagher, D. (2001) 'Delirium: The role of psychiatry.' *Advances in Psychiatric Treatment 7*, 6, 433–443.

Migliorelli, R., Teson, A., Sabe, L., Petracchi, M., Leiguarda, R. and Starkstein, S.E. (1995) 'Prevalence and correlates of dysthymia and major depression among patients with Alzheimer's disease.' *American Journal of Psychiatry 152*, 1, 37–44.

Moore, K. and Haralambous, B. (2007) 'Barriers to reducing the use of restraints in residential elder care facilities.' *Journal of Advanced Nursing 58*, 6, 532–540.

Nguyen, Q.A. and Paton, C. (2008) 'The use of aromatherapy to treat behavioural problems in dementia.' *International Journal of Geriatric Psychiatry 23*, 4, 337–346.

Olin, J.T., Katz, I.R., Meyers, B.S., Schneider, L.S. and Lebowitz, B.D. (2002) 'Provisional diagnostic criteria for depression of Alzheimer disease: Rationale and background.' *American Journal of Geriatric Psychiatry 10*, 2, 129–141.

Pelletier, I.C. and Landreville, P. (2007) 'Discomfort and agitation in older adults with dementia.' *BMC Geriatrics 7*, 27–34.

Raglio, A., Bellelli, G., Traficante, D., Gianotti, M.T. *et al.* (2008) 'Efficacy of music therapy in the treatment of behavioural and psychiatric symptoms of dementia.' *Alzheimer Disease and Associated Disorders 22*, 2, 158–162.

Ragneskog, H., Brane, G., Karlsson, I. and Kihlgren, M. (1996) 'Influence of dinner music on food intake and symptoms common in dementia.' *Scandinavian Journal of Caring Sciences 10*, 1, 11–17.

Rao, V. and Lyketsos, C.G. (2000) 'The benefits and risks of ECT for patients with primary dementia who also suffer from depression.' *International Journal of Geriatric Psychiatry 15*, 8, 729–735.

Richeson, N.E. (2003) 'Effects of animal-assisted therapy on agitated behaviors and social interactions of older adults with dementia.' *American Journal of Alzheimer's Disease and Other Dementias 18*, 6, 353–358.

Rossby, L., Beck, C. and Heakcock, P. (1992) 'Disruptive behaviors of a cognitively impaired nursing home resident.' *Archives of Psychiatric Nursing 6*, 2, 98–107.

Rozzini, L., Vicini Chilovi, B., Bertoletti, E., Trabucchi, M. and Padovani, A. (2007) 'Acetylcholinesterase inhibitors and depressive symptoms in patients with mild to moderate Alzheimer's Disease.' *Aging Clinical and Experimental Research 19*, 3, 220–223.

Ryden, M.B., Bossenmaier, M. and McLachlan, C. (1991) 'Aggressive behavior in cognitively impaired nursing home residents.' *Research in Nursing & Health 14*, 2, 87–95.

Savoie, M. (2008) 'Pain in severe dementia: How to assess.' *Canadian Review of Alzheimer's Disease and Other Dementias 11*, 3, 21–26.

Schreiner, A.S. (2001) 'Aggressive behaviors among demented nursing home residents in Japan.' *International Journal of Geriatric Psychiatry 16*, 2, 209–215.

Shanmugham, B., Karp, J., Drayer, R., Reynolds, C.F. and Alexopoulos, G. (2005) 'Evidence-based pharmacologic interventions for geriatric depression.' *Psychiatric Clinics of North America 28*, 4, 821–835.

Snowden, M., Sato, K. and Roy-Byrne, P. (2003) 'Assessment and treatment of nursing home residents with depression or behavioural symptoms associated with dementia: A review of the literature.' *Journal of the American Geriatrics Society 51*, 9, 1305–1317.

Tabloski, P., McKinnon-Howe, L. and Remington, T. (1995) 'Effects of calming music on the level of agitation in cognitively impaired nursing home residents.' *American Journal of Alzheimer's Care and Related Disorders and Research 10*, 1, 10–15.

Testad, I., Aasland, M. and Aarsland, D. (2005) 'The effect of staff training on the use of restraint in dementia: A single-blind randomised controlled trial.' *International Journal of Geriatric Psychiatry 20*, 6, 587–590.

Thomas, D.W., Heitman, R.J. and Alexander, T. (1997) 'The effects of music on bathing cooperation for residents with dementia.' *Journal of Music Therapy 34*, 4, 246–259.

Vollmer, C., Rich, C. and Robinson, S. (2007) 'How to prevent delirium: A practical approach.' *Nursing 37*, 8 (August 26–28).

von Gunten, A., Alnawaqil, A., Abderhalden, C., Needham, I. and Schupbach, B. (2008) 'Vocally disruptive behavior in the elderly: A systematic review.' *International Psychogeriatric Association 20*, 4, 653–672.

Chapter 14

WANDER-WALKING AND PEOPLE WITH DEMENTIA

Jan Dewing and Heather Wilkinson

INTRODUCTION

Wandering (or wander-walking) in people with dementia is a phenomenon that is poorly understood. Consequently, it is challenging for practitioners to implement evidence-based practice. Interventions to respond to the person who is wandering tend to be initiated after inaccurate or incomplete assessment and are not always appropriate for the wandering that is being lived out. The good news is that some of the evidence base on wandering is now reasonably developed, considering how recently wandering has been the focus of research, and can be used to guide assessment and interventions across a range of care settings. Additionally, knowledge about assistive technology (AT) in regards to wandering is an area opening up for further research. At the current time, little is known about the best way to assess for AT, or the application of and outcomes from AT in the case of people with dementia who wander or wander-walk. This chapter aims to provide an overview of wandering: what it is, how it can be assessed and the possible application of assistive technologies as one set of interventions in a therapeutic response to wandering. We will also consider people with learning disabilities and dementia. The chapter will make it clear that the debate that lies at the heart of making use of assistive technologies is essentially an ethical one and some of what we believe are the central ethical issues will be discussed later in the chapter.

Before beginning, we introduce a note on terminology. In the UK the term 'wandering' tends to be considered as a negative label. Consequently, there has been a push in some quarters to substitute the term 'walking' (Marshall and Allan 2006). However, this is etymologically inaccurate. Wandering is a distinct form of ambulation or locomotion. It does not constitute every type of walking that people with or without dementia engage in. For example, whilst we might use the terms interchangeably, we would know that strolling, rambling or paddling in the sea were different types of walking and that walking is the larger category to which these sub-types belong. Hence wandering is a type of walking, not walking *per se*. People with dementia may wander but not all ambulation or locomotion is wandering. Readers may thus like to substitute the term 'wander-walking'.

In this chapter we will describe the attributes of wandering or wander-walking as found in the literature and offer an overview of the current state of knowledge around assessment and interventions on wandering as relevant to this chapter. This is necessary background to understanding how AT can make a useful contribution as part of the interventions for responding to wandering. Central to this is an appreciation that wandering needs to be more systematically assessed and responded to across the diverse groups of people with dementia, including people with intellectual disabilities. We will then focus on discussing the main ethical concerns associated with using AT to respond to wandering.

DESCRIBING THE ATTRIBUTES OF WANDERING

For professionals working in dementia care, wandering will be something that is regularly encountered across different care settings from community to acute care and long-term care facilities. This is because it affects most people with dementia at some point during their dementia journey. However, as Lai and Arthur (2003) report, it is difficult to secure accurate figures on the numbers of people with dementia who wander. Klein *et al.* (1999) propose wandering occurs in 17.4 per cent of persons with dementia and is significantly more prevalent in persons with Alzheimer's types of dementia. Ryan (2000), in a small qualitative study, found wandering is the primary cause for families seeking a nursing home placement in 25 per cent of cases, whilst Nolan, Ingram and Watson (2002) report 58 per cent of families find wandering in the home problematic. Klein *et al.* (1999) and Teri, Larson and Reifler (1988) estimate the prevalence of wandering to vary from 17 per cent in community-dwelling persons to 50 per cent respectively. Ballard *et al.* (1991), in a survey, find wandering and getting lost outside of the home is a problem for families in 37 per cent of subjects. Studies examining the prevalence of dementia or dementia-related concerns in ethnic and indigenous groups are few. However, Sink *et al.* (2004), in a US study from a sample of 700 people from black and latino ethnic groups, found a higher prevalence of dementia-related behaviours (67%) than those from the white group. Cohen-Mansfield and Billig (1986) found 73 per cent of residents exhibited agitated behaviours daily and 39 per cent wandered by pacing back and forth (Cohen-Mansfield, Marx and Rosenthal 1989). Algase *et al.* (1997) found almost all residents with dementia wandered at some point. Then Beattie, Song and La Gore (2005) report that levels of wandering tend to be similar across nursing homes and assisted-living facilities.

Although wandering is something most professionals are familiar with, it is equally something that professionals in many countries are not as yet considering in evidence-based ways. We need to be able to distinguish other forms of walking from wandering and then distinguish the different entities of wandering from each other as wandering, in the case of people with dementia, is not a single entity. There are different types and patterns of wandering and people have different lived experiences of wandering. Before we can use any interventions, including AT, with the hope of successful outcomes, we need to know what the phenomenon is that is being responded to.

It is now generally accepted that wandering takes on three patterns or types – lapping, pacing or random – and occurs in cycles which tend to repeat (Algase 2006). Further, wandering can have different intensity levels, whereby some people wander less distance and have fewer cycles and the cycles are of shorter time duration than for other people. However, there is no national or international agreed definition(s) of wandering (Hermans, Htay and McShane 2007). Dewing (2007) reports more than a hundred definitions of wandering between 1979 and 2007 although recognising that several of the more recently empirically devised definitions are being used more frequently. Most definitions describe wandering as a problem behaviour and one that is meaningless or aimless. Algase has long called for an agreed definition of wandering. She has offered regular revisions of definitions based on research findings. Many definitions have often been underpinned by subjective, negative assumptions about dementia. More recently, Algase, Moore and Vandeweerd (2007) propose what they refer to as an objective and empirically founded definition: 'a syndrome of dementia-related locomotion behaviour having a frequent, repetitive, temporally-disordered and/or spatially-disoriented nature that is manifested in lapping, random, and/or pacing patterns, some of which are associated with eloping, eloping attempts, or getting lost unless accompanied'.

This definition is objective compared with previous ones where wandering was generally described as meaningless and aimless. It is important to acknowledge that research has overwhelmingly considered wandering as a behaviour. This conceptualisation has placed some limitations on the body of research to date; significantly wandering has been exclusively researched as an observable behaviour and researched in isolation from other behaviours. However, human activity or behaviour does not occur in isolation. Thus most people with dementia, when they wander, are also engaged in other activities. Further, what is observed as behaviour to others is a complex experience to the person living it. Dewing (2007, p.210) suggests wandering is 'the embodied manifestation of the ways in which a person living with an advancing dementia actively creates integrated meanings encompassing relationships with self, others and objects within named spaces and lived time'. Dewing's research also identifies a number of attributes of wandering, as experienced by older people, which distinguishes it from descriptions generated in behavioural-oriented research (see Box 14.1).

Box 14.1 The phenomenon of wandering

Relationships
- Little or low connection or sense of belonging to the current place and the people there: a lack of familiarity

and/or
- A strong sense of belonging to another place or people somewhere else.
- A strong recurrent desire to be elsewhere, get away or simply to leave the current place.
- Feelings of being alone or not with others who matter.
- A strong recurrent need to actively touch, hold and move about and otherwise explore objects

and/or
- A need to repeatedly enquire about objects within a named space, what they are for and how they work.

The body
- Moving about space and actively engaging with working things out through the body.
- Keeping going as a way of keeping the brain working.
- A searching desire or drive.
- A deep sense of waiting and/or a strong desire to leave.

Space
- A feeling of either being at home, in a temporary home for now

or

- A feeling of not being at home which influences feelings of needing to go.
- A need for enough space to explore and enough freedom to explore it or not or and either (1) space that is either small, structured and boundaried or (2) open, unstructured with flexible boundaries.
- Perceptions of space that lack personal meaning and continuity.

Time
- Sense of chronological time slipping away.
- A deep desire or longing for other/past times and the associations with this time.
- A dislike or anxiety about impending darkness towards darkness and night.

Assessing wandering is still relatively underdeveloped with limited screening and assessment tools available. Further, risk assessment of wandering is still poorly understood and the ordering of risk into possible or low, probable or medium and actual or high risk is generally not happening. All people who wander are considered the same, usually high, risk. This has implications for interventions, including how and when AT is introduced and used. The other aspect here is that introduction of AT with wandering is often associated with increasing risk. Thus, there is a danger that AT will be considered as an intervention for risk management rather than something to improve quality of life. Once the association with risk management is made, AT becomes identified with containment or ultimately with restraint.

THE VOICE OF PEOPLE WITH DEMENTIA

There are only very few accounts concerning wandering and dementia from the UK. In the first Robinson *et al.* (2007), through a small focus group, asked a number of people with dementia and their care partners about wandering and AT. The small number of participants with dementia expressed caution regarding the use of unfamiliar AT. For these participants, exercise and distraction therapies were considered to be the most acceptable interventions and raised no ethical concerns. Other forms of interventions were considered acceptable except for physical restraints, which were considered unacceptable. For all care partners, balancing risk and risk assessment was an important theme in the management of wandering. However, it is not clear what risk was being balanced with.

Dewing (2006), through email conversations via an international dementia network, collected views on wandering amongst seven people living with dementia. Enabling rather than preventing wandering seems to be a key message for practitioners and managers, as the three examples from the conversations here illustrate:

> I worry my home will be made so safe it will bore me. I imagine from what I know from my own work [teaching] that I will keep on learning and do this through exploring. If indoors is not exciting, well outdoors might just do it! I am concerned *now* about the risks I put myself in. But guess that won't apply later.

> I want to be allowed to safely do so [wander], and I'd like to be allowed to safely wander out of doors... When I am at risk of getting lost, I'd like to be fitted with a bracelet that continually broadcasts my whereabouts. If I do get lost, it would be able to locate me within an average thirty minutes' time. I would happily trade being marked and followed electronically in exchange for my continuing ability to move about my community. When I must be kept indoors, I'd like to have well-lighted areas to wander in, and an ever-changing array of safe items in the environment for me to discover and investigate. I'd like to be able to handle them, play with them, and possibly be able to keep them as trophies of my exploration. Such 'discovery' is inherently rewarding and essential to a positive life.

> I've been going out practically every day of my life for one thing or another. It's just what you do... A house and family doesn't run itself. I can't imagine not doing that. I might not know what I'm doing. At this point in time, if I get to that point myself, I would think I will still go out and about. I hate being cooped up. It would be easier to help me than stop me.

It seems that, for some people, AT is an option they would be willing to accept; surveillance or monitoring is seen as being worthwhile if it enables freedom of movement. But by no means are the few voices here claimed to be representative of all people with dementia. There is a moral imperative that professionals listen to and treat as a valid source of evidence the views and experiences of people with dementia. If people with dementia are willing to accept AT, practitioners and managers have a responsibility not to let any negative values and beliefs they hold become barriers in the workplace. Hughes (2008), amongst others, argues that people with dementia need to be included in the debates around ethics of AT. Although

AT covers a broad range of interventions from low to high technology, it is the 'electronic tagging,' surveillance or monitoring that tends to dominate and grab the headlines. It may be that for people with dementia their ethical priorities concerning AT become reordered and what would be most important in their pre-dementia life becomes altered as they live with dementia in the present and face a future with dementia.

RESPONDING TO WANDERING

Traditional management strategies

Traditional interventions have been focused on preventing all types of wandering (i.e. lapping, pacing and random wandering) regardless of type, pattern, intensity and actual risk. Interventions have centred around applying overt or covert physical and chemical restraint to the person or applying aspects of restraint in the environment such as locked doors, double-handled doors and complex baffle locks. In effect, interventions have been severe, applied to all the patient or resident population and generally not evaluated. Because of the severity and widespread application, they interfered with human rights for freedom of movement and choice (Dewing 2008a; Hughes and Louwe 2002). Technology here has been used to prevent and restrain rather than assist and enable.

Current response strategies

In the UK these are generally organised into pharmacological or non-pharmacological interventions. Non-pharmacological interventions consist of either subjective or non-subjective barriers and some other therapeutic interventions. A subjective barrier is an object or device that the person with dementia perceives and believes to be a real barrier. A non-subjective barrier is a real physically present barrier and experienced by all as such (e.g. door locks).

Pharmacological and non-pharmacological interventions

Broader pharmacological interventions for people with dementia have been discussed in another chapter. People with dementia who wander are still more likely to be restrained via pharmacology. While there seems to be a consensus in the literature that, in the majority of cases, non-pharmacological approaches may work just as well and have fewer side effects, in practice clinicians often resort to drugs as the first line of treatment.

Siders *et al.* (2004), in a systematic review of non-pharmacological interventions for wandering (from 31 studies), report on six categories of interventions: subjective barriers; walking/exercise; specialised environments; behavioural methods; music; and alarms. In a more recent systematic review Robinson *et al.* (2007) conclude there is no robust evidence so far to recommend the use of any non-pharmacological intervention to reduce or prevent wandering in people with dementia. From the ten studies in the review, three were about the multi-sensory environment, one about music therapy, one about exercise, two about special care units, two on aromatherapy and one on a specific behavioural intervention. The researchers call for further research to determine the clinical and cost-effectiveness of non-pharmacological interventions that both enable (although they say 'allow') safe wandering and ones that are ethically acceptable by carers and people with dementia. Hermans *et al.* (2007) set out to evaluate the effectiveness and safety of non-pharmacological interventions in reducing wandering in the home setting. As no randomised controlled trials were found, there was nothing to report. The evidence base here is currently of limited guidance.

Practitioners and policy makers need to approach interventions on a case-by-case basis. The contribution of AT within this needs to be considered as one part of a response and never expected to be an option that can replace caregiver input (Cahill *et al.* 2007; Neville, McMinn and Cave 2006). Any single AT intervention (e.g. a hand-held or wrist-watch-type global positioning system (GPS) locator) needs the person with dementia to consent to its use (either informed or process consent (Dewing 2008b)); to be involved in learning how to use it or accepting its presence; and in its review and evaluation. Rasquin *et al.* (2007) show in a single case study that even simple technology can be too challenging to use for both an older person with dementia and their carer. Each piece of AT will have a time-limited span of usefulness and will then need to be changed or withdrawn.

Subjective and non-subjective barriers
Based on research that shows cognitively impaired people tend to change their responses to stimuli (e.g. sounds, images, smells), research of visual and other selective barriers (such as mirrors, camouflage, grids/stripes of tape on the floor, floor patterns (Hewawasam 1996)) has taken place to see if these subjective barriers reduce wandering. Price, Hermans and Grimley Evans (2000), in a systematic review, found that interventions tended to be based on subjective exit modifications which were aimed at preventing people making attempts to leave. No randomised controlled or controlled trials were found and all other experimental studies did not meet the review

criteria and thus were excluded. The authors therefore conclude there is no evidence that subjective barriers prevent wandering in cognitively impaired people. Later, Algase (2006) suggested that the few experimental studies to manage wandering that are sufficiently rigorous indicate mounting evidence for effectiveness of subjective barriers. However, effectiveness in preventing wandering and effectiveness in responding to wandering can mean different things.

PEOPLE WITH AN INTELLECTUAL DISABILITY – DEMENTIA AND WANDERING

In this section we examine the meaning of wander-walking for someone growing older with an intellectual disability and how this can be a very different experience resulting in different service approaches than for an older person in the general population. We begin with a demographic overview before focusing on wandering when it is considered as a 'challenging' behaviour and some of the possible responses.

Growing older and dementia for people with an intellectual disability

There have been significant shifts in the demographics of people with an intellectual disability, mostly following improvements in medical and social support, and as a group people with an intellectual disability are now living further into old age (Baird and Sadovnik 1987; Janicki, McCallion and Dalton 2000). Subsequently the number of people with an intellectual disability will continue to grow by over 1 per cent a year over the next ten years (Department of Health 2001; Scottish Executive 2000).

Such shifts in life expectancy bring with them associated increases in the numbers of people with an intellectual disability experiencing age-related illnesses, such as dementia. Dementia generally affects people with intellectual disability in the same manner as it does other older people, although, as Tyrell, Cosgrove and McCarron (2001) state, adults with Down's syndrome are at greater overall risk of being affected by dementia, often but not exclusively Alzheimer's disease, and are often affected at an earlier age with a sharper decline and loss of skills within a shorter period of time. Often the loss of daily living skills is more apparent than memory loss in the early stages. Diagnosis can be problematic and often occurs much later than for people in the general population or there may be misdiagnosis (Prasher and Krishna 1993). Although statistics are not consistent (Lai and Williams 1989; Prasher and Krishna 1993; Tyrell *et al.* 2001), this is clearly a specific health issue for people with Down's syndrome as they age, and a matter of concern for their carers who need to be aware of different presentations and issues associated with dementia in people with Down's syndrome.

Many people with an intellectual disability in the UK live with their families, or within a continuum of formal care settings from segregated specialist provision specifically for older people to services for older people with an intellectual disability, either as part of general services for older people or in the context of more individualised routes of care (Heller 1999). Dementia is of particular concern for service planners and practitioners as the increased likelihood of the rapid progression of dementia in the individual places considerable extra demands on services (Wilkinson and Janicki 2000; Wilkinson *et al.* 2004). Despite the clear demographic imperative for understanding the needs of people with Down's syndrome and dementia, there is a dearth of policy guidance for this group in the UK (Forbat and Wilkinson 2008). Information and evidence on how best to provide services that are needs-led, multidisciplinary and supportive are missing (Watchman 2007).

When focusing on the experience of growing older with an intellectual disability and what this can mean in practice, the issue of wandering is an example of how exploring issues associated with providing care for people with intellectual disabilities and dementia highlights lessons that can be shared. One particular area within this is restraint and wandering.

Dementia and wandering for people with an intellectual disability

As outlined earlier in this chapter, wandering is often considered problem behaviour. For someone with an intellectual disability there are two key differences: first, 'wandering' may have been an activity or behaviour that they have engaged in throughout their life and is not necessarily something that is only associated with growing older or with the onset of dementia; second, behaviours and activities that people with an intellectual disability engage in that are problematic for staff or carers are often labelled as 'challenging' and receive a particular response, which may have previously included restraint. The literature on restraints for this population relates to 'challenging behaviours' and wandering is rarely specified and there are no systematic reviews.

Use of restraint

Sturmey (2009a, 2009b) clearly outlines the problematic nature of why and how restraints are used with people with intellectual disabilities. An analysis of injuries related to restraint of people with intellectual disabilities found that where planned and as part of a behaviour programme the rate of injury was lower than when used during a crisis (Williams 2009). Despite these concerns, a recent survey of 509 English social service units highlighted common use of pharmacological, physical and mechanical restraints with people with intellectual disabilities (Health Care Commission and the Commission for Social Care Inspection 2007). The range of restraints used with people with intellectual disabilities covers a spectrum of 'restrictive behavioural practices' that 'limit a person's movements, access to their personal possessions or that otherwise restrict their liberties' (Sturmey 2009a, p.105). The review work undertaken by Sturmey highlighted the difficulty in determining the exact prevalence of restricted behavioural practices but the data he analysed from The Healthcare Commision and Commision for Social Care Inspection (2007) survey found that 'approximately 80% reported using PRN medication and approximately half reported using personal and mechanical restraints'. (Sturmey 2009a, p.107). The views of service users around the use of restraints (Jones and Kroese 2006), whilst not specifically in relation to wandering, were mixed, although they indicated the need for staff training on when and how to use restraint and that generally greater communication would be a potentially effective alternative. Recent work in the US (Sanders 2009) places dignity and respect at the centre of good care and argues that the use of physical restraints is contrary to such treatment. Evidence indicated that learning encompassing staff awareness and training, alternative strategies and management support could reduce significantly the use of restraint by staff with service users with intellectual disabilities.

Case study: William

William is a 54-year-old man with Down's syndrome who was diagnosed with Alzheimer's type dementia three years ago. He receives residential care and lives in a large house with seven other men. At this stage of his dementia he is extremely mobile, wandering around his environment for most of the day (as well as during the night when his sleep is disturbed). Over the previous month he has become more adventurous and has 'escaped' from the house, taking himself to the local town which involves crossing various roads and navigating kerbs and uneven ground. On one occasion the police returned him to his home and on others general members of the public escorted him. Staff from the home also formed 'search parties'. After the most recent event, a multi-disciplinary meeting with police representation was convened, the subject being how to manage the situation.

The issues were:

- William wandered around his environment but now had developed an urgency to go outside, taking every opportunity to 'escape' out of either the front or back door.

- The doors were unlocked.

- The staffing levels were not sufficient to offer William 1:1 support.

- William was vulnerable and 'at risk' due to his Inability to perceive danger on the roads and his increased risk of falling due to his compromised balance reactions, gait pattern and his tendency to get lost, common issues associated with Alzheimer's disease within this client group.

Ideas from the staff:

- Locking the doors – despite the existing policy.

- Creating a system that allowed the other men to exit the house when they wanted to but alerted the staff team when William left.

- Providing extra hours of support staff time to offer William the increased observation he required.

- Referring to the physiotherapist to supply a 'lap strap' for either a wheelchair and/or his armchair which would increase his safety and enable the staff to keep an eye on him.

Resolutions considered:

- After much discussion the issue of locking the doors was partly resolved by locking the back door and hanging the key next to the door. This enabled the other men to use it; however, William was unable to correlate the sequence of getting the key then opening the door. A baffle lock was considered but felt to be inappropriate because it would attract William's interest and negatively impact on him and everyone else living there. The front door remained unlocked as it could not be locked due to the policy of the residential home as well as deprivation of liberty legislation.

- The front door was fitted with an alarm which sounded as the door was opened.

- Some extra hours were resourced which gave William 1:1 time.

- The physiotherapist accepted referral for assessment of William's needs. The idea of a lap strap was firmly discounted as this constituted a form of restraint and therefore legally and ethically wrong. It was suggested to the staff that keeping William fixed in one spot would decrease his mobility and increase his anxiety, agitation and stress.

- It was agreed to work with his need to mobilise and explore by enabling him to do this in a structured and accompanied way.

Plan:

The physiotherapist carried out an assessment and asked the care staff to share their observations of William's wandering. They started a weekly exercise group in the house. This was predominantly for William. However, some of the other men joined in too, making it a social event as well as therapeutic intervention. It was also decided to form a 'walking group'. William and a few of the men would, every week, go on a structured walk out and about in the community. This was led initially by the physiotherapist and included the extra help resourced for William so he had 1:1 support. From the beginning this became a true 'ramble' with points of interest pointed out and 'trophies' from the environment collected to take back and either have a discussion about and/or make collages, etc. from. William approached both these interventions with enthusiasm.

After six weeks the activities were evaluated. The effect on William was reported as being very positive; on the days he had his exercise or walk he was less frustrated in the evenings and was less inclined to make attempts to 'escape'. This is similar to findings by Holmberg (1997) in regard to a walking group. It was decided that the staff employed in the home would continue facilitating the group and that the extra support gained for William would be used to facilitate him to wander-walk outside for a designated time every day. The staff's values and beliefs also began to change to see how wandering need not be the negative behaviour they assumed it was; conversely, it was the consequences of ill-informed responses to wandering that caused the negativity.

ETHICAL CONCERNS WITH ASSISTIVE TECHNOLOGIES

The use of AT is becoming a more prominent feature in all our lives. To begin with it is necessary to look more broadly at how technology, especially electronic surveillance measures, are gradually becoming a part of our way of life. Although some debate is taking place about the ethics around this, it is almost after the event, and the technological tide continues to move forward. We both love and hate technology and both want to be under surveillance for security and not under surveillance for personal freedom (Archer 2006; Welsh *et al.* 2003). Its use with any potentially vulnerable group needs careful debate. For older people with dementia this is necessary partially because of the historical background and associated values and beliefs about dementia and dementia care within the context of ageing. This can be epitomised by the theme of keeping people with dementia safe in parallel with risk avoidance. A backdrop such as this led to AT being used as another method to prevent and restrain people and their freedom of movement. With the development and diversification of AT it will be necessary to have a broad definition of AT. Nelson, Powell-Cope and Gavin-Dreschnack (2004) consider the use of AT to promote safe mobility and reduce falls and wandering and discuss devices and equipment such as hip protectors, wheelchair anti-tippers, fall alarms and patient hoists. According to Goodacre, McCreadie and Flanagan (2007) the factors that affect a property's adaptability include property type and specific design and construction features.

Hussain and Brown (1987) used two-dimensional visual barriers to decrease exit seeking for eight men with dementia using a masking-tape grid pattern placed on the floor in front of exit doors. Then Namazi, Rosner and Calkins (1989) used three-dimensional cloth barriers to conceal door handles. Feliciano *et al.* (2004) undertook a case study method to examine the use of a cloth barrier to decrease entry into a restricted area by a developmentally disabled woman with bipolar disorder and probable dementia. A strip of turquoise fleece cloth (38 cm by 104 cm) that matched the door colour was attached to the entryway with 35-cm strips of material located at the participant's eye level. This was used because the participant was never observed to glance at the floor. Significant decreases in entries were observed. Later on, this was reinforced, and attempted entries were given lack of social reinforcement.

It is likely, however, that electronic AT will continue to be the focus of attention in regards to wandering. Bjorneby, Duff and Maki (2003) suggest seven core principles for all AT. AT should:

1. give the feeling of independence to the person
2. support the person in making choices
3. have a positive impact on their life
4. support existing or current skills rather than lost skills

5. support the self-image of the person and not focus on their disability

6. be part of previously used solutions preferred by the person

7. be easy to access and use technologically.

These principles can be used as part of assessment and discussion about ethical concerns associated with the use of AT for wandering. Hughes (2008) suggests there are two main forms of surveillance for wandering: boundary alarms and tracking systems. Boundary alarms are set to alert staff or caregivers when a person transgresses from what is considered a safe to a less safe area. Miskelly (2004) piloted a system of electronic tagging with three people centred on wearing of a wrist watch and found it was tolerated. Altus *et al.* (2000) undertook a six-month pilot evaluation of a specific electronic device designed to help caregivers quickly locate a person who had eloped. The study included case studies of seven people. An opinion survey of family caregivers, professional caregivers and search and rescue workers showed that respondents were positively impressed by the device. Case studies revealed that the equipment was easy to use, effective and helpful. Cost was seen as a drawback. The issue of introducing AT, especially expensive AT, needs consideration. This is not only because of maintenance and repair needs, but because of the funding issue and the issue about who needs to locate and retrieve the person if this is necessary. In many cases the cost and searching is borne by families.

Skilful assessment including observation and accompanying the person is needed to decide on where the boundaries lie. Tracking systems make use of global positioning systems and mobile phone technologies. Both forms of surveillance require the person to carry or wear a device of some sort. This may be, for example, in the style of a wrist watch (Miskelly 2004), within a phone, or an electronic chip positioned in an item of clothing or footwear. With regard to surveillance and monitoring, the negative association with electronic tagging and criminality is already rooted in public consciousness (Hughes 2008). This is something that will need some good PR to achieve a distance between the two.

There is increased opportunity for both indirect and direct abuse through, for example, the withdrawal of staff and financial resources from the care of people with complex needs. It needs to be remembered that all AT for surveillance requires staff input for assessment, monitoring and evaluation purposes. How much monitoring is needed before AT becomes an invasion of privacy is an important question for any team to debate. Implementing AT has ethical implications for human rights and civil liberties. Thus, risk assessment must look at risk versus benefit (human rights and civil liberties) strategies. A central concern seems to be around consent (Hughes and Louwe 2002) with many services getting round this by drawing on 'proxy' consent. An area very much overlooked is the environment. Attending to providing more dementia-sensitive and friendly environments can reduce the need for some AT in some people. For example, better colour contrast and signage can mean transgression of boundaries is reduced. Electronic tagging and tracking devices may be seen as a way of creating a more secure environment for vulnerable individuals. There continues to be a view that older people need to be watched and increased anxiety when this cannot happen. Recognition that this is not ethically desirable nor practically achievable needs to be factored in to debates. Further, AT does not have 'magical' powers. Ultimately, it does not prevent people who wander from wandering, from becoming lost, from getting hurt and sustaining injuries, though it may raise the alarm and enable easier location. Currently, many settings have CCTV on all the time and yet no one is watching it and there is no recorded data. It is a comfort for staff and yet a very misleading one for the welfare of people with dementia.

CONCLUSIONS

These are stated as a series of bullet points which set out the implications for practice and policy:

- Wandering usually cannot be prevented without breaking legal and ethical codes to some extent.

- Risk assessment must be based on core ethical principles.

- Wandering needs to be better understood and assessed.

- Current evidence of the effectiveness of non-pharmacological interventions including subjective and non-subjective barriers is of limited use in guiding practice and policy.

- AT needs to be considered as part of a multi-dimensional approach to responding to wandering.

- People with dementia, in many cases, may accept AT as a means of enabling greater personal freedom and freedom of movement.

- The most appropriate type of AT needs to be introduced at the right time to assist continuation of personal freedoms.

- Any AT intervention is of time-limited effectiveness.

- AT should not be seen as a universal 'fix all' nor a risk-prevention tool.

The future for research and practice in regards to wandering is set within a context that is becoming more risk averse and more litigious and yet one where human rights are supposedly of increasing importance in social and legal decision-making systems (Dewing 2008a). These rights must include people with dementia. Our energies, often put into preventing and controlling all wandering to avoid possible consequences, need to be redirected to facilitating safer wandering and promotion of rights and freedoms as the ultimate priority unless the person with dementia has and continues to express a different priority.

REFERENCES

Algase, D. (2006) 'What's new about wandering behaviour? An assessment of recent studies.' *International Journal of Older People Nursing 1*, 4, 226–234.

Algase, D.L., Kupferschmid, B., Beel-Bates, C.A. and Beattie, E.R. (1997) 'Estimates of stability of daily wandering behaviour among cognitively impaired long term care residents.' *Nursing Research 46*, 3, 172–178.

Algase, D.L., Moore, D.H. and Vandeweerd, C. (2007) 'Mapping the maze of terms and definitions in dementia-related wandering.' *Aging & Mental Health 6*, 686–698.

Altus, D.E., Mathews, R.M., Xaverius, P.K., Engelman, K.K. and Nolan, B.A.D. (2000) 'Evaluating an electronic monitoring system for people who wander.' *American Journal of Alzheimer's Disease and Other Dementias 15*, 2, 121–125.

Archer, B. (2006) 'Assistive technology: A balancing act.' *British Journal of Healthcare Computing and Information Management 23*, 8, 19–20.

Baird, P. and Sadovnik, A.D. (1987) 'Life expectancy in Down syndrome.' *Journal of Paediatrics 110*, 849–854.

Ballard, C.G., Mohan, R.N.C., Bannister, C., Handy, S. and Patel, A. (1991) 'Wandering in dementia sufferers.' *International Journal of Geriatric Psychiatry 6*, 611–614.

Beattie, E.R.A., Song, J.A. and La Gore, S. (2005) 'A comparison of wandering behaviour in nursing home and assisted living facilities.' *Research and Theory for Nursing Practice: An International Journal 19*, 20, 181–196.

Bjorneby, S., Duff, P. and Maki, O. (2003) 'Developing Assistive Technology for People with Dementia.' In G. Craddock (ed.) *Assistive Technology – Shaping the Future.* London: IOS Press.

Cahill, S., Macijauskiene, J., Nygard, A.M., Faulkner, J.P. and Hagan, I. (2007) 'Technology in dementia care.' *Technology and Disability 19*, 55–60.

Cohen-Mansfield, J. and Billig, N. (1986) 'Agitated behaviours in the elderly: A conceptual review.' *Journal of the American Geriatric Society 34*, 711–721.

Cohen-Mansfield, J., Marx, M.S. and Rosenthal, A.S. (1989) 'A description of agitation in a nursing home.' *Journal of Gerontology 44*, 3, M77–M84.

Department of Health (2001) *Valuing People: A New Strategy for Learning Disability for the 21st Century.* London: Department of Health.

Dewing, J. (2006) 'Wandering into the future: Reconceptualizing wandering "a natural and good thing".' *International Journal of Older People Nursing 1*, 4, 239–249.

Dewing, J. (2007) 'An exploration of wandering in older persons with a dementia through radical reflection and participation.' PhD thesis, University of Manchester.

Dewing, J. (2008a) 'Guest editorial: The right to walk – An older person's human right.' *International Journal of Older People Nursing 3*, 1–2.

Dewing, J. (2008b) 'Process consent and research with older persons living with dementia.' *Association of Research Ethics Journal 4*, 2, 59–64.

Emerson, E. (2002) 'The Prevalence of Use of Reactive Management Strategies in Community-Based Services in the UK.' In D. Allen (ed.) *Ethical Approaches to Physical Interventions: Responding to Challenging Behaviour in People with Intellectual Disabilities.* Plymstock: BILD Publishers.

Feliciano, L., Vore, J., LeBlanc, L.A. and Baker, J.C. (2004) 'Decreasing entry into a restricted area using a visual barrier.' *Journal of Applied Behavior Analysis 37*, 1, 107–110.

Forbat, L., and Wilkinson, H. (2008) 'Where should people with dementia live? Using the views of service users to inform models of care.' *British Journal of Learning Disabilities 36*, 1, 6–12.

Goodacre, K., McCreadie, C. and Flanagan, S. (2007) 'Enabling older people to stay at home: How adaptable are existing properties?' *British Journal of Occupational Therapy 70*, 1, 5–15.

Health Care Commission and the Commission for Social Care Inspection (2007) *A Life Like No Other.* London: Healthcare Commission.

Heller, T. (1999) 'Emerging Models.' In S.S. Herr and G. Weber (eds) *Aging, Rights and Quality of Life: Prospects for Older People with Developmental Disabilities.* Baltimore, MA: Paul H. Brookes.

Hermans, D.G., Htay, U.H. and McShane, R. (2007) 'Non-pharmacological interventions for wandering of people with dementia in the domestic setting.' *Cochrane Database Systematic Reviews*, Jan 24, 1.

Hewawasam, L. (1996) 'Floor patterns limit wandering of people with Alzheimer's.' *Nursing Times 92*, 22, 41–44.

Holmberg, S. (1997) 'A walking program for wanderers: Volunteer training and development of an evening walker's group.' *Geriatric Nursing 18*, 160–165.

Hughes, J. and Louwe, S. (2002) 'Electronic tagging of people with dementia who wander.' *British Medical Journal 325*, 847–848.

Hughes, R. (2008) 'Safer walking? Issues and ethics in the use of electronic surveillance of people with dementia.' *Journal of Assistive Technologies 2*, 1, 45–48.

Hussain, R.A. and Brown, D.C. (1987) 'Use of two-dimensional grid patterns to limit hazardous ambulation in demented patients.' *Journal of Gerontology 42*, 558–560.

Janicki, M.P., McCallion, P. and Dalton, A. (2000) 'Supporting People with Dementia in Community Settings.' In M.P. Janicki and E.F. Ansello (eds) *Community Supports for Aging Adults with Lifelong Disabilities.* New York: Paul H. Brookes.

Jones, P. and Kroese, B.S. (2006) 'Service users' views of physical procedures in secure settings for people with learning disabilities.' *British Journal of Learning Disabilities 35*, 50–54.

Klein, D.A., Steinberg, M., Galik, E., Steele, C. *et al.* (1999) 'Wandering behaviour in community-residing persons with dementia.' *International Journal of Geriatric Psychiatry 14*, 4, 272–279.

Lai, C.K.Y. and Arthur, D.G. (2003) 'Wandering behaviour in people with dementia.' *Journal of Advanced Nursing 44*, 2, 173–182.

Lai, F. and Williams, R.S. (1989) 'A prospective study of Alzheimer disease in Down syndrome.' *Archives of Neurology 46*, 849–853.

Marshall, M. and Allan, K. (2006) *Dementia: Walking not Wandering.* London: Hawker.

Miskelly, F. (2004) 'A novel system of electronic tagging in patients with dementia and wandering.' *Age and Ageing 33*, 3, 304–306.

Namazi, K.H., Rosner, T.T. and Calkins, M.P. (1989) 'Visual barriers to prevent ambulatory Alzheimer's patients from exiting through an emergency door.' *Gerontologist 29*, 5, 669–702.

Nelson, A., Powell-Cope, G. and Gavin-Dreschnack, D. (2004) 'Technology to promote safe mobility in the elderly.' *Nursing Clinics North America 39*, 3, 649–671.

Neville, C.C., McMinn, B. and Cave, P. (2006) 'Implementing the wandering evidence: Key issues for nurses and home carers.' *International Journal of Older People Nursing 1*, 4, 235–238.

Nolan, M., Ingram, P. and Watson, R. (2002) 'Working with family carers of people with dementia: "Negotiated" coping as an essential outcome.' *Dementia: The International Journal of Social Research and Practice 2*, 1, 75–93.

Prasher, V. and Krishna, V.H.R. (1993) 'Age-of-onset and duration of dementia in people with Down Syndrome: Integration of 98 reported cases in the literature.' *International Journal of Geriatric Psychiatry 8*, 915–922.

Price, J.D., Hermans, D.G. and Grimley Evans, J. (2000) 'Subjective barriers to prevent wandering of cognitively impaired people.' *Cochrane Database Systematic Reviews 4.*

Rasquin, S.M.C., Willems, C., de Vieger, S., Geers, R.P.J. and Soede, M. (2007) 'The use of technical devices to support outdoor mobility of dementia patients.' *Technology and Disability 19,* 113–120.

Robinson, L., Hutchings, D., Corner, L., Beyer, F. *et al.* (2007) 'A systematic literature review of the effectiveness of non-pharmacological interventions to prevent wandering in dementia and evaluation of the ethical implications and acceptability of their use.' *Evidence Based Nursing 10,* 1, 15.

Ryan, A.A. (2000) 'Nursing home placement: An exploration of the experiences of family carers.' *Journal of Advanced Nursing 32,* 5, 1187–1195.

Sanders, K. (2009) 'The effects of an action plan, staff training, management support and monitoring on restraint use and costs of work-related injuries.' *Journal of Applied Research in Intellectual Disabilities 22,* 216–220.

Scottish Executive (2000) *The Same as You? A Review of Service for People with a Learning Disability.* Edinburgh: The Stationery Office.

Siders, C., Nelson, A., Brown, L.M., Joseph, I., Algase, D. and Beattie, E. (2004) 'Evidence for implementing non-pharmacological interventions for wandering.' *Rehabilitation Nursing 29,* 6, 195–206.

Sink, K.M., Covinsky, K.E., Newcomer, R. and Yaffe, K. (2004) 'Ethnic differences in the prevalence and pattern of dementia related behaviours.' *Journal of the American Geriatric Society 52,* 1277–1283.

Sturmey, P. (2009a) 'Editorial: It is time to reduce and safely eliminate restrictive behavioural practices.' *Journal of Applied Research in Intellectual Disabilities 22,* 105–110.

Sturmey, P. (2009b) 'Restraint, seclusion and PRN medication in English Services for people with learning disabilities administered by the National Health Service: An analysis of the 2007 National Audit Survey.' *Journal of Applied Research in Intellectual Disabilities 22,* 140–144.

Teri, L., Larson, E.B. and Reifler, B.V. (1988) 'Behavioural disturbance in dementia of the Alzheimer's type.' *Journal of the American Geriatric Society 36,* 1–6.

Tyrell, J., Cosgrave, M. and McCarron, M. (2001) 'Dementia in people with Down's syndrome.' *International Journal of Geriatric Psychiatry 16,* 1168–1174.

Watchman, K. (2007) 'Dementia and Down syndrome: The diagnosis and support needed.' *Learning Disability Practice 10,* 2, 10–14.

Welsh, A., Hassiotis, G., O'Mahoney, G. and Deahl, M. (2003) 'Big brother is watching you – The ethical implications of electronic surveillance measures in the elderly with dementia and in adults with learning difficulties.' *Aging and Mental Health 7,* 5, 372–375S.

Wilkinson, H. and Janicki, M.P. (2000) 'The Edinburgh Principles with accompanying guidelines and recommendation.' *Journal of Intellectual Disability Research 46,* 3, 279–284.

Wilkinson, H., Kerr, D., Rae, C. and Cunningham, C. (2004) *Home for Good? Preparing to Support People with Learning Difficulties in Residential Settings When They Develop Dementia.* Brighton: Pavilion Publishing/Joseph Rowntree Foundation.

Williams, D.E. (2009) 'Restraint safety: An analysis of injuries related to restraint of people with intellectual disabilities.' *Journal of Applied Research in Intellectual Disabilities 22,* 135–139

Chapter 15

PREVENTING FALLS AND AVOIDING RESTRAINT

Samuel R. Nyman and David Oliver

INTRODUCTION

A frequent reason given by staff for restraining older people is to prevent falls (e.g. Hamers, Gulpers and Strik 2004). Falls have been defined as 'an unexpected event in which the participants come to rest on the ground, floor, or lower level' (Lamb *et al.* 2005, p.1619). Whilst falls are prevalent and a cause of morbidity and mortality for older people in the community (Kannus *et al.* 2005; Skelton and Todd 2004), the prevalence and consequences of falls are much higher for older people who are residents of long-term care institutions (care/nursing/residential homes) and hospital inpatients (Australian Commission on Safety and Quality in Healthcare 2005; National Patient Safety Agency (NPSA) 2007b; Oliver 2007; Registered Nurses' Association of Ontario (RNAO) 2005). In nursing homes falls are three times more likely than in the community because of greater frailty and more accurate reporting (Bowman, Whistler and Ellerby 2004; Rubenstein, Josephson and Robbins 1994). One in two residents will fall each year, and of these around half will fall more than once (Kannus *et al.* 2005), with incidence rates of 0.6–3.6 falls per bed (mean = 1.7) (Rubenstein 2006). In hospitals falls are the most frequent (30%) incident reported to the NPSA for inpatient services in England and Wales (NPSA 2007b). US figures suggest 2–12 per cent of inpatients fall, with incidence rates of 2.2–17.1 falls per 1000 patient days (Coussement *et al.* 2008), and UK figures suggest incidence rates of 2.1–8.4 falls per 1000 bed days (Healey, *et al* 2008b)

Falls can result in impaired mobility, loss of independence (Kannus *et al.* 2005; Murphy and Isaacs 1982), and fear of falling, which can lead to premature curtailment of activities and reduced quality of life (Lachman *et al.* 1998; Zijlstra *et al.* 2007). This is particularly so in the significant minority of falls that result in fracture, most often of the hip, that are also associated with premature death (Laxton *et al.* 1997; NPSA 2007b; Todd *et al.* 1995). For care home residents approximately 10–25 per cent of falls result in fracture or laceration, and one in five falls result in death (Rubenstein 2006; Rubenstein *et al.* 1994). Falls are also costly as they necessitate hospital admissions and long-term care. For example, inpatient falls in the US result in an extra 12 days in hospital costing an extra $4233 (Bates *et al.* 1995).

The prevention of falls in hospitals and care homes is therefore of great importance and has been highlighted in a number of guidelines and good practice resources (e.g. Australian Commission on Safety and Quality in Healthcare 2005; NPSA 2007b; RNAO 2005). In this chapter we review the evidence for the use or removal of restraint to prevent falls. We have included bedrails in our discussion of the evidence, as they may be considered a form of restraint if used to stop someone who wants to get out of bed from doing so. The use of bedrails is relevant, as for example, in an observational study with nurses in acute hospitals in England and Wales, the reason cited by nurses for using full bedrails was fall prevention in 74.4 per cent of cases where bedrails were raised and 'absence of falls risk' for not raising bedrails in 92 per cent of 'controls' (Healey, Cronberg and Oliver 2009). Of note is that the evidence we review mainly stems from studies in the US concerning the use of mechanical restraint, which is not accepted practice in the UK (Healey and Paine 2008). In the UK more subtle forms of restraint may be used, such as telling someone not to do something, or placing a person in a low chair or a table up against their chair to stop them from getting up (Healey and Paine 2008). Whilst further research is required into the extent that these more subtle forms of restraint affect falls rates, healthcare providers in the UK can consider the consequences of such improvised restraint in light of the evidence from mechanical restraint. We then review the wider evidence for restraints and bedrails to cause physical injury and other harms, possible alternative strategies to restraint for preventing falls, and conclude with best practice guidelines on the use of restraint in preventing falls. First, we comment on the quality of studies using/removing restraint to prevent falls.

QUALITY OF THE EVIDENCE BASE

The evidence base for the use or removal of restraint in preventing falls derives from observational and quasi-experimental studies of either a series of restraint-related injuries, case-control studies (comparing patients with and without bedrails/restraints) or 'before and after' studies of bedrail/ restraint minimisation. No randomised controlled trial (RCT) has been conducted to ascertain the effectiveness of the use or removal of restraint to reduce the number of falls, fall-related injuries or fallers (older people who fall). This is partly because an RCT of restraint application or removal would be inherently difficult to perform, especially in the frail, often unwell and cognitively impaired groups in which restraint is generally employed. Not only would consent be difficult to obtain, but the devices are already in widespread use in practice which could potentially 'contaminate' control groups, and staff would find it difficult to apply or remove devices against their own clinical judgement and may also be concerned over threats of complaint or litigation (Oliver 2007). Because of the absence of an RCT in this area, most systematic reviews and guidelines on falls prevention based narrowly on evidence from RCTs and meta-analyses do not inform about the use or removal of restraint (Chang *et al.* 2004; Feder *et al.* 2000; Gillespie *et al.* 2003; Kannus *et al.* 2005; National Collaborating Centre for Nursing and Supportive Care 2004; Rubenstein 2006; Shekelle *et al.* 2003; Tinetti 2003). However, there is growing acknowledgement that high quality studies of non-RCT design may still provide a reasonable quality of evidence, especially when RCTs are difficult to carry out of specific interventions or in specific populations (e.g. Guyatt *et al.* 2008; Ogilvie *et al.* 2005).

EVIDENCE BASE FOR RESTRAINT TO CAUSE OR PREVENT FALLS

Whilst restraints may be successfully removed, with a 92 per cent reduction in restraint use in one study (Werner *et al.* 1994), will the rate of falls increase or decrease with the removal of restraints? A systematic review of strategies to prevent falls and injuries in hospitals and care homes identified only five studies of restraint/bedrail application or removal with outcome data which allowed the calculation of falls rate ratios or relative risk of falling (Oliver *et al.* 2007). Four of these studies related only to mechanical restraint (vest, belts, cuffs, etc.) and one related to bedrail reduction. The studies identified were generally of moderate methodological quality, and were either prospective with historical controls (n = 2) or observational cohorts (n = 3). Whilst the pooled statistics were a rate ratio of 0.59 (95% confidence interval = 0.19–1.77) for reducing falls and a relative risk of 0.83 (95% confidence interval = 0.42–1.66) for reducing the number of fallers, the significant heterogeneity in the results for both falls ($I^2 = 99\%$) and fallers ($I^2 = 95\%$) resulted in a non-significant change in the rate of falls and fallers from removal of restraints. Only one study investigated the impact of removing mechanical restraint on fracture rates, and so future studies are required including this outcome. Also, the studies were clinically heterogeneous in terms of setting, population and intervention, so that pooling them for meta-analysis may have been methodologically imperfect (Cameron and Kurrle 2007) and meta-regression found no significant effect for the prevalence of dementia on effect sizes. The reviewers concluded that the five studies on the use of restraint did not provide evidence for either the use or removal of restraint (Oliver *et al.* 2007).

Chemical or pharmaceutical restraint

A recent report in relation to people with dementia in care homes expressed concern over the widespread inappropriate prescription of antipsychotics as a form of chemical restraint (All-Party Parliamentary Group on Dementia (APPG) 2008). Whether used as restraint or not, side effects of such drugs are excessive sedation, dizziness and unsteadiness, which increase the risk of falls and injuries (APPG 2008; Leipzig, Cumming and Tinetti 1999; Woolcott *et al.* 2008). Psychotropic medication is therefore to be avoided as a form of restraint, because it has been consistently recommended that its use be gradually withdrawn to prevent falls (Rubenstein 2006; Scott 2007; Skelton and Todd 2004; Tinetti 2003). An RCT has also found that reducing psychotropic medications in conjunction with a programme of exercise resulted in a 66 per cent reduction in falls, although participants experienced difficulty with withdrawing and not re-starting their medication (Campbell *et al.* 1999).

Bedrails

A recent systematic review investigated the effect of removing bedrails on the rate of falls in hospitals and nursing homes (Healey *et al.* 2008a). Included were five pre and post studies, three case-control and cohort studies, and 16 retrospective surveys, case series and case reports. For the pre and post studies, each significantly reduced the use of bedrails which resulted in either no difference in the rate of falls (n = 1/5), a significant increase in falls (n = 2/5), a significant increase in multiple falls (n = 1/5) or a significant reduction in falls for those patients chosen for bedrail removal, but where the rate of falls was still significantly higher than the rate of falls in those with bilateral bedrails (n = 1/5). In addition there was a significant increase in falls in a subset of older people with a visual impairment (n = 1) and inpatients with a history of stroke (n = 1). A case-control study found a significant reduction in risk of falls if bedrails were raised (n = 1/3), although two cohort studies found no significant difference in rates of falls or injuries (n = 2/3). For the retrospective surveys, case series and case reports, only 1/16 studies found a significant difference in the proportion of injuries: falls from bed were less likely to result in injury, especially head injury, if bedrails were raised (NPSA 2007b).

Thus, the systematic review found a trend for bedrails to actually prevent falls or injury, and although there was no conclusive evidence on the effect of the removal of bedrails, it suggested that studies aimed at eliminating or drastically curtailing bedrail use could lead to significant increases in falls. The studies reviewed were limited in that they made crude comparisons between older people with or without bedrails in use, as those with bedrails in place may have been more at risk of falls (e.g. less mobile, incontinent and more cognitively impaired). In addition it was impossible to separate the effects of removal of bedrails from patients for whom they may not have been appropriate from the effects of removal of bedrails from patients for whom they were appropriate, and changes in practice or other measures to prevent falls may have been adopted by staff, complicating interpretation of the results (Healey *et al.* 2008a).

The findings of the above systematic reviews on restraints and bedrails are consistent with an earlier systematic review (Evans, Wood and Lambert 2003), the US and UK guideline paper on the prevention of falls and its updated version (American Geriatrics Society (AGS), British Geriatrics Society (BGS) and American Academy of Orthopaedic Surgeons (AAOS) Panel on Falls Prevention 2001; Rubenstein *et al.* 2003) and recent World Health Organization (WHO) reports, that stated there was no evidence for the use of restraints, whether mechanically, pharmaceutically or with bedrails, to prevent falls (Kalache, Fu and Yoshida 2007; Skelton and Todd 2004). Indeed, the recently updated Cochrane Review on falls prevention interventions in hospitals and care homes found no firm basis for the use or removal of restraint due to a lack of research (Cameron 2008).

EVIDENCE BASE FOR RESTRAINT TO CAUSE OTHER INJURIES BESIDES FALLS

It has been noted that whilst restraints have not been shown to prevent falls, there is evidence from non-controlled trials and trials on falls risk for restraints to be associated with more injurious falls (AGS *et al.* 2001; Scott 2007; Skelton and Todd 2004). There is also the potential for mechanical restraint to lead to an increased risk of: loss of muscle tone, muscle strength and function; pressure area; incontinence; stiffness; agitation and confusion; worsening of delirium; feelings of frustration, anxiety and boredom; and feelings of being imprisoned or punished (Frengley and Mion 1998). A systematic review investigated whether the use of mechanical restraint causes injury (Evans *et al.* 2003). Evans *et al.* concluded that restraint can cause severe injury and death: hospital inpatients under restraint were more at risk of not being discharged home (odds ratio = 12.42), nosocomial infection (infection whilst in hospital) (odds ratio = 3.46) and death during their hospital stay (odds ratio = 11.24). However, because many of the studies were retrospective or based on death records, it is impossible to separate correlation from causation (e.g. being critically ill in the American settings could be associated with both mechanical restraint use and with poor health outcomes).

A recent systematic review identified 12 studies regarding the prevalence of direct injuries from bedrails (Healey *et al.* 2008a). Fatal entrapments in bedrails and falls from bed when bedrails broke or became detached appeared to be caused by bedrail equipment being poorly assembled, not maintained or obsolete (see Medicines and Healthcare products Regulatory Agency (MHRA) 2006; NPSA 2007a). However, no study used a comparison group and it is therefore impossible to estimate the risk of injury from potential falls in those patients had bedrails not been used (Healey *et al.* 2008a). One study within the systematic review (NPSA 2007b) indicated that, based on a random sample of 500 patient safety incident reports containing the keyword bedrail or synonyms, around 1246 reports of injury from bedrails, usually bruises or grazes to lower limbs, would be found within the 643,151 (0.19%) reports of patient safety incidents received in 2005 from hospitals in England and Wales.

EVIDENCE BASE FOR PREVENTING FALLS IN HOSPITALS AND CARE HOMES WITHOUT USING RESTRAINT

If restraints are to be withdrawn how else can falls be prevented? A WHO systematic review documented the evidence for preventing falls in hospitals and care homes (Skelton and Todd 2004), which has been supported by more recent WHO reports on falls prevention (Kalache *et al.* 2007; Scott 2007). They used four categories of evidence: RCT or meta-analysis of RCTs (A), non-controlled trial or trial on falls risk and not falls rates (B), non-experimental data (C) and expert opinion (D). For hospital inpatients, the WHO report found no evidence for the use of multifactorial interventions but grade B evidence for the benefits of alternative strategies to restraint such as using lower beds, placing mats on the floor, safe transfer and exercise training, and alarm devices. Grade C evidence was found for hospital discharge risk assessment and planning, and grade D evidence for the use of bed alarms but not the use of identification bracelets (Skelton and Todd 2004). These alternative strategies to restraint showed promise, and indeed the updated Cochrane Review on falls prevention with more recent trials has found evidence for multifactorial interventions to reduce falls rates (but not injuries), and that these interventions are generally more effective in hospitals with longer patient stays (Cameron 2008).

For care homes, the WHO report documented that multifactorial interventions have grade A evidence for preventing falls, which have included staff and resident education, medication review, environmental adaptation, supply and repair of walking aids, physical activity and the use of hip protectors (Skelton and Todd 2004). For single interventions, there is grade A evidence for the prescription of vitamin D and calcium supplements. Grade B evidence was found for other single interventions: gait training and advice on appropriate use of assistive devices, medication review (especially psychotropics), nutritional supplements, staff education, physical activity, environmental adaptation, post-fall problem-solving sessions and hip protectors. More recently, the updated Cochrane Review on falls prevention found that effective interventions with care home residents are those targeting individual risk factors, medication review and the prescription of vitamin D with calcium in residents who are deficient, but other interventions targeting single risk factors and hip protectors do not have a clear evidence base (Cameron 2008).

Of note is the evidence for preventing falls with those who suffer from delirium and/or dementia who become confused and/or agitated, because of the higher prevalence of these conditions in inpatients and residents and their increased risk of falls (Shaw 2002; Young and Inouye 2007). Whilst another review did not find dementia to moderate the effectiveness of falls prevention strategies (Oliver *et al.* 2007), for those with a cognitive impairment current falls prevention strategies appear ineffective for care home residents and those in hospital because of a fall (Kalache *et al.* 2007). Current advice is that, for patients who are confused and/or agitated, mechanical and pharmaceutical restraints are to be avoided as they are associated with higher levels of delirium and agitation, and injury with the hyperactive type (Young and Inouye 2007). Alternatives to the use of restraint in managing confusion and agitation include immediate identification and treatment of medical conditions such as infections, constipation and sleep deprivation, the withdrawal of medications and the provision of a clock/watch and reading glasses (Young and Inouye 2007).

BEST PRACTICE ADVICE ON THE USE OF RESTRAINT
Restraints and bedrails are to be avoided in any situation where they may be inappropriately used to compensate for inadequacies in staff

levels, supervision or management of behavioural disturbance/medical comorbidity (Oliver 2007). Indeed, as falls are markers of underlying disorders easily identifiable by a careful assessment after a fall, which in turn can be treated to reduce disability (NPSA 2007b; Rubenstein et al. 1994), addressing the medical needs of older people will reduce their risk of falls as a secondary benefit (Oliver 2007). The use of restraint has been reduced in a number of studies with no increase in falls and so efforts are required to prevent falls in other ways (Lord et al. 2007) and provide adequate staffing and care (see Kalache et al. 2007; Prevention of Falls Network Europe 2008). Alternatives to the use of restraint should be discussed with inpatients/residents, their relatives and staff, with acceptance that the use of restraint may be more detrimental than a possible fall (Rubenstein et al. 1994). Indeed, a setting with a zero rate of falls is likely to be overly controlling and not respectful of human rights (Oliver 2004).

Similar to guidelines on restraint for people with reduced mental capacity (e.g. Department for Constitutional Affairs 2007), the use of restraint and bedrails for the prevention of falls in older people should only be used as a last resort and when the potential benefits outweigh the potential costs (Evans et al. 2003; Healey and Paine 2008); should be prescribed on an individual case basis and only for a short time period (Lord et al. 2007); and only a minimal degree of restraint used, the need for restraint regularly reviewed, and the person restrained not isolated but continually observed (Evans et al. 2003). If bedrails are to be used, checks are required before use and regularly afterward to ensure that the bedrail is not an outmoded design, is correctly fitted, and in good working condition (MHRA 2006; NPSA 2007a; Oliver 2007). Indeed, for all types of restraint, it is advised that before use staff are educated about the dangers of restraint, correct use of restraints including manufacturers' recommendations for the devices and safe management of people under restraint (Evans et al. 2003).

CONCLUSION

Preventing falls is of high priority and frequently the main reason given for restraining an older person, especially those with a combination of falls risk factors such as postural instability, previous falls, confusion, restlessness and agitation. The evidence for mechanical restraints and bedrails to increase or reduce the risk of falls is limited and inconclusive, and so well-planned and executed observational/quasi-experimental studies are required to resolve the controversy over their use. The prescription of psychotropic medication should be minimised and not used as a means to prevent falls. Mechanical restraints and bedrails have been shown in a series of reports to cause injury and death, but their rates are unknown. Also, because studies have not used a comparator/denominator group, it is unknown whether injuries would have occurred without the use of restraint, and injuries from bedrails may stem from failure to use up-to-date equipment and fit them properly or using them on individuals unlikely to benefit. Efforts should be made to remove restraints and engage older people in evidence-based strategies to prevent falls, including treatment of medical conditions, multifactorial interventions and vitamin D and calcium supplements. Restraint should only be used as a last resort, and conducted by staff trained in its appropriate use.

REFERENCES

All-Party Parliamentary Group on Dementia (APPG) (2008) *Always a Last Resort: Inquiry into the Prescription of Antipsychotic Drugs to People with Dementia Living in Care Homes.* London: Alzheimer's Society.

American Geriatrics Society (AGS), British Geriatrics Society (BGS), and American Academy of Orthopaedic Surgeons (AAOS) Panel on Falls Prevention (2001) 'Guidelines for the prevention of falls in older persons.' *Journal of the American Geriatrics Society 49,* 5, 664–672.

Australian Commission on Safety and Quality in Healthcare (2005) *Preventing Falls and Harm from Falls in Older People: Best Practice Guidelines for Australian Hospitals and Residential Aged Care Facilities.* Canberra: Australian Commission.

Bates, D.W., Pruess, K., Souney, P. and Platt, R. (1995) 'Serious falls in hospitalized patients: Correlates and resource utilization.' *American Journal of Medicine 99,* 2, 137–143.

Bowman, C., Whistler, J. and Ellerby, M. (2004) 'A national census of care home residents.' *Age and Ageing 33,* 6, 561–566.

Cameron, I.D. (2008). 'Preventing falls and fractures: Harder to back a winner in residential aged care facilities and hospitals. The updated Cochrane Review. *Proceeding of the 3rd Australian and New Zealand Falls Prevention Conference, Melbourne, Australia,* 13–14.

Cameron, I.D. and Kurrle, S. (2007) 'Preventing falls in elderly people living in hospitals and care homes.' *British Medical Journal 334,* 7584, 53–54.

Campbell, A.J., Robertson, M.C., Gardner, M.M., Norton, R.N. and Buchner, D.M. (1999) 'Psychotropic medication withdrawal and a home-based exercise program to prevent falls: A randomized, controlled trial.' *Journal of the American Geriatrics Society 47,* 7, 850–853.

Chang, J.T., Morton, S.C., Rubenstein, L.Z., Mojica, W.A. *et al.* (2004) 'Interventions for the prevention of falls in older adults: Systematic review and meta-analysis of randomised clinical trials.' *British Medical Journal 328,* 7441, 680–683.

Coussement, J., De Paepe, L., Schwendimann, R., Denhaerynck, K., Dejaeger, E. and Milisen, K. (2008) 'Interventions for preventing falls in acute- and chronic-care hospitals: A systematic review and meta-analysis.' *Journal of the American Geriatrics Society 56,* 1, 29–36.

Department for Constitutional Affairs (2007) *Mental Capacity Act 2005: Code of Practice.* London: Stationery Office.

Evans, D., Wood, J. and Lambert, L. (2003) 'Patient injury and physical restraint devices: A systematic review.' *Journal of Advanced Nursing 41,* 3, 274–282.

Feder, G., Cryer, C., Donovan, S. and Carter, Y. (2000) 'Guidelines for the prevention of falls in people over 65.' *British Medical Journal 321,* 7267, 1007–1011.

Frengley, J. and Mion, L. (1998) 'Physical restraints in the acute-care setting: Issues and future direction.' *Clinics in Geriatric Medicine 14,* 4, 727–743.

Gillespie, L.D., Gillespie, W.J., Robertson, M.C., Lamb, S.E., Cumming, R.G. and Rowe, B.H. (2003) 'Interventions for preventing falls in elderly people.' *Cochrane Database of Systematic Reviews 4,* Art. No.: CD000340-DOI: 10.1002/14651858. CD000340.

Guyatt, G.H., Oxman, A.D., Vist, G.E., Kunz, R. *et al.* (2008) 'Analysis: Rating quality of evidence and strength of recommendations: GRADE: An emerging consensus on rating quality of evidence and strength of recommendations.' *British Medical Journal 336*, 7652, 924–926.

Hamers, J.P.H., Gulpers, M.J.M. and Strik, W. (2004) 'Use of physical restraints with cognitively impaired nursing home residents.' *Journal of Advanced Nursing 45*, 3, 246–251.

Healey, F. and Paine, T. (2008) *Let's Talk about Restraint: Rights, Risks and Responsibility.* London: Royal College of Nursing.

Healey, F., Oliver, D., Milne, A. and Connelly, J.B. (2008a) 'The effect of bedrails on falls and injury: A systematic review of clinical studies.' *Age and Ageing 37*, 4, 368–378.

Healey, F., Cronberg, A. and Oliver, D. (2009) Bedrail use in English and Welsh hospitals. *Journal of the American Geriatrics Society, 57*, 1887–1891.

Healey, F., Scobie, S., Oliver, D., Pryce, A., Thomson, R. and Glampson, B. (2008b) 'Falls in English and Welsh hospitals: A national observational study based on retrospective analysis of 12 months of patient safety incident reports.' *Quality and Safety in Health Care, 17,* 424–430.

Kalache, A., Fu, D. and Yoshida, S. (2007) *WHO Global Report on Falls Prevention in Older Age.* Geneva: World Health Organization.

Kannus, P., Sievanen, H., Palvanen, M., Jarvinen, T. and Parkkari, J. (2005) 'Prevention of falls and consequent injuries in elderly people.' *Lancet 366*, 9500, 1885–1893.

Lachman, M.E., Howland, J., Tennstedt, S., Jette, A., Assmann, S. and Peterson, E.W. (1998) 'Fear of falling and activity restriction: The survey of activities and fear of falling in the elderly (SAFE).' *Journal of Gerontology: Psychological Sciences 53N*, 1, P43–P50.

Lamb, S.E., Jørstad-Stein, E.C., Hauer, K. and Becker, C. (2005) 'Development of a common outcome data set for fall injury prevention trials: The Prevention of Falls Network Europe consensus.' *Journal of the American Geriatrics Society 53*, 9, 1618–1622.

Laxton, C.E., Freeman, C.J., Todd, C.J., Payne, B.V. *et al.* (1997) 'Morbidity at 3 months after hip fracture: Data from the East Anglian audit.' *Health Trends 29*, X, 55–60.

Leipzig, R.M., Cumming, R.G. and Tinetti, M.E. (1999) 'Drugs and falls in older people: A systematic review and meta-analysis: I. Psychotropic drugs.' *Journal of the American Geriatrics Society 47*, 1, 30–39.

Lord, S.R., Sherrington, C., Menz, H.B. and Close, J.C.T. (2007) *Falls in Older People: Risk Factors and Strategies for Prevention,* 2nd edn. Cambridge: Cambridge University Press.

Medicines and Healthcare products Regulatory Agency (MHRA) (2006) *Device Bulletin: Safe Use of Bed Rails* (Rep. No. DB2006(06)). London: Department of Health.

Murphy, J. and Isaacs, B. (1982) 'The post-fall syndrome: A study of 36 elderly patients.' *Gerontology 28*, 4, 265–270.

National Collaborating Centre for Nursing and Supportive Care (2004) *Clinical Practice Guideline for the Assessment and Prevention of Falls in Older People (Clinical Guideline 21).* London: National Institute for Clinical Excellence.

National Patient Safety Agency (NPSA) (2007a) *Safer Practice Notice 17: Using Bedrails Safely and Effectively.* London: National Health Service.

National Patient Safety Agency (NPSA) (2007b) *Slips, Trips and Falls in Hospital: The Third Report from the Patient Safety Observatory.* London: NPSA.

Ogilvie, D., Egan, M., Hamilton, V. and Petticrew, M. (2005) 'Systematic reviews of health effects of social interventions. 2. Best available evidence: How low should you go?' *Journal of Epidemiology and Community Health 59*, 10, 886–892.

Oliver, D. (2004) 'Prevention of falls in hospital inpatients: Agendas for research and practice.' *Age and Ageing 33*, 4, 328–330.

Oliver, D. (2007) 'Preventing falls and falls-injuries in hospitals and long-term care facilities.' *Reviews in Clinical Gerontology 17*, 2, 75–92.

Oliver, D., Connelly, J.B., Victor, C.R., Shaw, F.E. *et al.* (2007) 'Strategies to prevent falls and fractures in hospitals and care homes and effect of cognitive impairment: Systematic review and meta-analyses.' *British Medical Journal 334*, 7584, 82–85.

Prevention of Falls Network Europe (2008) 'Clinical Assessment Tool (CAT): Falls prevention assessment and intervention framework for health professionals.' Available at www.profane.eu.org/CAT, accessed 6 November 2009.

Registered Nurses' Association of Ontario (RNAO) (2005) *Prevention of Falls and Fall Injuries in the Older Adult: Nursing Best Practice Guidelines.* Toronto, ON: RNAO.

Rubenstein, L.Z. (2006) 'Falls in older people: Epidemiology, risk factors, and strategies for prevention.' *Age and Ageing 35*, suppl. 2, ii37–ii41.

Rubenstein, L.Z., Josephson, K.R. and Robbins, A.S. (1994) 'Falls in the nursing home.' *Annals of Internal Medicine 121*, 6, 442–451.

Rubenstein, L.Z., Kenny, R.A., Eccles, M., Martin, F., Tinetti, M.E. and the AGS/BGS/AAOS Panel on Falls Prevention (2003) 'Preventing falls in older people: New approaches and the development of clinical practice guidelines.' *Journal of the Royal College of Physicians of Edinburgh 33*, 262–272.

Scott, V. (2007) *A Global Report on Falls Prevention: Policy, Research and Practice.* Geneva: World Health Organization.

Shaw, F. E. (2002) 'Falls in cognitive impairment and dementia.' *Clinics in Geriatric Medicine 18*, 2, 159–173.

Shekelle, P.G., Maglione, M., Chang, J.T., Mojica, W. *et al.* (2003) *Falls Prevention Interventions in the Medicare Population.* Baltimore, MD: RAND.

Skelton, D.A. and Todd, C.J. (2004) *What Are the Main Risk Factors for Falls amongst Older People and What Are the Most Effective Interventions to Prevent These Falls?,* Copenhagen, Denmark: Health Evidence Network, World Health Organization.

Tinetti, M.E. (2003) 'Preventing falls in elderly persons.' *New England Journal of Medicine 348*, 1, 42–49.

Todd, C.J., Freeman, C.J., Camilleri-Ferrante, C., Palmer, C.R. *et al.* (1995) 'Differences in mortality after fracture of hip: The East Anglian audit.' *British Medical Journal 310*, 6984, 904–908.

Werner, P., Koroknay, V., Braun, J. and Cohen-Mansfield, J. (1994) 'Individualized care alternatives used in the process of removing physical restraints in the nursing home.' *Journal of the American Geriatrics Society 42*, 3, 321–325.

Woolcott, J.C., Richardson, K.R., Wiens, M.O., Patel, B. *et al.* (2008). 'A meta-analysis of the impact of medications on falling in older people.' *Proceedings of the 3rd Australian and New Zealand Falls Prevention Conference, Melbourne, Australia*, 25–26.

Young, J. and Inouye, S.K. (2007) 'Delirium in older people.' *British Medical Journal 334*, 7598, 842–846.

Zijlstra, G.A.R., van Haastregt, J.C.M., van Eijk, J.T.M., van Rossum, E., Stalenhoef, P.A. and Kempen, G.I.J.M. (2007) 'Prevalence and correlates of fear of falling, and associated avoidance of activity in the general population of community-living older people.' *Age and Ageing 36*, 3, 304–309.

Chapter 16

USING EVIDENCE-BASED KNOWLEDGE TO AVOID PHYSICAL RESTRAINT

Sascha Köpke, Gabriele Meyer,
Anja Gerlach and Antonie Haut

BACKGROUND

'Don't just do something, stand there!'

This largely quoted aphorism accurately summarises an important message of this chapter. The bottom line is that, as long as there is no convincing evidence for the effectiveness of the use of physical restraints with older people, the onus should be on those who intervene to show that their actions will result in a 'net improvement in human health' (Delamothe 2000). The use of physical restraints with older people has been reported as common practice in numerous countries (De Vries, Ligthart and Nikolaus 2004). International studies have reported prevalences between 2 and 70 per cent (De Vries *et al.* 2004; Evans *et al.* 2002; Hamers and Huizing 2005). Recently, our own epidemiological study on physical restraints showed a prevalence of 26 per cent in German nursing homes. Centre prevalence ranged from 4 to 59 per cent. The proportion of residents with at least one physical restraint cumulated to 40 per cent over the ten-month mean follow-up (Meyer *et al.* 2008).

The use of physical restraints has been claimed as a safety measure, primarily for the prevention of falls. Control of disruptive behaviour, safe use of medical devices and other reasons are also frequently reported (Hamers and Huizing 2005). On the other hand, questions have been raised about the justification for and consequences of the use of physical restraints. Considering the current evidence, it is questionable whether this practice can be justified in terms of controlling psychomotor agitation and reducing the risk of falling and fall-related injury (Evans *et al.* 2002; Healey *et al.* 2008). In residential care settings people with cognitive impairment and/

or challenging behaviour are more likely to be restrained than residents without cognitive problems (Evans *et al.* 2002; Meyer *et al.* 2008). The use of physical restraints has been shown to be associated with adverse outcomes, for example serious injuries and increased mortality (Evans *et al.* 2002). Also, other adverse events like reduced psychological wellbeing, lower cognitive performance and decreased mobility have been attributed to the use of physical restraints (Engberg, Castle and McCaffrey 2008; Evans *et al.* 2002), although the validity of these analyses is questionable (Healey *et al.* 2008).

A 'restraint-free' care environment has been demanded as the standard of care while anything less has been claimed as substandard (Flaherty 2004). Accordingly, in the past decades, strong efforts have been undertaken to reduce the use of physical restraints. Programmes to reduce the use of physical restraints with older people were first introduced in the United States (US) in the 1980s (Castle and Mor 1998).

Since then a number of studies have been conducted in hospitals and nursing homes, but mainly using methods and study designs prone to bias (Evans *et al.* 2002). Recently further trials have been conducted, mainly evaluating multi-faceted interventions to reduce the use of physical restraints (Capezuti *et al.* 2007; Huizing *et al.* 2006, 2009; Koczy *et al.* 2007; Lai *et al.* 2005; Testad, Aasland and Aarsland 2005). The interventions were designed as complex interventions, consisting of different components. These include, among others, educational sessions aimed to change nurses' attitudes to physical restraint use and information about and implementation of alternatives to the use of restraints. Disappointingly, the studies did not consistently result in clinically meaningful reductions of restraints. Thus, it might not be sufficient to educate nurses not to use restraints or to suggest or provide alternatives, although nurses desperately demand alternatives to the use of restraints. Considering the evidence on the effectiveness and safety of restraint use in older people, it might be the most sensible choice to 'just stand there'.

PHYSICAL RESTRAINT USE IN GERMAN NURSING HOMES

Until the late 1990s there were no reliable data on the use of physical restraints in German nursing homes. A questionnaire survey addressing nursing home staff in Munich reported a prevalence of 40 per cent of residents with physical restraints (Hoffmann and Klie 2004).

Since high quality epidemiological data on the frequency and continuity of restraints in German nursing homes were lacking, we recently performed a cross-sectional study on the prevalence of physical restraints in nursing homes and a 12-month cohort study on newly administered restraints and the frequency of restraint application. We also investigated factors associated with restraint use. Thirty nursing homes with 2367 residents in Hamburg, Germany, participated. Prevalence of restraints was obtained by direct observation of external investigators on three occasions on one day, psychoactive drugs (not reported in this chapter) were extracted from residents' charts and prospective data were documented by nurses (Meyer *et al.* 2008). Prevalence of residents with at least one physical restraint was 26.2 per cent (95% confidence interval (CI) 21.3 to 31.1). Centre prevalence ranged from 4.4 to 58.9 per cent. Bedrails were most often used (in 24.5% of residents). Fixed tables, belts and other restraints were comparatively rare. The proportion of people with at least one physical restraint after the first observation week of 26.3 per cent (21.3 to 31.3) cumulated to 39.5 per cent (33.3 to 45.7) at the end of follow-up (10.4 ± 3.3 months). The relative frequency of observation days of residents with at least one device ranged from 4.9 to 64.8 per cent between centres. The logistic regression analysis failed to identify centre characteristics that could explain differences between centres.

We can therefore conclude that the frequency of physical restraints in German nursing homes is substantial. Importantly, the observed pronounced centre variations suggest that standard care does not imply the use of restraints.

EFFORTS TO REDUCE PHYSICAL RESTRAINTS IN NURSING HOMES IN GERMANY

Although there has been discussion about the reduction of restraints in nursing home residents for some time, until recently no systematic supra-regional initiatives to reduce restraints have been developed in Germany.

Presently, a multidisciplinary and multifaceted intervention on physical restraint reduction is implemented in several regions of Germany (ReduFix 2006). The project is supported by the Federal Ministry of Family Affairs, Senior Citizens, Women and Youth. Unfortunately, nothing is known on the potential effectiveness of the approach. Also, no evaluation alongside the practice implementation will be performed. The results of a previously conducted randomised-controlled trial evaluating the intervention (Koczy *et al.* 2005) have not yet been published. First results accessible as grey literature indicate only small short-term effects and an unclear long-term effectiveness, despite strong efforts including education of nursing staff by experts from several disciplines, counselling, and provision of potentially alternative devices like sensor mats and hip protectors (ReduFix 2006). Therefore, from the perspective of evidence-based health care, the benefit of this project remains unclear, whereas harm in terms of waste of sparse nursing resources is likely.

In Germany, so far, no national guidelines strictly following methods of evidence-based practice guideline development have been developed for nursing topics. The German Network for the Development of Quality in Nursing has published so-called National Expert Standards on selected nursing issues (Deutsches Netzwerk für Qualitätsentwicklung in der Pflege (German Network for the Development of Quality in Nursing) 2007). These mono-disciplinary nursing expert standards lack rigorous methods for development, transparent reporting and clarity. Tools to allow structured implementation are not provided and the standards' effectiveness has not been evaluated (Meyer and Köpke 2006). Despite the lack of external evidence on their benefit, the recent modification of the German nursing care law demands the development and implementation of these nursing expert standards (Pflege-Weiterentwicklungsgesetz (Nursing care law) 2008). Therefore, an expert standard on physical restraints in the near future seems likely.

Another interdisciplinary initiative has developed a so-called 'quality level' on mobility and safety for residents of long-term care institutions with dementia. The quality handbook, covering 77 printed pages, is presently evaluated within a non-randomised controlled study. The quality level aims to enhance the mobility of residents, to reduce falls without increasing the frequency of restraints. The results will be welcomed, although validity will be limited due to lack of randomisation (BUKO-QS 2008).

In view of the high prevalence of restraints in nursing homes effective restraint minimisation approaches are urgently warranted. Considering the disappointing results of recent trials a paradigm shift seems necessary. The observed pronounced centre variations suggest that standard care does not imply the use of restraints. In the association analysis of our epidemiological study (Meyer *et al.* 2008) institutional characteristics like case mix and staffing did not explain centre differences in restraint use. Therefore, philosophy of care determining attitude and beliefs of nursing staff are most likely powerful determinants of routine restraint use. A carefully prepared evidence-based guideline may therefore help to overcome centre differences and enable restraint-free care in nursing homes in Germany and also internationally.

GUIDELINES ADDRESSING PHYSICAL RESTRAINTS IN NURSING HOMES

Guidelines, standards and other recommendations can serve as quality assurance instruments to promote knowledge-based care processes. Evidence-based guidelines intend to overcome practice variations with scientifically based recommendations (Köpke *et al.* 2008; Woolf *et al.* 1999). In Germany national evidence-based nursing guidelines are lacking.

The clinical effectiveness of guidelines, standards and recommendations targeting the avoidance of physical restraints in nursing homes has not been proved yet. Nevertheless, as part of complex interventions and quality assurance initiatives, they aim at reducing physical restraints. Legal action seems to have an impact on the frequency and handling of physical restraints as well as on the development of adequate quality assurance instruments (Castle and Mor 1998; Graber and Sloane 1995; Guttman, Altman and Karlan 1999; Hofinger *et al.* 2007). Still, they cannot be equated with guidelines or standards, which are professional recommendations and thus of different range and liability.

Recently we performed an extensive search of German and international guidelines, standards and other recommendations on the reduction of physical restraints in nursing homes covering four databases: PubMed, CINAHL, GeroLit and CareLit. In addition, an internet search (google.de/ch/at, metager.de, metacrawler.com) was conducted. Publications of 34 national and international health care organisations were also investigated. We searched for documents published in German, English within the last ten years. Most results were found on the internet, published in the past five years. The search identified 14 German and 29 international documents (US, n = 13; Australia, n = 5; Great Britain, n = 4; Switzerland, n = 3; France, n = 2; New Zealand, n = 1; Ireland, n = 1), published by professional, national accreditation, nursing, political and educational institutions as well as initiatives and federal ministries. Despite the wide variety of identified documents, results show that presently there is no publicly available evidence-based guideline for the avoidance of physical restraints in nursing homes. A systematic analysis of the documents evaluating their content and underlying methods regarding the recommendations for handling and avoiding physical restraints in nursing homes is in progress and results will be available in due course.

EVIDENCE-BASED PRACTICE GUIDELINE TO REDUCE PHYSICAL RESTRAINT

Clinical guidelines have been defined as 'systematically developed statements to assist practitioner and patient decisions about appropriate health care for specific clinical circumstances' (Field and Lohr 1990, p.38). Guidelines aim to reduce inappropriate variations in practice and to promote the delivery of high quality evidence-based health care by promoting interventions of proved benefit and discouraging ineffective ones, potentially resulting in relevant changes in patients' health outcomes (Woolf *et al.* 1999). Guidelines also aim to assist health care professionals in their work and to complement their knowledge and skills (Miller and Kearney 2004). Considering the above-mentioned problems regarding approaches to reduce or avoid restraints, an evidence-based practice guideline is likely to be an appropriate measure to reduce physical restraints and overcome centre variations. Therefore we are currently developing an evidence-based practice guideline on the use of physical restraints in nursing homes. The guideline aims to support nurses' decision-making processes and to subsequently reduce physical restraints in German nursing homes. For the first time, the project applies internationally discussed methods to the development of a nursing guideline in Germany.

Guideline development

A methodological framework has been set up and published (Köpke *et al.* 2008), based on internationally discussed methodological prerequisites for the development of evidence-based practice guidelines (Cluzeau *et al.* 2003; Grading of Recommendations Assessment, Development and Evaluation (GRADE) 2004; Scottish Intercollegiate Guidelines Network (SIGN) 2004). As a first step, we searched national and international databases and the internet for available guidelines in the field. Second, we conducted a survey asking patients' representatives to determine potential interventions and endpoints related to the reduction of restraints. Consumer involvement in clinical guidelines has been demanded, as consumers or their representatives might have different knowledge, understanding and experience from health care professionals (Field and Lohr 1990; van Wersch and Eccles 2001). Thus, eight national patient organisations were contacted.

As a further step, the multidisciplinary guideline development group was established. The group consisted of 16 experts from relevant fields: nursing management, geriatric medicine, family medicine, human rights, law, a dementia self-help organisation, an association for legal guidance, a nursing homes organisation, federal inspection boards on nursing home quality, and health insurance. Five nurse scientists of the Universities of Hamburg and Witten/Herdecke complemented the guideline development group and acted as a coordination group. The guideline development group met for five two-day meetings at the University of Hamburg. The meetings were organised by the coordination group and chaired by an experienced moderator.

As the methods have been published in detail elsewhere (Köpke *et al.* 2008), we will only briefly discuss the development process and focus on issues of special interest and adaptations made to the methodological framework during the guideline development process.

Training in evidence-based nursing
Most group members were not familiar with the methods of evidence-based nursing (EBN) and/or the process and methods of guideline development. Therefore the first meeting of the guideline development group included a one-day training on EBN and guideline development methods. The group members received a book on EBN (Behrens and Langer 2006) for advance preparation.

Interventions and endpoints
The guideline development group defined potential interventions and endpoints to be included in the guideline. The response of patients' organisations was included in the collection of interventions and endpoints which formed the basis of the systematic literature search (SIGN 2004).

Interventions
After an intensive discourse within the guideline development group 24 interventions for the reduction or avoidance of restraints were defined. The interventions comprised the following domains:

1. *Interventions directly targeting residents*
   These were occupational programmes, rehabilitation and exercise programmes, animal-assisted therapy, music interventions, electronic alarm systems, continence training, therapeutic touch and massage, aromatherapy, validation therapy, snoezelen (controlled multisensory stimulation), 'basal stimulation', reality orientation and cognitive stimulation, and reminiscence.

2. *Interventions targeting organisational aspects*
   These were educational programmes, person-centred care, special dementia care units and advanced geriatric nursing practice.

3. *Interventions targeting architecture and environmental arrangement*
   These were environmental modifications, special residential concepts, milieu therapy, phototherapy and light therapy, bright lighting, subjective and visual barriers, and specific night care.

Outcome measures

Following the GRADE approach, at the beginning of the guideline development process, a list of relevant outcomes was prepared based on the survey of patients' organisations. Outcomes were put into a hierarchical order according to their clinical relevance (Schünemann, Oxman and Fretheim 2006). Of these, apart from the obviously most important outcome, the use of physical restraints, only two further outcomes were initially considered relevant: dementia-related 'challenging behaviour' and falls. After thorough discussion the latter was not regarded as a valid outcome (see below).

Physical restraint

The number and intensity of physical restraints was defined as the most important endpoint. Evidence for the efficacy of interventions concerning the reduction of restraints was therefore considered as 'direct evidence' in the context of the guideline development.

Challenging behaviour

Challenging behaviours are common in nursing home residents with dementia. Several studies show strong associations between challenging behaviour and the use of restraints (Kirkevold and Engedal 2004; Werner 2002). Therefore challenging behaviour was defined as a valid secondary parameter as it considered a surrogate or 'indirect evidence' for the use of restraints.

Falls

After careful discussion the guideline development group decided that falls and fall-related injuries were not valid surrogate endpoints for the use of restraints. Although nurses regularly claim to use restraints to prevent falls (Hamers and Huizing 2005), it remains unclear if restraints can really prevent falls or if they even increase the number of falls or fall-related injuries (Evans *et al.* 2002). Unlike 'challenging behaviour' there is no obvious direct relation between falls and the application of restraints. Therefore interventions effectively reducing falls were not considered as 'indirect evidence' for the reduction of restraints.

Systematic review of the evidence

For each of the 24 interventions, we carried out a systematic literature review following the GRADE approach (Guyatt *et al.* 2008a). We searched the databases PubMed, CINAHL, and the Cochrane Library for 'direct evidence', i.e. evidence that the intervention had been shown to reduce the number or the intensity of restraints in nursing home residents. If there was no direct evidence, we searched for indirect evidence, i.e. evidence for the intervention's efficacy on the reduction of challenging behaviour in nursing home residents.

The evidence was rated considering 'four key elements': study design, study quality, consistency and directness (GRADE 2004). For studies aiming to reduce the number of restraints randomised-controlled trials (RCTs) or systematic review of RCTs provide the best evidence whereas observational studies usually have a limited internal validity. Therefore we followed the GRADE approach and assigned evidence from RCTs as high quality evidence, whereas evidence from observational studies and other evidence (e.g. case studies) was considered low and very low quality evidence. After this initial assignment, the studies were analysed for methodological quality, for consistency and directness, and upgraded or downgraded according to the recommendations of the GRADE working group (Guyatt *et al.* 2008b; Köpke *et al.* 2008), resulting in four definitions of quality of evidence: high, moderate, low and very low.

The results of the systematic review were presented in detail to the guideline development group using evidence tables (GRADE 2004). These allowed a quick overview on the evidence of each of the 24 interventions and included the description of the evidence, methodological quality of the included studies, results for effects and side effects and cost, if available.

Recommendations

Based on the systematic reviews and the presentation of the evidence, the guideline development group found recommendations for each of the 24 interventions using the 'nominal group technique' (Hutchings *et al.* 2006) led by an experienced moderator. The GRADE system offers two grades of recommendations: 'strong' and 'weak' in favour or against the intervention. The recommendations are based on the quality of evidence, but also on other factors such as the balance between desirable and undesirable effects or variability in preferences of different patient groups (Guyatt *et al.* 2008b). Strong recommendations are based on interventions where the desirable effects clearly outweigh the undesirable effects (or clearly do not). Weak recommendations indicate that the evidence suggests that desirable and undesirable effects are closely balanced (Guyatt *et al.* 2008b).

After detailed discussion, the guideline development group opted for a modification of the GRADE system. The strong and weak recommendations were rephrased and a neutral recommendation was added, leading to the following five-stage pattern of recommendations with according graphical representation:

↑↑ = Intervention is recommended
↑   = Intervention can be considered
↔   = No recommendation possible
↓   = Intervention is not recommended
↓↓ = Intervention is advised against

Results
After the five two-day meetings of the guideline development group, a first 280-page version of the evidence-based practice guideline was completed in September 2008, followed by a 25-page short version.

Quality of evidence
For none of the 24 interventions high quality direct evidence for the interventions' effectiveness on the reduction of restraints could be found. For a number of interventions there was also no high quality 'indirect evidence', i.e. evidence for the reduction of challenging behaviours. For two interventions (aromatherapy, bright lighting) evidence of moderate quality could be identified, and low or very low quality evidence was found for eight and seven interventions respectively, whereas for a further seven interventions no relevant evidence at all could be identified. The latter were electronic alarm systems, continence training, basal stimulation, reality orientation and cognitive stimulation, special residential concepts, specific night care and subjective and visual barriers.

Recommendations
Taking into account the poor evidence for the interventions, no strong recommendations could be expected. However, the guideline development group decided to make a single strong recommendation for 'educational

programmes', although with a narrow majority of 8 of 15 votes. Despite low quality evidence the group appreciated the fact that there was some direct evidence indicating positive effects for educational programmes. For seven further interventions the guideline development group consented on a weak recommendation in favour of the intervention. These were occupational programmes, music interventions, animal-assisted therapy, electronic alarm systems, special dementia care units, person-centred care and environmental modifications. For two interventions (phototherapy and light therapy, bright lighting) the group recommended (weakly) against the intervention. For 14 of the 24 interventions the group felt unable to provide a recommendation.

Problems and lessons learned
EBN skills
During the guideline development process some difficulties emerged. Although all members of the guideline development group had declared their willingness to participate in the development of an evidence-based guideline, some seemed to have strong resentments towards the approach of EBN. Thus time-consuming and exhausting discussions about EBN came up during all five group meetings. The one-day EBN training obviously failed to provide basic understanding and acceptance of the EBN approach. Therefore future guideline development projects should spend more efforts on the delivery of EBN skills and understanding.

Group process
The multidisciplinary guideline development group included representatives from different relevant professions with renowned expertise in their field. The interaction between the group members was not always easy and single group members often dominated the discussion. During the third group meeting the group temporarily threatened to fall apart, but after intensive discussion the conflict was resolved.

As a consequence, for the final two meetings a more experienced moderator was engaged, who made an important contribution to the successfully completed guideline development process.

The role of lay group members and other group members
Little is known about the optimal integration of lay group members. These persons, who are usually not very familiar with group discussions, are therefore supposedly less dominant group members within guideline development processes. Therefore we prospectively aimed to describe and

analyse the roles and interaction of the group (Haut *et al.* 2008). Process data were collected by unstructured observation and written documentation of each meeting concerning frequency, content and mode of the group members' contributions and their understanding of the guideline's aim and underlying methods. Observation protocols were content-analysed and used as the basis for an interview guide. In December 2008 individual interviews with the group members were conducted. First impressions point out the decisive role of a skilled moderator, the difficulties of the group members in understanding the methodology of EBN and the challenge of interdisciplinary interaction and communication within the group.

Further steps

Implementation aids

Currently, five experts from different disciplines who were not involved in guideline development are reviewing the first version of the guideline. The acceptability and comprehensibility of the guideline will be explored in four focus groups with nurses and residents' relatives. The focus group members will also review the guideline's short version and the relatives' version. In parallel, different guideline implementation aids will be developed. These include a structured education programme for nurses, a pocket guide for nurses and an information programme for residents and their representatives.

Evaluation

The evaluation of the guideline development process has been reported above. In a further step the guideline's efficacy will be evaluated in a cluster-randomised controlled trial of 40 German nursing homes. In the intervention group the guideline will be implemented using the implementation aids referred to above. The control group will receive brief information about professional and legal issues related to physical restraints. The primary endpoint is defined as the number of residents with at least one restraint after 12 months' follow-up.

Nationwide implementation

If the guideline's efficacy is proven, different strategies helping to implement the guideline in German nursing homes will be carried out. These include publication of the guideline and implementation aids via the internet. An audit instrument will also be developed and made available. The guideline will be updated regularly.

DISCUSSION

In recent years the use of physical restraints in nursing homes has been extensively discussed. However, restraints are still commonly used and regarded as an effective measure to reduce falls and fall-related injuries. Court decisions in Germany have regarded restraints as an appropriate measure to avoid injuries. Accordingly, nurses strongly demand alternative measures in order to be able to avoid restraints.

This evidence-based practice guideline makes clear that only weak or no recommendations can be drawn for specific interventions to avoid restraints. This is not common in the context of guidelines. Nevertheless, we are confident that the guideline is a significant contribution towards restraint-free care.

The systematic review on which this guideline is based points out two important implications. First, the review emphasises that restraints are not an adequate measure to prevent falls or fall-related injuries and that they can be avoided without negative consequences. Second, it shows that there is currently no evidence for the effectiveness of any intervention to reduce or avoid the use of restraints in nursing home residents. Coming back to the introductory aphorism, the guideline should encourage nurses to 'just stand there' and thereby relieve them from the burdening duty to 'do something'. Furthermore, all persons involved in decisions on the use of physical restraints, including nurses, relatives, legal guardians and judges, must realise that, loosely quoting Billy Bragg, 'the only way to avoid restraints is to avoid restraints'.

So far, there are no evidence-based guidelines addressing physical restraints in nursing home residents, although, as pointed out above, these might be a promising approach. This especially holds true if one considers recent approaches that have often failed to successfully reduce restraints. The results from the upcoming RCT will verify, if our assumption is right. But even if the study fails to prove the guideline's efficacy, the work carried out so far is still extremely valuable as it provides an exhaustive literature review that indicates a large number of questions for further research.

REFERENCES

Behrens, J. and Langer, G. (eds) (2006) *Evidence-Based Nursing and Caring*. Bern: Hans Huber.

BUKO-QS (Bundeskonferenz zur Qualitätssicherung im Gesundheits- und Pflegewesen e.V.) (ed.) (2008) *Qualitätsniveau I: Mobilität und Sicherheit bei Menschen mit demenziellen Einschränkungen in stationären Einrichtungen* (Quality level I: Mobility and safety of people with dementia restrictions in residential facilities). Bonn: Economica.

Capezuti, E., Wagner, L., Brush, B., Boltz, M. *et al.* (2007) 'Consequences of an intervention to reduce restrictive side rail use in nursing homes.' *Journal of the American Geriatrics Society 55*, 334–341.

Castle, N. and Mor, V. (1998) 'Physical restraint in nursing homes: A review of the literature since the Nursing Home Reform Act of 1987.' *Medical Care Research and Review 55*, 139–170.

Cluzeau, F.A., Burgers, J.S., Brouwers, M., Grol, R. *et al.* (2003) 'Writing group development and validation of an international appraisal instrument for assessing the quality of clinical practice guidelines: The AGREE project.' *Quality and Safety in Health Care 12*, 18–23.

Delamothe, T. (2000) 'Quality of websites: Kitemarking the west wind.' *British Medical Journal 7*, 321, 7265, 843–844.

Deutsches Netzwerk für Qualitätsentwicklung in der Pflege (German Network for the Development of Quality in Nursing) (2007) *Methodisches Vorgehen zur Entwicklung und Einführung von Expertenstandards in der Pflege* (Methodical steps for the development and implementation of expert standards in nursing care). Available at www.dnqp.de, accessed 6 November 2009.

De Vries, O., Ligthart, G. and Nikolaus, T. (2004) 'On behalf of the participants of the European Academy of Medicine of Ageing–Course III. Differences in period prevalence of the use of physical restraints in elderly inpatients of European hospitals and nursing homes.' *Journals of Gerontology. Series A, Biological Sciences and Medical Sciences 59*, M922–923.

Engberg, J., Castle, N. and McCaffrey, D. (2008) 'Physical restraint initiation in nursing homes and subsequent resident health.' *Gerontologist 48*, 442–452.

Evans, D., Wood, J., Lambert, L. and Fitzgerald, M. (2002) *Physical Restraint in Acute and Residential Care*. Adelaide: The Joanna Briggs Institute.

Field, M.J. and Lohr, K.N. (eds) (1990) *Clinical Practice Guidelines: Directions for a New Program*. Washington, DC: National Academy Press.

Flaherty, J. (2004) 'Zero tolerance for physical restraints: Difficult but not impossible.' *Journal of Gerontology 59A*, 919–920.

Graber, D.R. and Sloane, P.D. (1995) 'Nursing home survey deficiencies for physical restraint use.' *Medical Care 33*, 1051–1063.

Grading of Recommendations Assessment, Development and Evaluation (GRADE) (2004) 'Grading quality of evidence and strength of recommendations.' *British Medical Journal 328*, 1490–1494.

Guttman, R., Altman, R.D. and Karlan, M.S. (1999) 'Report of the Council on Scientific Affairs – Use of restraints for patients in nursing homes.' *Archives of Family Medicine 8*, 101–105.

Guyatt, G.H., Oxman, A.D., Vist, G.E., Kunz, R. *et al.* (2008a) 'GRADE: An emerging consensus. On rating quality of evidence and strength of recommendations.' *British Medical Journal 335*, 924–926.

Guyatt, G.H., Oxman, A.D., Kunz, R., Vist, G.E. *et al.* (2008b) 'What is "quality of evidence" and why is it important to clinicians?' *British Medical Journal 336*, 995–998.

Hamers, J. and Huizing, A. (2005) 'Why do we use physical restraints in the elderly?' *Zeitschrift für Gerontologie und Geriatrie 38*, 19–25.

Haut, A., Gerlach, A., Köpke, S. and Meyer, G. (2008) *Evaluation of a Guideline Development Group Process*. Abstract, 5th International G-I-N Conference, Helsinki, Finland.

Healey, F., Oliver, D., Milne, A. and Connelly, J. (2008) 'The effect of bedrails on falls and injury: A systematic review of clinical studies.' *Age and Ageing 37*, 368–378.

Hoffmann, B. and Klie, T. (eds) (2004) *Freiheitsentziehende Maßnahmen* (Physical restraints). Heidelberg: C.F. Müller.

Hofinger, V., Kreissl, R., Pelikan, C. and Pilgram, A. (2007) *Zur Implementation des Heimaufenthaltsgesetzes* (Implementation of the nursing home stay law). Vienna: Institut für Rechts- & Kriminalsoziologie. Available at www.irks.at/downloads/Zur%20Implementation%20des%20 HeimAufG_Endbericht.pdf, accessed 6 November 2009.

Huizing, A., Hamers, J., Gulpers, M. and Berger, M. (2006) 'Short-term effects of an educational intervention on physical restraint use: A cluster randomized trial.' *BMC Geriatrics 26*, 6–17.

Huizing, A.R., Hamers, J., Gulpers, M. and Berger, M. (2009) 'Preventing the use of physical restraints on residents newly admitted to psycho-geriatric nursing home wards: A cluster-randomized trial.' *International Journal of Nursing Studies 46*, 4, 459–469.

Hutchings, A., Raine, R., Sanderson, C. and Black, N. (2006) 'A comparison of formal consensus methods used for developing clinical guidelines.' *Journal of Health Services Research and Policy 11*, 218–224.

Kirkevold, Ø. and Engedal, K. (2004) 'A study into the use of restraint in nursing homes in Norway.' *British Journal of Nursing 13*, 902–905.

Koczy, P., Klie, T., Kron, M., Bredthauer, D. *et al.* (2005) 'Effektivität einer multifaktoriellen Intervention zur Reduktion von körpernaher Fixierung bei demenzerkrankten Heimbewohnern' (Effectiveness of a multifactorial intervention to reduce physical restraints in nursing home residents with dementia). *Zeitschrift für Gerontologie und Geriatrie 38*, 33–39.

Köpke, S., Meyer, G., Haut, A. and Gerlach, A. (2008) 'Methodenpapier zur Entwicklung einer Praxisleitlinie zur Vermeidung von freiheitseinschränkenden Maßnahmen in der beruflichen Altenpflege' (Methods paper on the development of a practice guideline for the avoidance of physical restraints in nursing homes). *Zeitschrift für Evidenz, Fortbildung und Qualität im Gesundheitswesen 102*, 45–53.

Lai, C., Wong, T., Chow, S., Kong, S. *et al.* (2007) 'Why is it so hard for nurses to take off the restraints?' *Gerontology 53*, 489.

Meyer, G. and Köpke, S. (2006) 'Expertenstandards in der Pflege – wirkungsvolle Instrumente zur Verbesserung der Pflegepraxis oder von ungewissem Nutzen?' (The German nursing expert standards: Powerful instruments to improve nursing practice or of doubtful benefit?). *Zeitschrift für Gerontologie und Geriatrie 39*, 211–216.

Meyer, G., Köpke, S., Haastert, B. and Mühlhauser, I. (2008) 'Restraint use among nursing home residents: cross-sectional study and prospective cohort study.' *Journal of Clinical Nursing 18*, 7, 981–990

Miller, M. and Kearney, N. (2004) 'Guidelines for clinical practice: Development, dissemination and implementation.' *International Journal of Nursing Studies 41*, 813–821.

Pflege-Weiterentwicklungsgesetz (Nursing care law) (2008) 'Bundesgesetzblatt Jahrgang 2008 Teil I Nr. 20.' Available at www.bgblportal.de/BGBL/bgbl1f/bgbl108s0874.pdf, accessed 6 November 2009.

ReduFix (2006) 'Reduktion von körpernaher Fixierung bei demenzerkrankten Heimbewohnern' (Reduction of physical restraints in nursing home residents with dementia). Available at www.efh-freiburg.de/Dokumente/agp/00%20Tagungsbericht.pdf, accessed 6 November 2009.

Schünemann, H.J., Oxman, A.D. and Fretheim, A. (2006) 'Improving the use of research evidence in guideline development: 6. Determining which outcomes are important.' *Health Research Policy and Systems/BioMed Central 4*, 1–6.

Scottish Intercollegiate Guidelines Network (SIGN) (2004) *SIGN 50: A Guideline Developers' Handbook 2004*. Edinburgh: SIGN. Available at www.sign.ac.uk/guidelines/fulltext/50/index.html, accessed 6 Novemeber 2009.

Testad, I., Aasland, A. and Aarsland, D. (2005) 'The effect of staff training on the use of restraint in dementia: A single-blind randomised controlled trial.' *International Journal of Geriatric Psychiatry 20*, 587–590.

van Wersch, A. and Eccles, M. (2001) 'Involvement of consumers in the development of evidence based clinical guidelines: Practical experiences from the North of England evidence based guideline development programme.' *Quality in Health Care 10*, 10–16.

Werner, P. (2002) 'Perceptions regarding the use of physical restraints with elderly persons: Comparison of Israeli health care nurses and social workers.' *Journal of Interprofessional Care 16*, 59–68.

Woolf, S.H., Grol, R., Hutchinson, A., Eccles, M. and Grimshaw, J. (1999) 'Clinical guidelines: Potential benefits, limitations, and harms of clinical guidelines.' *British Medical Journal 318*, 527–530.

Chapter 17

REDUCING RESTRAINT – The BENEFITS of EDUCATION and TRAINING

Ingelin Testad and Dag Aarsland

INTRODUCTION

The capacity to make medical treatment decisions (competency) is a fundamental aspect of personal autonomy, and refers to an individual's cognitive and emotional capacity to accept a proposed treatment, to refuse treatment or to select among treatment alternatives. Loss of competence is an inevitable consequence of neurodegenerative dementias; as memory, language and judgement abilities erode, persons with dementia lose the capacity to make medical health care decisions (Marson 2001). An assessment that someone lacks competency has major implications: it gives care staff influence over the person, it also gives care staff a duty to act on behalf of this person in *his best interest*, and it could potentially be abused (Nicholson, Cutter and Hotopf 2008). For someone to lack competency there must be a disturbance in the functioning of the brain, resulting in the ability to retain, use or weight information relevant to a decision or to communicate a choice. Assessment of capacity includes a *status approach*, where a person having reached a diagnostic threshold would be described as lacking capacity for all decisions, or a *functional approach*, where capacity needs to be reassessed for all decisions, particularly if the impairment fluctuates over time (Nicholson *et al.* 2008). And, finally, someone could lack competency in some areas but not in others. This means that, for someone living with dementia in a nursing home for example, having reached a diagnostic threshold and with loss of competency as a status they could still have the competency to make decisions with regards to activities of daily living (ADLs).

Use of restraint is the use of force to make someone do something they are resisting, as well as a restriction of a person's freedom of movement (Nicholson *et al.* 2008). Use of restraint towards a person lacking competency should be believed necessary to prevent harm and maintain health, be proportional to the likelihood and seriousness of harm and should be in the person's *best interest*. To make this decision is one of the major challenges when caring for residents with dementia in nursing homes, including the question: *to restrain or refrain?*

Ideally, a safe and restraint-free environment at all times and for all older people living in care homes is central to good quality care services. However, studies show that people with cognitive impairments in nursing homes are the most likely to be restrained physically (Bredthauer *et al.* 2005; Hamers, Gulpers and Strik 2004). Hamers *et al.* (2004), for example, found that physical restraints were used for 49 per cent of all residents.

Is a restraint-free environment possible and is it actually in the patient's *best interest* at all times? A review of studies of strategies for physical restraint minimization in the acute and residential settings found 13 studies identified in residential care, and only one of these was a randomized controlled trial (RCT) (Evans, Wood and Lambert 2002). Evans *et al.* (2002) concluded that physical restraint could be safely reduced in residential settings through a combination of education and expert clinical consultation. Two recent systematic reviews on clinical trials of the effect of continuing education and training for nursing home staff concluded that few such studies had been reported, and that methodological limitations such as non-randomized studies, small sample sizes and high attrition rates (Aylward *et al.* 2003; Kuske *et al.* 2007) preclude clear interpretations of the findings. Most notably, few studies employed long-term follow-up evaluation to ensure whether any effect is sustained beyond the intervention period, and many studies reported staff outcomes only. It is not therefore clear whether any staff-effect is transferred from theory into practice in terms of improved care or resident quality of life or behaviour. In addition to a previous pilot study from our group (Testad, Aasland and Aarsland 2005), where restraints were significantly reduced by more than 50 per cent, using the educational intervention 'relation-related care' (RRC) only one study has assessed whether reduction in the use of restraints can be achieved after staff education, using a simple pre-post design (Middlethon *et al.* 1999).

The RRC education and training programme provides a practical framework for staff to understand behaviour and reduce use of restraint (see Box 17.1). It consists of a two-day seminar and a seven-step guidance group illustrated in Tables 17.1 and 17.2 respectively (Testad, Ballard and Aarsland in press; Testad *et al.* 2005).

Box 17.1 Relation-related care (RRC): An innovative education and training programme to reduce the use of restraint

Relation-related care (RRC) has been designed to reduce use of restraint in nursing homes, as outlined in the case of Mr Barlow throughout this chapter.

Programme aims

Every decision to use restraint towards people with dementia in care homes should be carefully considered based on the individual's own need and circumstances.

Content

RRC consists of two major elements:

- a two-day seminar (Table 17.1)
- seven-step guidance group (Table 17.2).

RRC has been developed and used since 1999 and is structured into three main factors:

1. predisposing factors (dissemination of information, i.e. lectures, written materials)
2. enabling factors (resources to implement new skills, i.e. treatment guidelines)
3. reinforcing factors (reinforcing new skills, i.e. feedback, peer support).

This classification system was originally developed by Green *et al.* (1980) to examine educational interventions and behaviour change in health promotion (Aylward *et al.* 2003). A combination of these three factors is necessary to change the knowledge, attitudes and practices of care staff on a long-term basis (Aylward *et al.* 2003).

The intervention not only improves the interaction between the older people and care staff but also provides staff with tools to understand the situation from the perspective of the older person and to provide better person-centred care.

To ensure an individual's needs and preferences are met the RRC intervention also takes a whole systems and structures view. Thus the RRC includes a combination of predisposing factors, enabling factors and reinforcing factors. We included *all* care staff and leaders to facilitate the implementation of new skills, treatment guidelines, etc. to ensure that all older people are treated fairly and equally regardless of which members of staff are on duty at the time.

Table 17.1 Modules and content of the two-day training seminar

MODULES	CONTENT
Dementia	What is it?
Dementia and behavioural and psychological symptoms of dementia (BPSD)	Causes in the disease itself Causes in the physical or social environment Causes due to unmet needs
Treatment in dementia and BPSD	Psychosocial intervention Pharmacological intervention
Use of restraint	Definitions Structural restraint Interactional restraint Competency
Care staff issues	Perceptions Feelings Attitudes
Relationships between older people and staff	Structure and content Universal and special relationships Interaction and experience
Organizational and psychosocial environment	Physical environment Organizational environment Psychosocial environment

Table 17.2 Summary of seven-step guidance group

Step 1	Description of the situation
Step 2	Explanation and interpretation
Step 3	Recognizing and accepting care staff feelings towards the situation
Step 4	Reflection about the situation Tools: resident history and diary
Step 5	Problem solving
Step 6	Intervention
Step 7	Evaluation

The substantive part of this chapter draws on examples from the RRC training programme, to answer the question: *to restrain or refrain?* Underpinning the discussion is an exploration of best interests and whether 'every decision to use restraint towards residents with dementia in nursing homes should be carefully considered, based on each resident's individual need and situation' (Testad *et al.* in press). Specifically, we will focus on use of interactional restraint related to ADLs, as shown in the case of Mr Barlow.

Case study: Mr Barlow

Mr Barlow, a man of 79 with a diagnosis of Alzheimer's disease, was admitted to the nursing home when his wife was unable to care for him at home. He had become increasingly confused and aggressive and was not able to care for himself. He was also incontinent. When his wife tried to help him with dressing or with other necessary care, he would get angry with her. One day he tried to hit her, and their sons decided that he could not live at home any longer. His wife was grieving the fact that she could no longer keep him at home but understood the reasons why and was looking forward to getting help and have him 'well groomed' again.

That did not happen, for when care staff tried to help Mr Barlow with personal care, including showering and grooming, he would kick, hit and spit. The care staff did their utmost to care for him by holding his hands, so he would not hurt anyone, during personal care routines. Despite this, he did not look 'well groomed' at all. His wife was very upset and demanded that the care staff use force to give him the proper care she felt he deserved.

USE OF RESTRAINT IN NURSING HOMES

The RRC education and training programme defined restraint as any limitation on a person's freedom of movement (Hantikainen 1998). Specifically this includes:

- physical restraint (belts or other fixing to bed, belts or other fixing to chair, locked in a room)

- electronic surveillance (devices on patients that automatically lock the door, devices on patients that alarm the staff, devices to track patients, devices that sound when a patient leaves the bed)

- force or pressure in medical examination or treatment (mixing drugs in food or beverages, use of force to perform examination or treatment)

- force or pressure in ADLs (holding of hands, legs or head for washing or dressing/undressing, showering or bathing against the patient's verbal or physical resistance, forcing the patient to the bathroom, feeding a patient against his/her will).

Restraint was further classified into two groups: structural restraint and interactional restraint (Testad *et al.* in press). Structural restraints are measures of restraint outside the treatment and care giving activity, such as locked doors on the ward, electronic surveillance and bedrails, whereas interactional restraints are measures used between care staff and older people during the provision of treatment and care, such as force or pressure in medical examination or treatment or force or pressure during ADLs. In the case of Mr Barlow force or pressure during ADLs was used and is viewed as interactional restraint.

In a systematic review on reasons for restraining residents, agitation-related reasons for restraint use were reported in 90 per cent of the studies (Evans *et al.* 2002). Furthermore, Kirkevold, Sandvik and Engedal (2004) found that the strongest correlates to use of restraints were degree of dementia, dysfunction in ADLs and aggressive behaviour (Kirkevold, *et al.* 2004; Smith and Buckwalter 2005). Kirkevold, Laake and Engedal (2003) conducted a large survey in Norway consisting of 1398 wards and 25,108 residents (corresponding to 60% of all patients in institutions for older people in Norway), where they found that 78.7 per cent of the wards reported one or more types of restraint – physical restraints, electronic surveillance, force or pressure in medical examination or treatment, force or pressure in ADLs – during the last seven days. The most frequent use of restraint was related to ADLs (61.3%) and medical treatment (49.8%).

FORCED ADLS AND PROBLEM BEHAVIOUR

Case study: Mr Barlow

The wife of Mr Barlow wanted the care staff to use force in helping him with necessary care. But he kicks, hits and spits when they try to help him. By using force, they are able to do the most necessary care. Still, his wife worries a lot and talks to the care staff about the problem when she visits. She lets them know she is not happy about the situation; her husband is unshaved and sometimes he smells unpleasant too. Mr Barlow sits quietly as long as nobody bothers him and sometimes he looks away. 'It is almost like he knows,' his wife remarked one day.

Behavioural and psychological symptoms of dementia (BPSD) include syndromes of agitation: aggressive behaviour, physically non-aggressive behaviour, verbally agitated behaviour and hiding/hoarding behaviour (Cohen-Mansfield 1989). Several studies have explored the prevalence of

BPSD in various care settings with as many as 83 per cent (Smith 2005; Smith and Buckwalter 2005) to 95 per cent (Davis, Buckwalter and Burgio 1997) of people with dementia experiencing some form of BPSD. There are usually multiple causes of BPSD and different reasons why it is seen as a problem. For example, biological, psychological and social factors may contribute to agitation, including personality, personal history and physical and psychosocial environment. Other interacting factors such as pain or depression (Cohen-Mansfield and Werner 1999), overstimulation (Draper *et al*. 2000), loneliness (Hallberg 1995) and premorbid characteristics and history (Kolanowski, Litaker and Buettner 2005) may also influence people's behaviour. Disruptive behaviour will normally be a combination of the following three causes:

- the disease itself
- the physical or social environment
- unmet needs. (Algase *et al*. 1996)

Over the last decade, the concept of problem behaviour or agitation has developed in recognition that there may be a number of underlying causes for the behaviour (Volicer *et al*. 2006). Behaviour is also now seen as valuable information about people's condition and the communication of unmet need, so there has therefore been a move away from problematizing it.

Resistiveness to care can make people with dementia unmanageable at home and can make it difficult to care for people in nursing homes (Mahoney *et al*. 1999). When people resist care the task is often still carried on ('we are doing this for his own good') unless staff encounter violence, as in the case of Mr Barlow. These situations can further provoke aggression amongst older people with dementia and recourse of staff to use restraint.

FORCED ADLS AND COMPETENCY

Using restraint or force towards a patient lacking competency should only be believed necessary to prevent harm and maintain health. An important goal for staff is to assume competency in order to maintain as much of the individual's autonomy as possible (Testad 2004) (see Figure 17.1).

In the case of Mr Barlow he resisted care. Using a status approach on competency Mr Barlow had reached a diagnostic threshold that involves lack of competency. Is it still possible to assume competency related to ADLs and maintain some of Mr Barlow's autonomy?

The situation of Mr Barlow worsened. Staff could no longer agree on what was absolutely 'necessary' care and whether ADLs should be forced. They could not agree and staff became increasingly reluctant to approach

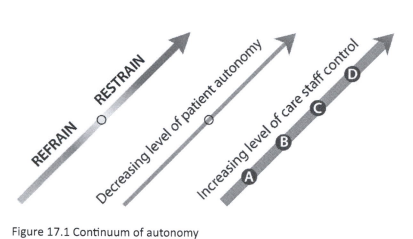

Figure 17.1 Continuum of autonomy
Source: Testad 2004

him. The situation escalated when, one morning, he refused to get out of bed.

USING THE RRC EDUCATION AND TRAINING PROGRAMME

The RRC provides a means of analysing and interpreting patterns of behaviour and the relationships between older people and care staff (see Box 17.1).

What is a situation?

A situation may be viewed in a number of ways: (1) universal, yet special; and it involves (2) previous experience and demands an action – interaction; and it has (3) a structure and a content (Martinsen 1993) (Figure 17.2).

The interpretation of the situation is contingent on the persons involved: care staff and the older person and their families and carers. Another challenge for staff relating to people with dementia is that they approach the situation through intellect and a problem-solving approach whereas older people with dementia approach situations more through their senses and feelings.

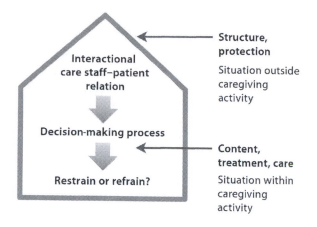

Figure 17.2 The situated context of restraint

Source: Testad 2004

1. Universal and special

There are certain universal aspects and basics in life such as love, trust and care. These fundamental aspects of a human being are universal and present in all situations and relationships. This will vary from one situation to another, depending on the relationships between those involved in the situation and the factors that make situations unique. Furthermore, each situation has its own special demand (Martinsen 1993). In the case of Mr Barlow the demand on the care staff was to care for him but he resisted offers of help.

2. Interaction; previous experience and actions

Regardless of what we choose to do in the situation – if we take action, if we choose to do nothing (which is also an action) – the resident situation will be influenced by the care staff, as the care staff will be influenced by the resident (Figure 17.3).

Furthermore, our actions are, amongst other things, based on experience. However, there are no guarantees that our experiences will lead to actions that are in the older people's best interest or serve their individual needs. And having good intentions is no guarantee either of what is in the individual's best interests. In the case of Mr Barlow care staff clearly did have good intentions, and they did take action; they did the best they could, based on their own experience. However, there was no way

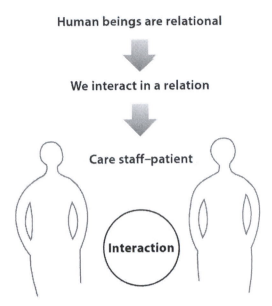

Figure 17.3 The relationship between older people and care staff
Source: Testad 2004

of knowing what was working and whether their actions were in the best interests of Mr Barlow.

3. Structure and content
The structure of the situation includes physical conditions such as the built environment, the type and size of organization and care staff–resident ratios. The structure of the situation is influenced by the content and the actions chosen. The content chosen is again based on the relationship between care staff and older people. This depends on what individuals bring into the situation (Martinsen 1993). Only focusing on the structure of the situation, and being occupied with 'doing' and getting control of the situation, will make it difficult to understand the 'being' of the older person, as an individual, and the way they may be communicating through behaviour. There is the risk of decisions being made that are not in accordance with older people's best interests and further risk of enhancing agitation and the inappropriate use of restraint.

Case study: Mr Barlow

When Mr Barlow was admitted to the nursing home, he was admitted to a special care unit, due to his 'problem behaviour'. There were only eight other older people in the unit and the care staff–client ratio was 0.8. However, counting the number of older people, staff and visitors, Mr Barlow was exposed to 30 new people in his first week. In addition, this was a whole new environment for him where he could no longer get up at night and find the bathroom, or the kitchen if he was thirsty, or his way outside if he wanted to take a walk.

To ensure decisions as to whether to *restrain or refrain?* are based on individual need the situation needs to be analysed further to explore staff understanding of the situation.

Understanding the situation

In the case of Mr Barlow, care staff might want 'something to be done'. This 'something' could involve more staff, having the patient medicated or voting for moving Mr Barlow to another unit – interventions that are not necessarily based upon the individual situation and need or in the person's best interests. Feelings are key to opening up and understanding the situation. Feelings are 'rational' because they can lead to recognition and understanding of the situation (Martinsen 1993).

Feelings can best be described as a continuum from positive to negative feelings, i.e. from empathy to disgust (Vatne and Fagermoen 2007). These feelings are seldom reflected upon, even more seldom recognized and very rarely reflected upon in a group of care staff. Furthermore, there is an assumption that care staff should not have negative feelings towards the patient, only 'right' feelings: being understanding, caring and willing to help. Feelings of anger and disgust towards the patient are not 'right' feelings and care staff may feel ashamed of their feelings and subsequently may be reluctant to share them with others (Vatne and Fagermoen 2007).

Restrain or refrain?

Case study: Mr Barlow

Mr Barlow used to be very particular about his appearance and the way he dressed. He did not like to undress in public, and never went to public baths. This used to be a family joke, as well as him being really grumpy in the morning. 'Don't talk to Dad before he has had two cups of coffee,' one of the sons said. At home Mr Barlow did not have a shower, only a bath. Mr Barlow was a gentle and kind man and his greatest interests were bird watching and classical music. He had a big music collection at home.

The decision to *restrain or refrain?* should consider all aspects of the situation: care staff, nursing home environment, the individual and their history and the way care staff and clients influence each other (Figure 17.4).

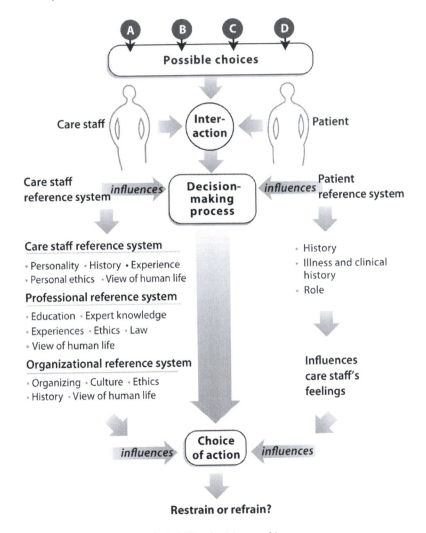

Figure 17.4 Restrain or refrain? The decision-making process

Source: Testad 2004

The decision to *restrain or refrain?* should consider three major areas: (1) maintaining as much of the person's autonomy as possible, (2) be proportional to the likelihood and seriousness of harm and (3) be believed necessary to prevent harm and maintain health and choose the least restrictive intervention.

Case study: Mr Barlow

Mr Barlow was given a cup of coffee in the morning, while the staff put food out for the birds outside his window and selected some music from his list of favourites. It was obvious that he enjoyed this. This care was carefully planned. At first he would resist going to the bath but, slowly, as the head nurse ensured the same procedure every morning, he started to relax. Staff started to relax and the routine was followed through with no or little pressure. When his wife came to visit, she would relax too and enjoy being with her husband. He looked well groomed, smelled nice, he stopped looking away and they could capture moments where he recognized her. One of the staff said, 'I enjoy having a cup of coffee with Mr Barlow in the morning and watching the birds. I feel I am a professional again, doing a good job and enjoying it too. Everybody wants to go to visit Mr Barlow now.' No force or pressure in ADLs were subsequently needed.

Recognizing Mr Barlow as a person with history enabled staff to identify which care arrangements were in his best interests. In doing so, staff assumed competency and therefore maintained some of Mr Barlow's autonomy. The use of force and restraint during ADLs was necessary at the beginning of the relationship between staff and Mr Barlow. However, a person-centred approach, considering Mr Barlow's individual needs and personal circumstances, fostered trust and there was no subsequent need to use restraint.

CONCLUSION

Education and continuous guidance for all staff is necessary to reduce the need for inappropriate restraint. To address whether to 'restrain or refrain' must be based on a careful assessment of an individual's best interests, clinical needs and personal circumstances.

REFERENCES

Algase, D.L., Beck, C., Kolanowski, A., Whall, A *et al.* (1996) 'Need-driven dementia-compromised behavior: An alternative view of disruptive behavior.' *American Journal of Alzheimer's Disease 11*, 10–19.

Aylward, S., Stolee, P., Keat, N. and Johncox, V. (2003) 'Effectiveness of continuing education in long-term care: A literature review.' *Gerontologist 43*, 259–271.

Bredthauer, D., Becker, C., Eichner, B., Koczy, P. and Nikolaus, T. (2005) 'Factors relating to the use of physical restraints in psychogeriatric care: A paradigm for elder abuse.' *Zeitschrift für Gerontology und Geriatrie 38*, 10–18.

Cohen-Mansfield, J. and Werner, P. (1999) 'Longitudinal predictors of non-aggressive agitated behaviors in the elderly.' *International Journal Geriatric Psychiatry 14*, 831–844.

Cohen-Mansfield, J., Marx, M.S. and Rosenthal, A.S. (1989) 'A description of agitation in a nursing home.' *Journals of Gerontology 44*, M77–84.

Davis, L.L., Buckwalter, K. and Burgio, L.D. (1997) 'Measuring problem behaviors in dementia: Developing a methodological agenda.' *Advances in Nursing Science 20*, 40–55.

Draper, B., Snowdon, J., Meares, S., Turner, J. *et al.* (2000) 'Case-controlled study of nursing home residents referred for treatment of vocally disruptive behavior.' *International Psychogeriatrics 12*, 333–344.

Evans, D., Wood, J. and Lambert, L. (2002) 'A review of physical restraint minimization in the acute and residential care settings.' *Journal of Advanced Nursing 40*, 616–625.

Green, L., Kreuter, M., Deeds, S. and Partridge, D. (1980) *Health Education Planning: A Diagnostic Approach.* Palo Alto, CA: Mayfield Press.

Hallberg, I.R. (1995) 'Clinical group supervision and supervised implementation of planned individualized care of severely demented people: Effects on nurses, provision of the care, and patients.' *Journal of Psychiatric and Mental Health Nursing 2*, 113–114.

Hamers, J.P., Gulpers, M.J. and Strik, W. (2004) 'Use of physical restraints with cognitively impaired nursing home residents.' *Journal of Advanced Nursing 45*, 246–251.

Hantikainen, V. (1998) 'Physical restraint: A descriptive study in Swiss nursing homes.' *Nursing Ethics 5*, 330–346.

Kirkevold, O., Laake, K. and Engedal, K. (2003) 'Use of constraints and surveillance in Norwegian wards for the elderly.' *International Journal of Geriatric Psychiatry 18*, 491–497.

Kirkevold, O., Sandvik, L. and Engedal, K. (2004) 'Use of constraints and their correlates in Norwegian nursing homes.' *International Journal of Geriatric Psychiatry 19*, 980–988.

Kolanowski, A.M., Litaker, M. and Buettner, L. (2005) 'Efficacy of theory-based activities for behavioral symptoms of dementia.' *Nursing Research 54*, 219–228.

Kuske, B., Hanns, S., Luck, T., Angermeyer, M.C., Behrens, J. and Riedel-Heller, S.G. (2007) 'Nursing home staff training in dementia care: A systematic review of evaluated programs.' *International Psychogeriatrics 19*, 818–841.

Mahoney, E.K., Hurley, A.C., Volicer, L., Bell, M., *et al.* (1999) 'Development and testing of the Resistiveness to Care Scale.' *Research in Nursing and Health 22*, 27–38.

Marson, D.C. (2001) 'Loss of competency in Alzheimer's disease: Conceptual and psychometric approaches.' *International Journal of Law and Psychiatry 24*, 267–283.

Martinsen, K. (1993) *Fra Marx til Løgstrup: Om etikk ogsanselighetisykepleien.* Oslo: Tano.

Middlethon, H., Keene, R., Johnson, C., Elkins, A. and Lee, A. (1999) 'Physical and pharmacological restraints in long-term care facilities.' *Journal of Gerontological Nursing 25*, 26–33.

Nicholson, T.R., Cutter, W. and Hotopf, M. (2008) 'Assessing mental capacity: The Mental Capacity Act.' *British Medical Journal 336*, 322–325.

Smith, M.B.K. (2005) 'Behaviors associated with dementia.' *American Journal of Nursing 105*, 40–52.

Smith, M. and Buckwalter, K. (2005) 'Behaviors associated with dementia: Whether resisting care or exhibiting apathy, an older adult with dementia is attempting communication. Nurses and other caregivers must learn to "hear" this language.' *American Journal of Nursing 105*, 40–52; quiz 53.

Testad, I. (2004) 'Mechanical restraints – Is there really no alternative?' Thesis, University of Oslo.

Testad, I., Aasland, A.M. and Aarsland, D. (2005) 'The effect of staff training on the use of restraint in dementia: A single-blind randomised controlled trial.' *International Journal of Geriatric Psychiatry 20*, 587–590.

Testad, I.B.K., Ballard, C. and Aarsland, D. (in press) 'The effect of staff training on agitation and use of restraint in nursing home residents with dementia: A single-blind randomised controlled trial.' *International Journal of Clinical Psychiatry* (submitted).

Vatne, S. and Fagermoen, M.S. (2007) 'To correct and to acknowledge: Two simultaneous and conflicting perspectives of limit-setting in mental health nursing.' *Journal of Psychiatric and Mental Health Nursing 14*, 41–48.

Volicer, L., Simard, J., Pupa, J.H., Medrek, R. and Riordan, M.E. (2006) 'Effects of continuous activity programming on behavioral symptoms of dementia.' *Journal of the American Medical Directors Association 7*, 426–431.

SELECT BIBLIOGRAPHY

Rhidian Hughes

All-Party Parliamentary Group on Dementia (2008) *Always a Last Resort: Inquiry into the Prescription of Antipsychotic Drugs to People with Dementia Living in Care Homes.* London: Stationery Office.

Allen, D. (2000) *Training Carers in Physical Interventions: Towards Evidence Based Practice.* Kidderminster: British Institute of Learning Disabilities.

Allen, D. (ed.) (2002) *Ethical Approaches to Physical Interventions: Responding to Challenging Behaviour in People with Intellectual Disabilities.* Kidderminster: British Institute of Learning Disabilities.

Alzheimer's Society (2007) *Safer Walking Technology.* London: Alzheimer's Society.

Australian Commission on Safety and Quality in Healthcare (2005) *Preventing Falls and Harm from Falls in Older People: Best Practice Guidelines for Australian Hospitals and Residential Aged Care Facilities.* Canberra: Australian Commission.

Australian Government, Department of Health and Ageing (2004) *Decision-Making Tool: Responding to Issues of Restraint in Aged Care.* Canberra: Australian Government, Department of Health and Ageing.

Bibby, P. (1994) *Personal Safety for Social Workers.* Farnham: Ashgate, in association with the Suzy Lamplugh Trust.

Bibby, P. (1995) *Personal Safety for Health Care Workers.* Farnham: Ashgate, in association with the Suzy Lamplugh Trust.

Braun, J.W. and Lipson, L. (1996) *Towards a Restraint-Free Environment: Reducing the Use of Physical and Chemical Restraints in Long-Term and Acute Care Settings.* Baltimore, MD: Health Professions Press.

Carlile of Berriew, Lord (2006) *An Independent Inquiry into the Use of Physical Restraint, Solitary Confinement and Forcible Strip Searching of Children in Prisons, Secure Training Centres and Local Authority Secure Children's Homes.* London: Howard League for Penal Reform.

Commission for Social Care Inspection (2007) *Rights, Risks and Restraints: An Exploration into the Use of Restraint in the Care of Older People.* London: Commission for Social Care Inspection.

Counsel and Care (2001) *Residents Taking Risks: Minimising the Use of Restraint – A Guide for Care Homes.* London: Counsel and Care.

Counsel and Care (2002) *Showing Restraint: Challenging the Use of Restraint in Care Homes.* London: Counsel and Care.

Dewing, J. (2006) 'Wandering into the future: Reconceptualizing wandering "a natural and good thing".' *International Journal of Older People Nursing 1*, 4, 239–249.

Ellis, J. (2007) 'Volunteer in a dementia-registered nursing home.' *Working with Older People 11*, 1, 28–31.

Evans, D. and Fitzgerald, M. (2002) 'The experience of physical restraint: A systematic review of qualitative research.' *Contemporary Nurse 13*, 2/3, 126–135.

Evans, D. and Fitzgerald, M. (2002) 'Reasons for physically restraining patients and residents: A systematic review and content analysis.' *Journal of International Nursing Studies 39*, 7, 735–743.

Evans, D., Wood, J. and Lambert, L. (2003) 'Patient injury and physical restraint devices: A systematic review.' *Journal of Advanced Nursing 41*, 3, 274–282.

Fisher, W.A. (1994) 'Restraint and seclusion: A review of the literature.' *American Journal of Psychiatry 151*, 11, 1584–1591.

Gillespie, L.D., Gillespie, W.J., Robertson, M.C., Lamb, S.E., Cumming, R.G. and Rowe, B.H. (2003) 'Interventions for preventing falls in elderly people.' *Cochrane Database of Systematic Reviews 4*, Art. No.: CD000340-DOI: 10.1002/14651858. CD000340.

Harris, J., Cornick, M., Jefferson, A. and Mills, R. (2008) *Physical Interventions: A Policy Framework*, 2nd edn. Kidderminster: British Institute of Learning Disabilities.

Hart, D. (2004) *Report on the Use of Physical Intervention Across Children's Services.* London: National Children's Bureau.

Haw, C. and Stubbs, J. (2007) 'Off-label use of antipsychotics: Are we mad?' *Expert Opinion in Drug Safety 6*, 5, 533–545.

Haw, C. and Yorston, G. (2004) 'Thomas Prichard and the non-restraint movement at the Northampton Asylum.' *Psychiatric Bulletin 28*, 4, 140–142.

Hermans, D.G., Htay, U.H., McShane, R. (2007) 'Non-pharmacological interventions for wandering of people with dementia in the domestic setting.' *Cochrane Database of Systematic Reviews 1.*

Hughes, C.M., Lapane, K.L., Mor, V., Ikegami, N. *et al.* (2000) 'The impact of legislation on psychotropic drug use in nursing homes: A cross-national perspective.' *Journal of the American Geriatrics Society 48*, 8, 931–937.

Hughes, J.C. and Louw, S.J. (2002) 'Electronic tagging of people with dementia who wander.' *British Medical Journal 325*, 7369, 847–848.

Hughes, R. (2008) 'Safer walking? Issues and ethics in the use of electronic surveillance of people with dementia.' *Journal of Assistive Technologies 2*, 1, 45–48.

Hughes, R. (ed.) (2009) *Reducing Restraints in Health and Social Care: Practice and Policy Perspectives.* London: Quay Books.

Irving, K. (2002) 'Governing the conduct of conduct: Are restraints inevitable?' *Journal of Advanced Nursing 40*, 4, 405–412.

Jukes, M. and Spencer, P. (2007) 'Neuman's Systems Model.' In M. Jukes and J. Aldridge (eds) *Person-Centred Practices: A Holistic and Integrated Approach.* London: Quay Books.

Kitwood, T. (1990) *Dementia Reconsidered: The Person Comes First.* Buckingham: Open University Press.

Leadbetter, D. and Paterson, B. (2009) 'Towards Restraint-Free Care.' In R. Hughes (ed.) *Reducing Restraints in Health and Social Care: Practice and Policy Perspectives.* London: Quay Books.

Marshall, M. and Allan, K. (2006) *Dementia: Walking not Wandering – Fresh Approaches to Understanding and Practice.* London: Hawker.

Mental Welfare Commission (2005) *Safe to Wander? Principles and Guidance on Good Practice in Caring for Residents with Dementia and Related Disorders where Consideration is Being Given to the Use of Wandering Technologies and Care Homes and Hospitals.* Edinburgh: Mental Welfare Commission.

Mental Welfare Commission (2006) *Rights, Risks and Limits to Freedom: Principles and Good Practice Guidance for Practitioners Considering Restraint in Residential Care Settings.* Edinburgh: Mental Welfare Commission.

National Collaborating Centre for Nursing and Supportive Care (2004) *Clinical Practice Guideline for the Assessment and Prevention of Falls in Older People (Clinical Guideline 21).* London: National Institute for Clinical Excellence.

National Patient Safety Agency (2005) *Bedrails – Reviewing the Evidence: A Systematic Literature Review.* London: National Patient Safety Agency.

Oliver, D. (2007) 'Preventing falls and falls-injuries in hospitals and long-term care facilities.' *Reviews in Clinical Gerontology 17*, 2, 75–92.

Paterson, B. (2006) 'Developing a perspective on restraint and the least intrusive intervention.' *British Journal of Nursing 15*, 22, 1235–1241.

Paterson, B., Bradley, P., Stark, C., Saddler, D., Leadbetter, D. and Allen, D. (2003) 'Deaths associated with restraint use in health and social care in the United Kingdom: The results of a preliminary survey.' *Journal of Psychiatric and Mental Health Nursing 10*, 1, 3–15.

Paterson, B., Leadbetter, D. and Bowie, V. (1999) 'Supporting staff exposed to violence at work: The role of psychological debriefing.' *International Journal of Nursing Studies 36*, 6, 479–486.

Royal College of Nursing (2008) *'Let's Talk about Restraint': Rights, Risks and Responsibility.* London: Royal College of Nursing.

Royal College of Psychiatrists (1998) *The Management of Violence in Clinical Settings: An Evidence Based Guideline.* London: Gaskell.

Sheard, D. (2008) *Being: An Approach to Life and Dementia.* London: Alzheimer's Society.

Skills for Care (2009) *Combating Violence Against Adult Social Care Staff and Volunteers.* London: Skills for Care. Available at www.skillsforcare.org.uk/developing_skills.aspx

Smith, G.M., Davis, R.H., Altenor, A., Tran, D. *et al.* (2008) 'Psychiatric use of unscheduled medications in the Pennsylvania State Hospital System: Effects of discontinuing the use of P.R.N. Orders.' *Community Mental Health Journal 44,* 4, 261–270.

Social Care Institute of Excellence (2009a) *Restraint in Care Homes for Older People.* London: Social Care Institute of Excellence.

Social Care Institute of Excellence (2009b) *Minimising the Use of 'Restraint' in Care Homes: Challenges, Dilemmas and Positive Approaches.* London: Social Care Institute of Excellence.

Strumpf, N.E., Robinson, J.P., Wagner, J.S. and Evans, L.K. (1998) *Restraint-Free Care: Individualized Approaches for Frail Elders.* New York: Springer.

Testad, I., Aasland, M. and Aarsland, D. (2005) 'The effect of staff training on the use of restraint in dementia: A single-blind randomised controlled trial.' *International Journal of Geriatric Psychiatry 20,* 6, 587–590.

Testad, I.B.K., Ballard, C. and Aarsland, D. (in press) 'The effect of staff training on agitation and use of restraint in nursing home residents with dementia: A single-blind randomised controlled trial.' *International Journal of Clinical Psychiatry* (submitted).

Turnbull, J. and Paterson, B. (1999) *Aggression and Violence: Approaches to Effective Management.* Basingstoke: Macmillan.

Wardhaugh, J. and Wilding, P. (1993) 'Towards an explanation of the corruption of care.' *Critical Social Policy 37,* 13, 4–31.

Welsh, S., Hassiotis, A., O'Mahoney, G. and Deahl, M. (2003) 'Big brother is watching you – The ethical implications of electronic surveillance measures in the elderly with dementia and in adults with learning difficulties.' *Aging and Mental Health 7,* 5, 372–375.

Yorston, G. and Haw, C. (2009) 'Historical Perspectives on Restraint.' In R. Hughes (ed.) *Reducing Restraints in Health and Social Care: Practice and Policy Perspectives.* London: Quay Books.

AFTERWORD

Barbara Pointon

I've been there.

I cared for my husband, Malcolm, for most of our 16-year journey, with his Alzheimer's as our fellow-traveller. As I reflect on the views expressed in this book, memories come flooding back of the many times I found myself on the horns of a dilemma: was an action (or non-action) by myself or others really 'restraint'? Glimpses of those situations reveal that there were few black-and-white absolutes but many shades of grey, each vignette throwing restraint into a different light.

To find a starting point for each one, rather like the Victorian young man being questioned by the father of the girl he wishes to marry, were my intentions honourable? Take for example Malcolm's determination to go for walks alone, often just as it was getting dark or beginning to rain, and also early in the morning, still in his dressing gown, whatever the weather. Because of his lack of visuo-spatial awareness (common in the great majority of people with Alzheimer's) he soon became disoriented, failed to recognise familiar landmarks and would get lost. In a state of high anxiety, I spent hours in the car, often in the dark, sweeping the countryside in widening circles. Reluctantly, I tried locking the front door, but Malcolm kicked the glass in and lifted secure garden gates off their hinges. A rota of kind neighbours took him for a long walk every day, but he still, very rightly, clung to his independence. It is impossible for family carers to be vigilant round the clock: I'd suddenly realise he wasn't in the house and, with the threatening hum from the M11 motorway only a mile away, would stand at the end of the drive wishing for an electronic gismo to tell me which way he had gone. In my view, it would not have been restraint or an infringement of his human rights: he would have had the freedom to walk alone and I the peace of mind of knowing where to retrieve him if necessary. There's no quality of life without some risk.

So it is good to read an open, informed debate on this thorny issue and that the intentions behind apparent restraint are considered to be more important than the devices themselves. The main psychological need of a patient in the severe stage of dementia is to feel both physically and emotionally safe. On being moved, because he did not know where he was in space, Malcolm had severe myoclonic jerking. He also suffered from tonic-clonic seizures, so we had to use lap-straps in his wheelchair (and indeed on the shower chair), softly padded bed-rails at night and a reclining chair. All devices to help him feel safe and to prevent him from becoming bed-bound or looking at the same bit of wall all day, which can be a form of restraint in itself.

But there were occasions when chemical restraint was used and it was certainly not in Malcolm's best interests. He was subjected to severe over-medication, both from myself and from professionals in hospital, respite care and carehome settings. During a long period of bizarre and aggressive behaviour, he became physically violent towards me and was prescribed Haloperidol (PRN), which I gave him, believing it was 'doing him good'. Only years later did I learn that perplexing behaviours have logical reasons, that they send us messages about the environment or disapproval of the way that person is being treated and that anti-psychotics should only be used in the last resort and in the short term. When I read the journal I kept at the time, I am truly ashamed about what I subjected him to through ignorance and now plead for every family carer to receive help in understanding and dealing more humanely with perplexing behaviour. Restraint is simply the wrong solution to the situation.

Professionals have a case to answer, too. Malcolm had a short stay in the mental hospital for re-assessment. I took in a man who could walk ten miles, and a few days later found a man unable to stand, zonked out and confined to a wheelchair because no one knew how to deal with his behaviour. In the two years he spent in a nursing home, he became increasingly rigid, could not bend in the middle and was confined to his bed with bed-rails. I just thought this was the next stage of the illness. Apparently his consultant had realised that it was sodium valproate causing the rigidity and several times recommended a reduction in dosage in line with severity of dementia. However, the GP had not actioned this because, as the staff told me, 'He's easier to manage now he's off his feet'. I had to make waves to get the dosage reduced and vowed to bring him home again. Both cases illustrate restraint for the benefit of the staff. It is essential that the whole workforce receives good quality training concerning behaviours and drugs in dementia.

A procedure can sometimes be wrongly interpreted. When Malcolm's swallowing mechanism became compromised, it sometimes took nearly an hour and a great deal of patience for me or paid care staff to feed him a small bowl of pureed food and 350ml of thickened juice by the teaspoonful. It is the most trustful thing in the world to open your mouth to be fed; Malcolm would refuse to take food from a new care worker and I would have to take over for a bit. Unknown to me, a new arrival, used to working in care homes, reported that I was force-feeding Malcolm to our district nurse who, naturally, immediately came to investigate. Unfortunately, she too, because it took so long, assumed the same. Deeply hurt by this false accusation, I explained how we took our cues from Malcolm, who by then was mute: to show that he had taken enough, he would either turn his head away or allow the food to run out of his mouth. Things are not always what they seem to be and each patient, carer and setting is unique.

In institutional settings I have observed where inflexible regimes themselves cause intentional or consequential restraint. Where, beginning as early as 6.30pm, residents had to be in bed by 9pm (because that was when the night shift came on) and not allowed to get up before 7am, so a farmer's wife who all her life had gone to bed late and got up at the crack of dawn was sedated for non-medical reasons. Where an older man with severe Parkinson's, dementia and swallowing problems, at the end of meals, was given his Parkinson's medication (which he pouched in his cheeks and subsequently slowly dribbled it all out again) rather than before meals (when there was a better chance of it being swallowed) because 'that is when we do the drug rounds', resulting in rapid deterioration.

Finally, there is a restraint more difficult to define. On one hand, I found that when Malcolm began to lose his speech and especially when he no longer recognised people, wider family and friends fell away. This isolation of the patient (and their carer) places restraints on their human need for social contact when neither can easily get out of the house. On the other hand, there was a restraint yet more curious. Some visitors in the last stages seemed to be restraining *themselves* – with Malcolm mute, immobile and severely demented, they'd pin themselves to the wall, or disappear behind a newspaper, unsure how to behave when normal channels of communication are blocked, perhaps thinking of Malcolm as 'a vegetable'. Despite outward appearances, the real Malcolm was still in there with intact sensory, emotional and spiritual needs. Holding or stroking a hand, giving a spontaneous hug, seeking eye-contact, talking to him about anything under the sun (the sound of a human voice is a basic need from our babyhood) or just being there, quietly close to him, all made him feel loved and cherished. Perhaps our basic humanity can only come into play when we understand more about the non-physical needs of the seriously ill and learn to let go of our normal inhibitions and self-restraint.

This thought-provoking book challenges us all to re-examine our personal attitudes when caring for older people. At its heart lies a desire to improve relationships, quality of life and holistic well-being. In striving for that goal, in a mysterious way, those same benefits tend to rub off onto the people offering care, whatever the setting. It's in everyone's best interests.

ABOUT THE CONTRIBUTORS

Dag Aarsland is Professor of Geriatric Medicine and Psychiatry at the Institute of Clinical Medicine, University of Bergen, and Director of Neuropsychiatric Research at the Norwegian Centre for Movement Disorders, Stavanger University Hospital, Norway. He is a board member of several professional societies including the Task Force on Criteria for Dementia in Parkinson's Disease and the Task Force on Psychosis in Parkinson's Disease Rating Scales for the Movement Disorder Society.

Aidan Altenor is Director of the Bureau of Community and Hospital Operations for the Pennsylvania Department of Public Welfare. He received his doctorate in Psychology from Lehigh University in Bethlehem, Pennsylvania, and completed a postdoctoral fellowship at the University of Pennsylvania in Clinical Psychology. Aidan is a licensed psychologist in Pennsylvania and a member of the American Psychological Association. He has extensive work experience as a clinical psychologist and has served as the chief executive officer at both Haverford and Norristown State Hospitals within the Pennsylvania State Hospital System. He has co-authored several professional publications and has presented nationally on seclusion and restraint reduction initiatives.

Donna M. Ashbridge is a 33-year veteran of Pennsylvania's State Hospital System and currently serves as Chief Executive Officer of the Danville State Hospital, Danville, Pennsylvania. She is a faculty member of the National Association of State Mental Health Program Directors for Technical Assistance on Seclusion and Restraint Reduction and has presented nationally on Pennsylvania's non-restraint approach. Danville State Hospital became the first hospital in Pennsylvania to fully eliminate the use of seclusion and mechanical restraints in 2003 and the hospital has not utilised mechanical restraints for over six years. She also served on the original 1997 statewide committee that drafted the policy to reduce the utilisation of seclusion and restraint in the state hospital system.

Stephen Clarke has been a training consultant for over ten years working in the health and social care sectors providing courses on staff safety, conflict management and behaviour management. His courses are particularly relevant to the needs of staff, providing strong health and safety perspectives balanced with the needs of the service user. He is a member of the Institute of Conflict Management, the Society of Educational Consultants and a professional member of the British Institute of Learning Disability, and holds the Certificate in Health and Safety.

Janet Davis has been a certified activities director since 1991, a certified activities consultant since 1997, and has more than 26 years' experience in long-term care.

In the first couple of years with the Pennsylvania Restraint Reduction Initiative Janet served as a primary educational consultant and facility liaison to six long-term care training facilities, bringing them to restraint-free status and facilitating their roles as training sites. In 2008 Janet co-developed a specialised dementia training programme, CAPStone – *Creative Approaches Person-centered Solutions*, assisting facilities in developing person-centred approaches to reduce challenging behaviours during bathing. She continues to work closely with facilities throughout Pennsylvania and the rest of the nation providing presenting programmes and consultation on physical restraint reduction, fall prevention/management, bed and side rail safety and activity programming for residents with dementia.

Robert H. Davis is Associate Medical Director of the Office of Mental Health and Substance Abuse Services, Pennsylvania. He is a graduate of Wilkes University and the Pennsylvania State University College of Medicine. He is certified by the American Board of Psychiatry and Neurology in Geriatric Psychiatry and the American Board of Forensic Psychiatry. He is a fellow of the American Psychiatric Association and a clinical associate professor in the Department of Psychiatry at the Pennsylvania State College of Medicine. Robert has lectured on the treatment of individuals with mental illness who are incarcerated in the criminal justice system, and he has lectured and written on the use of alternatives to seclusion and restraint in treatment settings and the use of unscheduled psychiatric medications (*statim* and *pro re nata* medications).

Jan Dewing works as an independent consultant nurse. She is also a visiting professor in Aged Care and Practice Development at the University of Wollongong, New South Wales, Australia, as well as an honorary research fellow at the University of Ulster, Northern Ireland, and a visiting fellow at Northumbria University. In aged care, Jan's research interests are around developing person-centred cultures, active learning and wandering.

Jim Ellis is a retired university lecturer now working as a volunteer in dementia care. Drawing on his academic research he developed therapeutic applications for his wife and other nursing home residents. He has written numerous articles based on his experience of psychological care in the community, nursing home and hospital.

David Evans is a senior lecturer and Program Director for Research Degrees at the University of South Australia. He gained his nursing qualification at the Royal Adelaide Hospital and his PhD from the University of Adelaide. He has active research interests in the areas of evidence-based practice and systematic reviews and is currently focusing on the care of people with delirium and dementia.

Chris Gastmans, Professor of Medical Ethics at the Catholic University of Leuven (Faculty of Medicine, Centre for Biomedical Ethics and Law), Belgium, is teaching and undertaking research in the field of end of life ethics, elderly care ethics and empirical ethics. He chairs several ethics committees in hospitals in Flanders. Chris is involved in national and European research projects on ethics codes in nursing, suicide in the elderly, involvement of nurses in euthanasia and other end of life decisions, and institutional ethics policies on euthanasia. In 2002 he was elected Secretary-

General of the European Association of Centres for Medical Ethics (EACME). For more information see www.cbmer.be.

Beryl D. Goldman is Director for Kendal Outreach, Pennslvania, where she plays a critical role in facilitating restraint-free policies and care practices. Currently, she oversees the Pennsylvania Restraint Reduction Initiative and the implementation portion of the Pennsylvania Department of Health's Best Practices Project. She also led the implementation for a one-year project, Models to Improve Care, sponsored by the Ohio Department of Health. In addition, Beryl serves as the outreach leader for the national Hospital Bed Safety Workgroup, which includes representatives of academia, the health care industry and government working together for safety. Beryl has been published in *Journal of Aging and Social Policy, Geriatric Nursing, Journal of Gerontological Nursing, Generations, Long Term Care News, The Gerontologist* and *Ethical and Legal Dilemmas in Occupational Therapy*.

Anja Gerlach is a research fellow at the University of Hamburg, Unit of Health Sciences and Education. She is engaged in a project on the development and evaluation of practice guidelines on physical restraints in nursing homes. This involves literature reviews, fieldwork and assessing best practice strategies on the reduction of physical restraint. Formerly she was involved in a research project on abuse and neglect in professional and informal care.

Baroness Greengross: Sally Greengross OBE has been a crossbench (independent) member of the House of Lords since 2000 and chairs three all-party parliamentary groups: Corporate Social Responsibility, Intergenerational Futures: Old and Young Together, and Continence Care. Sally is Chief Executive of the International Longevity Centre, UK. She is Chair of the Advisory Groups for the English Longitudinal Study on Ageing and the New Dynamics of Ageing, Commissioner for the Equality and Human Rights Commission, Trustee of the Resolution Foundation, President of the Pensions Policy Institute, President of the College of Occupational Therapists and Honorary Vice President of the Royal Society for the Promotion of Health. Sally was Director General of Age Concern England from 1987 until 2000, and is now their Vice President. Until 2000 she was Joint Chair of the Age Concern Institute of Gerontology at King's College London, and Secretary General of Eurolink Age. Sally holds honorary doctorates from seven UK universities.

Antonie Haut is a research fellow at the University of Witten-Herdecke, Institute of Nursing Research. She is engaged in a project on the development and evaluation of practice guidelines on physical restraint in nursing homes, involving literature reviews, interviewing members of the guideline development group and surveying nurses' and relatives' attitudes about their beliefs on physical restraint.

Carmel M. Hughes, is Professor of Primary Care Pharmacy at the School of Pharmacy, Queen's University Belfast. She is a former Harkness Fellow in Health Care Policy and was the only pharmacist to have been appointed to a National Primary Care Career Scientist Fellowship. Her primary research interests are the quality of care (focusing on medicines) in older people, particularly in long-term care settings and evidence-based practice.

Rhidian Hughes was a university researcher for many years before working at the Commission for Social Care Inspection during its existence between 2004 and 2009. At the CSCI he was responsible for a host of studies including one on the restraint of older people (*Rights, Risks and Restraints: An Exploration into the Use of Restraint in the Care of Older People*). He holds honorary positions as a visiting senior lecturer at Guy's, King's and St Thomas' School of Medicine and a visiting senior research fellow at the Institute of Gerontology, King's College London. He has written a number of articles on restraint and has edited *Reducing Restraints in Health and Social Care: Practice and Policy Perspectives* (Quay Books) and *Ageing in East Asia: Challenges and Policies for the Twenty-First Century* (Routledge) with Tsung-hsi Fu.

Kate Irving works as a lecturer in nursing in Dublin City University, Ireland. She competed her Nursing degree in 1998 at Leeds Metropolitan University and worked in aged care for three years before going to Australia to commence her PhD at Curtin University of Technology. The title of the PhD was 'Case studies in restraint use: A Foucaultian approach'. Since completing her PhD she has settled in Dublin City University where she teaches aspects of dementia care, research and communication and heads up two academic practice initiatives. Both are aimed at increasing our understanding of and response to early dementia through early screening and supportive intervention and by seeking to foreground the voice of the person with dementia.

Sascha Köpke is a senior researcher at the University of Hamburg, Unit of Health Sciences and Education. He has been involved in several projects addressing nursing home care. Projects have focused on fall prevention, fall risk assessment and the epidemiology and reduction of physical restraints. His second main research field is decision support for people with multiple sclerosis.

Kate L. Lapane, is Professor and Chair at Virginia Commonwealth University in the Department of Epidemiology and Community Health. Kate is an epidemiologist whose contributions to the field of pharmacoepidemiology have been substantial. The overarching theme of her applied research is to improve the health outcomes of older people through the understanding of risks and benefits of medications in patients systematically excluded from clinical trials.

Suparna Madan is a geriatric psychiatrist and Clinical Assistant Professor in Geriatric Psychiatry at the University of Calgary in Alberta, Canada. She is Head of the Division of Geriatric Psychiatry and Program Medical Director for Geriatric Mental Health for Alberta Health Services in Calgary. Her clinical interests include inpatient geriatric psychiatry and geriatric consultation-liaison psychiatry. Prior research interests include music therapy and more recently delirium prevention and development of continuing medical education projects using an electronic health record.

Gabriele Meyer is Professor of Clinical Nursing Research at the University of Witten-Herdecke, Institute of Nursing Research. Her main research interests are in the prevention of accidental falls and fall-related fractures in older people, epidemiology and reduction of physical restraint, evidence-based diagnostics with focus on assessment instruments, epidemiology of fractures, and evidence-based consumer/patient information.

Samuel R. Nyman has a BSc, MSc (research methods) and PhD, all in psychology. He has published from his Economic and Social Research Council-funded PhD that evaluated a falls prevention website, and from a literature review funded by Help the Aged on communicating falls prevention advice. In addition to his work on preventing falls in older people, he has conducted research investigating the emotional support needs of people with sight loss. He is currently a postdoctoral research fellow investigating older people's views of assistive technology in detecting falls, and is a co-editor of *Generations Review*, the online newsletter for the British Society of Gerontology.

David Oliver is Visiting Professor of Medicine for Older People at City University, London, a consultant physician at the Royal Berkshire Hospital, and National Secretary of the British Geriatrics Society. He has developed and run clinical services for the prevention of falls and fractures and has a longstanding research interest in the prevention of falls, with numerous publications including systematic reviews on falls prevention interventions, falls risk assessments, bedrails and restraints. He has worked with the Department of Health, Healthcare Commission and National Patient Safety Agency advising on falls prevention.

Barbara Pointon lectured in music, but took early retirement to care for her husband who was diagnosed at 51 with Alzheimer's Disease – a 16-year journey documented in ITV's film *Malcolm and Barbara...Love's Farewell* (2007). She campaigns for a better understanding of people with dementia and their carers, and was awarded Member of the Order of the British Empire in 2006. She is an ambassador for the Alzheimer's Society and also for the charity 'For Dementia' (Admiral Nurses). Having contributed to the National Dementia, End of Life and Carers' Strategies, she is actively involved in the training of health and social care workforces in hands-on dementia care.

Pat Rowe is a registered nurse with over 30 years of clinical and administrative experience in psychiatry and geriatric nursing. Her interests include educating caregivers to provide person-centred care and to develop creative strategies to manage dementia-associated behaviours. She is currently employed as a geriatric mental health consultant with Alberta Health Services in Calgary, Alberta, Canada.

Karen Russell has 30 years of nursing experience in acute and long-term care settings, practising as a staff nurse, admissions coordinator and staff development coordinator. She has served as a regional director for the Pennsylvania Restraint Reduction Initiative since July 1998; her expertise is in physical restraint reduction including bed and side rail safety, fall management, comprehensive assessment processes, including in-depth environmental assessments, as well as individual resident analysis, pressure ulcer prevention and resident–family–staff relationships. Karen has worked with the Quality Improvement organisations in Wisconsin, South Carolina, Pennsylvania, West Virginia and Nebraska. She has also presented to national conferences including the American Society on Aging, the American Association of Homes and Services for the Aging and the American Association of Nurse Assessment Coordinators.

Gregory M. Smith currently serves as Chief Executive Officer of the Allentown State Hospital, Allentown, Pennsylvania. He has presented internationally on Pennsylvania's non-restraint approach to psychiatric care and services and has co-authored several professional publications on this topic. Gregory is a faculty member of the National Association of State Mental Health Program Directors for Technical Assistance on Seclusion and Restraint Reduction. He also administers the Pennsylvania State Hospital risk management system and issues a monthly report on adverse events and restraint use, which can be found at www.dpw.state.pa.us/PartnersProviders/ MentalHealthSubstanceAbuse/StateHospitals.

Ingelin Testad is Director of the Centre for Research at Stavanger Teaching Nursing Home, Leader of Health Science Research at the Norwegian Centre for Movement Disorders, Stavanger University Hospital, and Project Manager of the Medical Centre in Aging, Stavanger University Hospital.

Joan Ferlo Todd serves as a senior nurse consultant and analyst with the US Food and Drug Administration. She evaluates and analyses medical device adverse event reports and publishes device safety articles associated with hospital beds, breast implants and physical medicine devices. She is the co-lead of the FDA's steering committee for hospital bed safety and a member of the International Electrotechnical Commission's workgroup (IEC 60601-2-52) that develops international standards for medical beds. She has 16 years of clinical experience in intensive care and medical-surgical nursing, as well as eight years of experience in the medical device bed industry.

Heather Wilkinson is Co-Director of the Centre for Research on Families and Relationships, as well as Research Director for the School of Health in Social Science, University of Edinburgh. Her research interests centre on issues of inclusion and quality of life for people with dementia and for people with a learning disability and dementia. Current research projects examine night-time care, care homes and practice development for staff working with older people. She is actively involved in developing methods for including people with dementia in research and policy and was a founder member of the Scottish Dementia Working Group.

Jane Williams has spent her career divided between the care of older people and, for the last 15 years, has focused on stroke care and the development of a local stroke service. She is Consultant Nurse in Stroke Care delivering clinical care, education and training, leadership, and development, delivery and evaluation of an evidence-based stroke service within Portsmouth Hospitals NHS Trust. She is involved in many national working parties and has completed a PhD on decision-making processes and the involvements of carers and relatives.

Sheena Wyllie has for the past ten years been working in private care homes, the last five of these with Barchester Healthcare. Sheena's career in health care commenced more than 30 years ago as a student nurse and she has enjoyed many varied roles in the NHS and other services. Sheena is currently Director of Dementia Services and has led the development of the Memory Lane programme and dementia care services across the company. This has involved initiating change management, leadership programmes and supporting teams to make a difference to the individual lives of people with dementia.

SUBJECT INDEX

AUTHOR INDEX

Made in the USA
Lexington, KY
10 March 2012